TNS

TNS

The Newest Profession

Steve Salerno

William Morrow and Company, Inc.
New York

Copyright © 1985 by Steve Salerno

Library of Congress Catalog Card Number: 85-61786

ISBN: 0-688-04997-4

Printed in the United States of America

First Edition

1 2 3 4 5 6 7 8 9 10

BOOK DESIGN BY JAMES UDELL

Contents

Sales Miscellany

Estimated percentage of the sales force that generates four fifths of the gross national sales product: 20.

1

Au Revoir, *Willy Loman*

The Old . . .

Item: There's this joke about the used-car dealer.

Said car dealer is showing his brother around the lot for the first time when in walks a little old grandmotherly type. She volunteers that her husband passed away a year ago, she just got her driver's license, and she's in the market for a nice, reliable used car. Spotting an easy mark, the dealer tries to interest her in a repainted taxicab, but grandma, as it develops, has a surprisingly good eye for detail—she notices the yellow paint on the doorjambs and some suspicious-looking puddles of fluid underneath the chassis.

So the car dealer guides her to a fairly spiffy specimen, a late-model Chevy. "And the best thing is, it's only got thirty thousand miles on it," he gushes. Grandma likes the car, but hesitates, saying that she wants her son to return with her later in the week to examine the vehicle more closely. The dealer grows adamant, claiming the Chevy is a one-day special, that several other people have already expressed interest. He concludes by snorting, "Look, lady, we both know it's the perfect car for you, but I'm not gonna hold it without a deposit. If you want it, and you want it at this price, I need to see cash, *now*." Reluctantly, the old woman agrees, forking over the money.

Afterward, the dealer confesses mirthfully to his brother that the Chevy's odometer had been turned back from eighty-five thousand miles, and the car's front end is badly in need of repair. "That little old lady thought she was such a sharp cookie, but I showed her a thing or two, huh?" he gloats.

The brother is incredulous.

"How could you do such a thing?" he demands. "I don't know if it occurred to you, but that sweet old lady was about the same age as our mother. Would you have sold that clunker to Mom?"

"Hell no!" the dealer replies indignantly. "Mom trusts me— I coulda sold *her* the taxi!"

Item: On April 13, 1984, during the taping of the popular game show *Family Feud,* Richard Dawson asks a young woman what kind of person one would least like to see at the door. Without a heartbeat's hesitation, the woman says, "Salesman."

It is the number-one answer.

Nor was this the first contribution the show had made to the vilification of the sales trade. A year or so before, Dawson had asked contestants to name a profession for which a good liar would be ideally suited.

Once again, the top response—overwhelmingly so—was salesman.

Cut to: Woody Allen's comedy classic *Take the Money and Run.* In one scene, Allen's character, a pathetically incompetent petty thief named Virgil, has misbehaved in prison. As a result, the narrator informs us in a deadly serious voice, Virgil "is severely tortured. For three days and nights, he is locked in a room with an insurance salesman. . . ."

. . . And the New

At a fashionable shop on New York's Park Avenue South, on a lovely spring morning, Max and his wife, Mavis, have come to select a nice dress for the cocktail party they're both attending next Saturday night. They are here, rather than twenty or so blocks farther uptown, because their budget is limited, and this particular area of Manhattan has a reputation for selling goods at discount. Mavis wants something fashionable—she's prepared to go as high as $150—but that's it. Max has heard good things about this shop and the people who work there. Still, having just done business with a car dealer who made the prospect of next week's root-canal surgery seem attractive, Max looks forward to meeting another salesperson with about as much enthusiasm as Robert Vesco looked forward to meeting another process server.

But Max is to be pleasantly surprised. Though the sales-woman who greets them is smiling, it is not in the cloying, sac-charin manner he has always associated with members of her trade. She seems businesslike but casual, and honestly friendly: *real*.

Max's first impression is that she is not a very threatening figure.

The impression is heightened once she begins to speak. She does not bellow, "May I help you?" Rather, in a light, pleasant tone of voice—and pretty much all in one breath—she says her name is Michelle, invites them to browse freely through her shop, and suggests that they fetch her if and when there's any-thing special she can find for them. She waits a mere instant before she pirouettes and retreats behind the counter.

Accustomed to salespeople who home in on you like cruise missiles, with mouth and mannerisms ablaze, Max turns to Mavis and smiles.

"Gee, honey," he says, "wasn't that a refreshing change of pace?" He takes a deep breath and begins to relax.

Before long Max's wife finds a lovely silk dress. They sum-mon Michelle, and the conversation goes more or less as fol-lows.

"This is really nice," says Mavis.

"Isn't it?" Michelle affirms, nodding. She continues nodding as she turns her gaze to Max. And Max finds himself nodding and smiling along with her.

But as Mavis holds the dress against her, surveying her re-flection in the full-length mirror, she grimaces. "Do you think," she asks Michelle, "this is a little too dressy for an ordinary Sat-urday night party?"

The saleswoman looks pensive. "Hmmm. I suppose that de-

11

pends—but what do you think?" Barely pausing, she adds, "You'd probably be able to get a better idea of the full effect if you tried it on, don't you agree?" Ever so gingerly, Michelle reaches over and takes the dress, motioning for Mavis to follow.

Max begins to feel a little apprehensive—after all, he doesn't yet know how much this is going to cost him. But on the other hand, why worry? Michelle hasn't yet done anything to pique his normal distrust of salespeople. In fact, thus far she's been the epitome of graciousness. Enthusiastic without being giddy or affected; concerned, but hardly obsequious. Overall, she strikes a nice balance between interested and deferential. If the damned thing's too expensive, he'll just tell her when the time comes. She's not one of those hard-sell types who'd make things uncomfortable for you. In the meantime, let her have her fun.

Mavis returns wearing not just the dress, but a broad grin. She looks, in fact, as radiant and fulfilled as a mother-to-be. Michelle looks very nearly so.

"Oh, honey, it's so gorgeous," Mavis blurts, still halfway across the store from her husband. Max has to admit it looks pretty good. "But," she says, sighing as she reaches him, "I'm still a little worried about it being too formal."

At this point, Michelle reaches down to the woman's waist to adjust the dress's belt, an exquisitely feminine rendering of diaphanous lace. "There," she says, calling Mavis's attention once more to the mirror in front of her, "that's better, don't you think? It looked a little off line."

Mavis studies the image before her, starting with the belt and panning first upward and then down, looking pleased beyond words. But when the querulous expression returns a moment later, Michelle—by now very much attuned to Mavis's concerns—asks, "Do you know what everyone else is wearing?"

Mavis shrugs.

"How many people are coming?"

"I think twenty couples."

"Do you think it's possible that at least a few ladies might wear something as nice, or nearly as nice, as this?"

Mavis ponders that for a moment. Then she summons her broadest smile of the day. It is a special kind of smile, an affirmation.

Michelle seems pleased—just as she has seemed, through-out, to be a participant in each of Mavis's emotional phases: frowning when Mavis frowned, nodding when Mavis nodded, ever in sync with the woman's unfolding emotional cycle.

"I guess even if nobody else does wear anything quite this fancy . . ." Mavis's voice trails off, but Michelle is quick to supply the missing words: ". . . there's nothing wrong with feeling like the belle of the ball, right?"

Max resists the temptation to ask what it's going to cost for his wife to be the belle of the ball. The remark, he reasons, would sound curt and gratuitous, given Michelle's behavior thus far. But his wife has apparently been reading his thoughts.

"Look, Michelle," she begins, sheepishly, "I really love this dress. But I have a feeling it's going to cost a lot of money." Max marvels at the tone of his wife's voice, which borders on squeamish. Clearly, Mavis is cool to the prospect of ruining the constructive rapport she has established with Michelle—as though merely raising the issue of price might be a personal affront to this cheerful ally who has helped her through her tense decision.

Michelle sighs. "I know how you feel," she says, sounding very much as though she does, indeed, know how Mavis feels. "It happens to me, too. Every time I find something special, something I really *adore,* I expect it to be expensive." She leaves it at that, forcing her patron to come directly to the heart of the matter.

"Well . . . how expensive is it?" says Mavis, half biting her lip.

"It's three hundred and five dollars," says Michelle. She is very natural and warm, treading that most delicate of lines between empathy and optimism: not so optimistic that she seems presumptuous, nor so full of empathy that her manner could be construed as an apology for the price.

Mavis looks at her husband, and Max is acutely aware that the whole thing has been dumped in his lap. His wife is sold. She simply wants him to rubber-stamp the deal.

Under his spouse's imploring gaze (Michelle, meanwhile, is once again fussing with the frills of the dress, wearing the same kind of smile you might see on the face of a mother appraising her only daughter in her bridal gown), Max feels the sudden, heavy onset of that pressure he hadn't expected to feel at this shop, with this saleswoman. He begins to assess his options.

On the one hand, the dress is definitely over budget. Both of them agreed beforehand: no more than $150.

But they can hardly blame Michelle for that. It isn't as if she harpooned them on the way in and dragged Mavis over to the most expensive rack. His wife discovered this delightful little gem all by herself. Michelle was off somewhere else, doing her own thing. She had no way of knowing what kind of dress they were going to wind up with. Presumably, she'd have shown them the same courtesy even if they managed to unearth something for sixteen bucks.

After a few moments of oppressive silence, Max hears his own voice say, "Three hundred dollars is a lot of money." But he doesn't sound very convincing, least of all to himself. There's a curious numbness to the words, a decided lilt in final inflection that makes it seem more like a question than a judgment.

Another moment of silence. Max's remark has obviously not been interpreted as the definitive statement on the subject. Michelle has now stopped fussing with the dress, and is looking at him expectantly. Max can't be sure—it's probably just his imagination—but somewhere in the depths of her eyes he thinks he sees just a glimmer of defiance, as though she were daring him: *Go ahead. . . . I want to hear you come right out and tell your wife that she can't be the envy of every other woman at the party.*

Suddenly Michelle chooses to alleviate the uncomfortable quiet. Out of the blue, in that same sunny tone of voice with which she'd first greeted them, she asks Mavis, "If you did wear this kind of dress, what sort of pocketbook would you use with it?"

Mavis shrugs again. Michelle smiles and escorts her to the handbag counter a few yards away. They talk between themselves for a few minutes, picking up this or that bag and holding it next to the dress. When they return five minutes later, each of them is holding a pocketbook.

"We decided we need a man's opinion," says Michelle. "Do you think this one goes better. . . ?" She indicates the bag

Mavis is holding. The price tags says $48. ". . . or do you prefer this other one?" She taps the pocketbook in front of her. Its tag says $28.95. Before allowing Max much of a chance to reply, she adds, "I like this one just as well, and it saves you twenty dollars. Nothing wrong, is there, with economizing where you can?"

"There sure isn't," says Max emphatically, and before you know it, Michelle has whisked Mavis away to the register, dress and pocketbook in hand.

• • •

TNS. The New Salesmanship. Inobtrusively—using nothing but her natural warmth, plus careful cultivation of the sentiments she was given to work with—the saleswoman in the above anecdote helped Max and Mavis exceed their budget by 100 percent. (More, if you count the pocketbook.) This is not necessarily to be construed as an indictment of what Michelle did, by the way; there's no denying that Max and Mavis went home happy. (Well, Mavis did, anyway.)

And the saleswoman certainly can't be faulted for being pushy; if you reread the scene, you'll note that Michelle introduced very few of her own opinions into the discussion. Instead, she simply seized upon things said and done by Max and Mavis that were helpful to the ultimate objective of closing the sale. She affirmed or rephrased or redirected as necessary, reinforcing a positive sentiment here, confounding or circumnavigating a negative one there.

Her presentation relied not just on an appealing demeanor—a demeanor refined and perfected through countless hours watching herself on videotape, hunting for the slightest nuance of haughtiness or condescension, exploring the subtlest subtleties of facial expressions and body language—but on a variety of state-of-the-art selling tactics so inobtrusive that they probably didn't strike you as tactics at all. For instance, the culmination of those efforts was Closing on the Minor Point. That is to say, she did not sell them the *dress*; why run the risk of having the whole deal collapse amid a protracted cost-benefit discussion of the high price of the dress? Rather, she extricated herself from a tense moment by focusing attention instead on a twenty-eight-dollar accessory. What Michelle sold them—the item she actually closed on—was a handbag. The three-hundred-dollar dress just happened to come with it.

It's a little bit like being on vacation with the family in California, and having your kid ask you whether you'd rather go to Disneyland on Tuesday or Wednesday. He's assumed the major decision—which is, of course, to go to Disneyland at all—and merely left you with the relatively inconsequential prerogative of choosing a day.

If you've shopped for a VCR lately, you may have experienced firsthand the popularity of this particular technique with salespeople who work for video specialty stores. When they think they've got you fairly close to committing on a given machine, they'll kind of nudge you over toward the mouth-watering racks of movies and ask which rental film or two you'd like to take home with you for a night, free of charge, "just to get you started in the wonderful world of video." They assume the sale of the five-hundred-dollar recorder, and instead leave you with a choice between a couple of items that are free.

Which would you rather do? Buy something for five hundred dollars? Or choose between two items that are free?

Sound fluky? Consider that this same technique is used daily not just to sell dresses and VCRs, but by some of America's highest-paid sales professionals to close transactions running to seven or eight figures. E. H. Boullioun, who sat at the helm of Boeing's sales organization during the company's salad days, would wrap up the sale of a dozen jumbo jets by asking the buyer about upholstery colors. It worked for Boullioun, just as it continues to work today for Avon salespeople who close a customer by asking which free gift she'd prefer with her $12.50 purchase. And Closing on the Minor Point is merely one of a whole battery of techniques deployed by TNS adherents.

The world of sales has changed immeasurably since the days of belligerence and "blue sky" ("blue sky" refers to claims that are so outrageously idyllic as to warrant comparison with the untroubled feeling of a cloudless summer day). But, whether they're selling aircraft or Avon, new-breed salespeople do the things they do for a reason. Very little is left to instinct. Though they may impress as casual—sometimes undisciplined—nothing could be farther from the truth. Though they may violate every one of your beliefs about professional salespeople—and that is part of their charm—they are, in fact, consummate salespeople for whom the word "professional" barely suffices.

The New Salesmanship—at once simple and intricate, brash and understated, warm and aloof, selfish and altruistic—is very possibly like nothing you have ever encountered.

This book, then, is a look at selling in contemporary America. Not a How-to, but a What-Is. We'll examine the subject in the broadest possible sense: the mythology and the reality of where selling has been, where it's headed, what life is like for today's breed of salesperson, and—last but certainly not least—how all of this relates to you.

A Few Basic Myths—Explored, Explained, Exploded

That the sales profession has something less than a stellar public image is no great revelation. To most people, ever since the reeking sludge that once covered the earth combined by chance in just such a way to produce the first used-car dealer, selling has always been a shadowy, Mephistophelian activity. Traditionally, salespeople are thought not only to screw their customers, but to take great pride in doing it regularly and often.

A very successful Chevrolet salesman I know once worked himself into a frenzy when somebody reeled off the car-dealer joke at a cocktail party. He thought it an unfair and awful caricature. Yet all caricatures are, of course, rooted in fact. The outrageously funny sketches of President Reagan's hair are outrageously funny, after all, only because our chief executive's hair does happen to bob up and form a noticeable clump on one side of his head. Otherwise, the grotesque exaggerations penciled by satirists would make no sense, and no one would be amused.

In the same vein, while it is doubtful that many salespeople have actually conned their mothers, I am personally acquainted with at least two fellows who've done jobs on relatives not far removed from their immediate families, and a third who swindled his sister out of four or five grand on a land deal. So, at least in one sense—and there are other senses, as we'll shortly see—the public's jaundiced perception of the trade in which I toiled for over a decade did not evolve in a vacuum. (Then again, perhaps it did, since it is the image of the Man from Electrolux that frequently comes to mind when one hears the word *salesman*.)

In the past, selling's image problems have reached to the highest levels of American business. Speaking of the representatives of a large and well-known industrial sales outfit, a friend once remarked that he had "more ethics in my little pinkie finger than they have in their entire nationwide operation."

The stigma on sales is, in fact, institutionalized in the English language. Check some of the synonyms given for the word *sell* in the current *Roget's Thesaurus,* which reflects popular, connotative usage:

> *sell,* vend, dispose of, auction, hawk, dump, unload . . .

The presentation of the word *salesman* is no less illuminating. It is lumped together with such flattering synonyms as *huckster, hawker, moneychanger, faker,* and *costermonger.* Overall, it is probably safe to say that when the word *salesman* is used by those outside the trade (and not infrequently inside), its use is pejorative.

Enter the U.S. government, which saw fit to involve itself in the perpetuation of the myth of the salesperson by way of a commissioned study on the sales personality. A top contender, as I recall, for Senator William Proxmire's Golden Fleece Award (an annual commemoration of the most ambitious waste of taxpayers' dollars), the study used some seventy-odd pages of bar charts and graphs to confirm what its researchers had proposed going in: that salespeople are aggressive. Not long after the momentous federal survey, confessed contract killer and mob sting man Sonny Gibson took it a step further.

"All good salesmen have something in common," proposed Gibson in his spellbinding autobiography, *Mafia Kingpin.* "They're greedy and they're crooked. *That's what makes good salesmen*" (italics mine).

Nonetheless, there is ample evidence that better salespeople have seldom relied for their success on dishonest and immoral tactics. There was always an instinctive if not conscious recognition of the fact that in good selling, things had to work for mutual benefit. Both the salesperson and the customer had to end up happy. Above all, the customer could not be made to feel threatened.

The fact is that down through the ages—surprise of surprises—most superior salespeople have actually professed to like their fellow human beings. The operative word in the last sentence is . . . *superior.* (Caught you, didn't I? You thought I was going to say *professed.*) They enjoyed working with people, and derived tremendous satisfaction from the mutual rewards of the salesperson/client relationship.

In his book entitled *Getting Back to the Basics of Selling,* former salesman and venture capitalist Matthew J. Culligan cites a study undertaken by an unnamed major corporation that sought to determine what customers found most impressive about its top sales workers. Says the author, "The only characteristic they all had was the somewhat ill-defined one of niceness." Culligan goes on to say, "Time after time, customers rated the top salespeople as 'nice.'"

So. On the one hand, we have Matthew Culligan telling us that top salespeople are really swell. On the other hand, there is Sonny Gibson, telling us that for all intents and purposes, going from a salesperson to a hit man is a step up in life.

Which is the myth and which is the reality?

Well, the two viewpoints are not necessarily incompatible. Gibson's circle of friends probably did not include too many people from more enlightened sales organizations like IBM and Dupont. (And even if it did, this, remember, was several decades ago, when selling, even at the top levels, was nothing like what it is today.) Odds are the mafioso-cum-author's characterization of "good salesmen" refers more to your high-powered door-to-door go-getters—many of whom, even now, continue to resist the burgeoning professionalism of the trade—than to the decorous corporate types Culligan had in mind.* So in this case, at least, there's a little myth and a little reality to each position.

* *There's actually another question here, having to do with whether or not such characteristics as greed and crookedness by definition preclude one's coming across as "nice." But for now, we'll leave that in abeyance.*

Yet down through the ages, the public has tended almost unanimously to side with Gibson. And they continue to do so even today, as salesmanship undergoes dramatic changes.

Why?

There are actually a number of reasons, not the least of which is that the average salesman encountered by the average customer on an average day is not really a professional salesman at all. Rather, he is just an ordinary person who happens to be selling at that particular moment. In no way is he representative of the state of the art.

The majority of salespeople are neither career-minded nor successful—not eminently so, in any case. A popular sales axiom poses that in any given sales environment, 80 percent of the production comes from just 20 percent of the sales reps. (The 80/20 ratio is a near-ubiquitous rule of thumb with applications throughout the sales sphere. It is also said that 80 percent of an individual salesman's volume is provided by 20 percent of his customers, and that the average salesman spends just one fifth of his time selling, and the balance of it preparing to sell.) Sales trainer extraordinaire Tom Hopkins estimates that only a quarter of the total sales force is well versed in the more enlightened approaches. Don Chinery, president of Hirsch USA, which underwent Xerox's comprehensive sales-training program some years back, says that the odds of your encountering a true sales standout are even more remote than one out of four.

"Most of them work in high-tech environments, or sell high-ticket items," says Chinery, "so the odds of the average consumer running into them more often than once every few years—or at all—are pretty long."

The nonserious, nonprofessional salespeople fall into several overlapping categories: people who dislike regimentation, people who like to socialize, people who like to work outdoors, people who have other interests they wish to pursue and need the relatively large amount of free time sales work affords, people who get a kick out of the standard sales perks (company cars, expense accounts, tax write-offs, and so on), people who simply can't find other work, people who—I kid you not—are looking for an employee discount on a fairly substantial product they're looking to buy (although the IRS is cracking down in this regard, and it will soon be necessary to declare the discount as income). Sales is one of those jobs people just seem to fall into. I fell into it, after graduating from college and discovering that the business community was unwilling to prostrate itself before a twenty-year-old whose most noteworthy achievement had been the consumption of a full quart bottle of Yago Sangria during a four-minute recess between classes. I was fortunate, by the way. Many of my college buddies were driving taxis. (Now, they're unemployed).

There are few concrete prerequisites for entry-level sales positions (unlesss, that is, IBM is your quarry, in which case you'd better come armed with a college degree and a minimum 3.5 grade-point average). Even in today's super-technological society, it remains possible for a total novice to land a trainee sales job at a Savin or a Minolta or, depending on how things are going at Savin and Minolta, Xerox. With luck and a certain minimal effort, that trainee can bring home twenty-five thousand dollars his first year. I earned almost twenty thousand dollars during my first full year in sales a decade ago, when my grasp of sales mechanics was abysmal—I held the customer's interest about as well as I held my sangria.

Needless to say, today's young salespeople have an easier time selling exciting new office products to efficiency-minded, early-adopter businessmen than I had selling tacky mirrors to the denizens of Brooklyn's Bed-Stuy ghetto. Their financial prospects are far brighter, so much so that a rank beginner who handles himself well at the job interview can frequently wangle a draw against commission, and be good for a guaranteed four hundred dollars per week, plus car, right off the bat. François Levy joined AT&T at a training salary of twenty-two thousand dollars. After going on commissions at the six-month point, he finished the year at sixty thousand dollars. Levy's background— retail clothing sales—gave no sign of the greatness he would achieve. Though he is the exception, not the rule, Levy is living proof of the earnings potential that exists for many sales novices.

For these and other reasons, there are a lot of people wandering around with sample cases who have precious little idea what the hell they're doing. They approach the job with insoucient abandon; they have fun, meet people, get laid, and occasionally sell something. They move from sales organization to sales organization to the musicians' union and back again. They eke out a modest living, and often leave their employers holding the bag for thousands of dollars in back draw they were never able to "beat." Beating your draw, I should explain, means earning enough in commissions to offset money the company has advanced to you in the form of guaranteed pay. If, hypothetically, your employer is paying you a $1,500 monthly draw, and you're on a 10 percent flat-commission schedule selling a $1,000 item, by month's end you'll have to sell at least fifteen of those items in order to beat your draw. If you sell but twelve, you technically earn just $1,200; but your boss has already paid you $1,500 in guaranteed draw, so you're the proud owner of what's known as a $300 "negative." If this goes on for a while, you'll be fired, which explains the aforementioned bag employers get stuck holding.

Because you're never legally responsible for amounts advanced to you, and because, until recently, few employers bothered to check references on entry-level sales applications, it was not terribly uncommon for psuedosalespeople to drift from firm to firm, collecting their overdraws, failing to produce, getting fired, and moving on to repeat the cycle in perpetuity. Shortly before I left sales, a company for which one of my friends worked interviewed a fifty-five-year-old gent named Gary. Gary claimed to be embarking on a sales career after two decades of teaching high-school political science. The boss knew that former teachers have been known to make excellent salespeople. (He might have been thinking of Sharon Snowden, who left teaching to become a top producer for Sharp, and later, a six-figure rep for Lanier Business Products. Or Geraldine Young, who broke both the sex and color barriers in industrial distribution.) So he hired Gary, only to discover months later—and thousands of dollars too late—that this was not his first, but more like his *fifteenth* attempt at a career in sales. Gary had run up a two-thousand-dollar deficit with his former employer, and nearly a grand with the firm before that. At last report, the company was toying with the idea of taking Gary to court. Fraud or some such thing. I doubt anything came of it.

As you may have guessed, the turnover in the sales field is astounding. Buy today's newspaper and tuck it away somewhere. Unearth it a month from now, open it to the classified section next to the current day's edition. Locate the *S* heading and compare the ads under SALES HELP WANTED. Seventy-five percent of the advertisements will be identical in both papers. And it's not that the ads are there again—it's that they're there *always,* day in and day out, week after week. Anticipating a huge turnover, employers are forever hiring.

In the past, employers contributed to this in large measure by implementing hiring criteria that all but guaranteed the jobs would go to the wrong people. Companies wanted assertive, so they hired an obnoxious boor; confident, so they hired a braggart; gregarious, so they chose some smooth-talking sharpie. Given a clear choice between subtlety and overkill, they invariably opted for the latter.

Less often, hiring decisions would be informed by the precursors of the modern psychological-profile test. Though today considered highly reliable and given much credence by those responsible for formulating sales policy, back in the fifties and sixties such tests demonstrated the most insipid kind of screening techniques. Crafted partly from Freud, partly from a seminal form of Dianetics, and mostly from hunger, they featured questions that ran something like this:

At a party, what I like to do most is . . .
(a) garrote the hostess
(b) blow my nose into the hors d'oeuvres
(c) sit in the corner and play with my navel
(d) mingle and get to know as many people as possible

The upshot of all this is that there was often little relation between what was going on at the top of the sales world—where the million-dollar producers worked—and what went on in the trenches, where you and I were likely to meet the people who would help to formulate our impressions of the field.

This is changing as TNS methodology takes hold throughout the world of sales. "It's certainly improved," says Xerox's Myron Howard, one of the corporation's top thirty national account managers. "I don't get quite the same body language at parties when people find out I'm a salesman. In fact, more and more it's becoming something that people will actually be impressed by." And more help is on the way. Major business schools like Harvard and Wharton are now offering sales curricula, which adds unimpeachable legitimacy to what has always been a tainted undertaking.

So, then, to sum up: While the mythology suggests that there was always something inherently evil about the process of selling (and thus, by extension, about those who engaged in that process), the facts are less damning. Selling—though it certainly wouldn't have ranked up there with missionary work—was never quite as bad as it was cracked up to be. At least at the upper echelons of the trade, where the real money changed hands, there were definite pockets of wisdom and warmth. They may have been few and far between, and they may have had little effect on the conduct of selling as a whole. But they were there. Even in the bad old days.

All of this takes on added meaning as we forge ahead into a second piece of American folklore: the notion of the "born salesman."

Are Salesmen Born or Made?
This is a toughie, and you'll find strong feelings on both sides. (Indeed, some people seem to argue both sides. Consider the intriguing catch-22 position taken by Zig Ziglar, one of the high priests of the contemporary sales-training movement. Zig's message to his seminar audiences, delivered in a mood of high spirituality, is that they were "born to win." Which, of course, means they really needn't have shown up for the seminar. But then again, they wouldn't have known that unless they attended.)

As a rule, though, those inside sales organizations tend to think salespeople are born, or at least predisposed. "There's a certain type of individual who's going to have the fortitude to last in this business, and then there's others who won't," says Marvin Edelstein, eastern regional manager for Burroughs Corporation. "You can train people who don't have certain basic sales qualities like stick-to-itiveness, and the ability to cope with rejection—but they'll never really achieve for you."

Those in sales training, on the other hand—and not surprisingly—tend to adopt the opposite view. "Our research shows that a salesman is only as good as his ability to deal correctly with sales situations as they happen," says Betsy Moser of Xerox Learning Systems. Her company has conducted several studies which, she says, demonstrate that most of the factors stereotypically identified with sales achievement are actually irrelevant to the process of closing a sale. "And that is an ability which, we feel, can very definitely be nurtured in individuals of a wide variety of backgrounds."

With certain reservations, I tend to go along with those of Moser's inclination, even though my own mother, bless her heart, is wont to refer to me as a born salesman. (She does so fondly, I suppose, but then, you know how mothers are: "I want you all to meet my son, John—he's in banking," said Mrs. Dillinger.) In so doing, Mom conveniently forgets that I didn't really come out of my shell until I was nearly twenty-one; hell, I seldom came out of my *room* until I was past fifteen.

Somewhat more graphic is the case of Tom Hopkins, generally conceded to be America's foremost individual sales trainer. Sales-related articles penned by journalists unfamiliar with the trade often preface Tom's name with phrases like "that archetypal born salesman. . . ." Yet Tom himself is the first to admit that his formative years—parts of which were spent in that archetypal wellspring of sales talent, the steelworkers' union— provided no clue whatever to the selling heroics he would one day achieve. One of Hopkins's favorite lines is "There was a time when I didn't know the difference between the 'close' you put on a customer and the clothes you put on your back." (Tom also says, "No woman ever went into the delivery room, put her legs up into the stirrups, and gave birth to a salesman.") It was only after a prolonged period of floundering in the real estate trade that Tom enrolled in a course taught by master sales theorist J. Douglas Edwards, and blossomed. Today, with a million-plus in annual income, Tom is obviously able to put some very nice clothes on his back.

Granted, some cases are hard to call. At age thirteen, Markita Andrews, a serious contender for the title of World's Greatest Living Seller of Girl Scout Cookies, has not had the opportunity to attend too many courses in sophisticated sales techniques. So at least some of what has enabled Markita to sell her 15,500 boxes of chocolate swirls and peanut-butter delights must be natural talent. But some of her youthful insights—"You can't just chat," she told one interviewer, "you have to ask for the order"—sound far too professionally precocious to be the result simply of genes. Markita has clearly done some reading, or at least some serious thinking, on the subject. Introspectively, perhaps, she has trained herself.

Still, to those who remain unconvinced, I strongly recommend attending a seminar conducted by Rodney Queen. I had the pleasure of attending just such a seminar not long ago. Queen was introduced to the group as "a top-ranking sales executive" with IEC, a subsidiary of one of the prime cogs in the massive West Coast defense machine.

At first glance, Queen seemed perhaps the single most unlikely person to be teaching finesse to in-home salespeople, let alone to have actually been an exceptional in-home salesman himself. Rodney, you see, has a moderate-to-severe nervous tic. His conversation is marred by sporadic coughing, throat-clearing, and knuckle-cracking, and he seems unable to stand still for more than a second at a time. I confess that when he first strode to the front of the room, took his place at the podium, and began his distracting routine, I thought it might be a put-on, an ice breaker of the sort not uncommonly used to start intensive, all-day sales seminars. I don't think I was alone in this perception. In fact, nobody knew quite how to react. The room was soon filled with the telltale gagging sounds that occur when people are having great difficulty suppressing laughter they suspect might be somehow inappropriate. Undaunted, Queen launched into his story, and within minutes the audience was spellbound.

Seems Rodney had been summoned to Vietnam from the cotton fields of South Carolina in late 1967. After three years overseas, he returned from Southeast Asia physically intact but afflicted with a neurological disorder which, he assured us, was far worse than what we were presently witnessing.

Like many boys from the deep South, he went back to what

he'd done before the draft. As so often happens with people who go on to become selling greats, it was the sheer dismalness of the life-style he rediscovered in his Carolina home that made him determined to find something—*anything*—else to do with his life.

"I worked in a cotton mill," said Queen, in a broad, faltering drawl, "and when you work in a cotton mill, you develop pra-*sah*-slay one burning goal in life—to get the hell out of that cotton mill."

Eventually Rodney managed to scrape together a few bucks. Recruiting some co-workers from the mills, he launched himself in what he perceived was an industry whose time had come: the residential security business. For the first half year Queen sold little. (Actually, six months seems to be a fairly standard incubation period among super-salesmen. Tom Hopkins says it took him about that long just to realize he didn't know what he was doing.) "It would take me two hours to get through the same presentation most guys could make in maybe forty minutes," Queen said. But he persevered, learning both salesmanship and human nature the hard way—through trial and error. His speech improved somewhat. Sales picked up. Queen added more salespeople, with whom he shared the lessons of his front-line experience. Soon a number of Queen's one-time cotton-field cronies were making their sales calls in brand new Mercedeses. And within six years, Rodney was able to sell the fruits of his labor to his present employer, IEC, a subsidiary of NYSE-listed Figgie International, for a sum of money he characterizes as "almost obscene." Today, Rodney Queen resides in a sprawling home on Southern California's Lido Isle, a peninsula about which an admiring colleague asks rhetorically, "Is there a more expensive piece of property anywhere in the world?"

Sure, it's possible on one level to view Queen's Cinderella story as a *vindication* of the "born salesman" theory. His dogged sense of self-determination, coupled with his refusal to quickly give up in the face of early rejection, would seem to indicate the presence of innate salesmanship attributes. But it is equally possible that Rodney Queen's dedication to the cause was the result of simple stubbornness. Anyone who has ever been within earshot of an intransigent teenager understands that stubbornness and salesmanship are not the same thing. A good salesman is never stubborn; he knows not only when it's time to quit, but when it's in his long-term best interest to make short-term concessions.

In addition, Queen was something less than a sales natural. His initial presentations were flawed by countless breaches of the most basic tenets of good selling. This is not surprising, since nothing in Queen's background could be construed as presaging sales greatness. Indeed, given his speech impediment and employment history, he would probably strike you as more likely to end up as the kind of disoriented, disenfranchised, disillusioned Vietnam vet that TV news people delight in finding for special reports.

The saga of Rodney Queen, far from being relatively unique, is actually par for the course among top-selling salespeople. A good percentage of America's standout sales performers have come to their riches by way of rags, and publications of all description regularly feature their inspiring stories. If you want to examine a whole bunch of them at once, just pick up any copy of *Success* or *Entrepreneur*. Each issue typically contains a half dozen or so ads, masquerading as articles or profiles, that read pretty much as follows:

> (photo:) Man in bermuda shorts leaning on shiny new Mercedes Benz. Behind him is the white sandy beach of some exotic-looking island. Above his head is a sign that says THE ROAD TO SALES SUCCESS . . .
> (copy:) *This man's name is Tony Megabux. Nine hours ago, Tony was flat broke. Then he discovered The Formula. Now he drives this gorgeous Mercedes (his Rolls is in the shop), owns a villa in Majorca, . . . (and so on).*

The body of the text differs from case to case, of course. But the last few lines are almost always the same:

> . . . *and so if you'll send just $9.95 for Tony's new book,* The Secrets of the Secrets of Knowing All the Secrets . . .

Such advertisements imply that the relationship between Tony's financial triumph and the information being offered is a hard-and-fast reality. Even if the information itself is strong and sound, the premise—that you can easily duplicate Tony's success—is not infallible. But examined solely for their vivid, Horatio Alger narratives, ads like the above do demonstrate one important thing: While it is true that there are some traits that can be identified in successful salespeople *after the fact,* it is equally true that there is no way of predicting whether your teenage nephew Harold would make a good textile salesman. There are just too many variables. Too many people have defied the personality stereotypes and gone on to become superlative sales performers. Tom Hopkins was down and out at twenty and well on his way to being a millionaire at twenty-one—how can you know such things ahead of time?

Fine, but if All This Is True, Why Do So Many Salespeople— Particularly from the Old School—Seem So Much Alike?

I've done a lot of asking on this one, and have yet to hear a convincing answer. But I'd like to venture a theory of my own. (Okay, I'm no Joyce Brothers, but during my decade in sales in New York, I saw a lot of people develop, both professionally and personally.)

Picture yourself a novice salesperson in the world of selling as it was twenty or thirty years ago. Your new employer has no training program to speak of. This being the era of Vince Lombardi and all, there is an overwhelming, all-pervasive emphasis on The Bottom Line. Winning is the only thing. You've got to adapt—figure out what the hell you're going to do—and you've got to do it fast. Or else you're gone.

Ultimately, you do what baby ducks do when they're tossed into a foreign environment away from their mothers; you pattern yourself after the most dominant authority figure available. Which usually tends to be the star of the staff. By emulating him, you cope.

But there is a problem, and that problem is that the role model is just so thoroughly . . . bizarre. This isn't a simple case of pretending to be somebody you aren't for a few hours each day. It is a case of having to surrender most, if not all, of your sensitivities, of having to forego all that you've been taught, since childhood, about the golden rule—a case of having to

29

check your morals at the door as you punch your time card each morning. This is method acting of the most intense kind, a kind that demands an almost schizophrenic response. You have to come to work willing to do what has to be done to close the sale. And the only way to live with yourself after work is to convince yourself that the person who is doing all these nefarious things—the salesperson—isn't you. It is somebody else.

Psychologists will tell you that in any given case of untreated schizophrenia, the submissive side will eventually yield to the aggressive side, especially in stressful circumstances. And so sooner or later, the salesman becomes the alter ego he has adopted for selling purposes.

When I was a teenager, I heard that veteran horror-film actor Bela Lugosi capped off several years of erratic behavior by insisting on being buried in his Dracula cape. So it is with your veteran salesman and his acquired persona.

There is a term, *suspension of disbelief,* used principally by writers and dramatists. It is every fiction writer's dream to achieve a 100 percent suspension of disbelief, wherein every reader is so involved in the story that it is no longer just a story, but something that is unfolding in real life, right in the middle of the reader's living room. It's the same in sales work: You must be totally convincing to be successful. An ancient sales dictum poses, you can't sell it if you don't believe it. Since, in the pre-consumerist America of the first half of this century, many products were downright god-awful, and since the average presentation relied on a combination of cajolery, intimidation, and outright deceit, salespeople were put in the position of creating for themselves an artificially sanguine view of their product, their company, their sales pitch, their likelihood of changing the customer's life for the better. They had to rationalize; being (arguably) human, with feelings and sensitivities, they'd have found it hard to sleep at night unless they learned to see their product for what it wasn't.

Their disbelief, in short, needed to be suspended. Therefore, salespeople learned to fantasize (often spontaneously) all sorts of supportive data, anecdotal material, testimonial dialogue, and so forth. After a while, they got unbelievably good at it.

Case in point: Residents of New York City's Harlem seem to

either love or hate dogs. Those that love them, love them profoundly. "Strewn" is an overused word, but it can be said that the apartments of Harlem's dog lovers are literally strewn with dog pictures, dog novelties, dog toys, dog memorabilia, and dogs themselves. Somewhere along the line, an alert colleague of mine who sold mirrors got in the habit of telling uptown dog owners this ridiculous, made-up story about one of his "first customers," a poor, bedridden old lady who loved her dog so much that she installed a mirror in the hallway so she could enjoy watching her pet cavort around the small apartment. When the dog died, the story went, she continued to get pleasure out of that mirror, recalling how she used to watch him.

It was, of course, a terrible, mawkish tale, but it went over well, as expected, and the salesman made frequent use of it. Gradually, the dog acquired a breed (Great Dane, no less) and a name (Baron). The old woman got an address in a well-known middle-class Harlem housing development.

Before long, according to the salesman-cum-storyteller, his tale's imagery grew so vivid as to seem real. He was genuinely able to envision a skinny old recluse confined to her bed, staring lovingly into this mirror as her gargantuan pet gamboled about the living room, knocking over furniture.

Then something really strange happened. It dawned on him, as he told the tale for the umpteenth time one afternoon, that he actually *believed* it all; somewhere along the line he had forgotten that it was nothing but a fantastic, heart-rending lie.

That was the day he decided to get out of sales. "I figured if my sense of reality was shot to hell," he now observes wryly, "my sense of values was the next to go."

It's worth noting that the man who *has* lost his sense of values can be dangerous indeed when he falls in with the wrong crowd. He's liable to do anything, so atrophied are his natural inhibitions. After four or five years of total immersion in a medium that values only the bottom line—and insists on complete mental dedication to the cause—it's easy to lose sight of a sense of right and wrong.

A former sales manager for IBM once observed that placing a naïve young salesman into the environment of the typical home-improvement company was not unlike sentencing a petty car thief to Attica: The guy is bound to come out far worse than he went in. In days of yore, impressionable young sales apprentices entered the trade and soon fell under the wing of veteran salespeople who had found a way of rationalizing their qualms about screwing the customer.

Thus, selling created salespeople, not the other way around. The so-called sales personality was a result, not a cause, of an individual's sales activities.

If so many salesmen from the old school seem disconcertingly alike, it's probably because they've all followed that same surrogate duck for so long.

Recent studies, however, have confirmed that if there is indeed such a thing as a "sales type," it is not a single thing, but one that embraces several categories of people. As much as sixty years ago, in fact, psychologist Edward Strong concluded on the basis of an exhaustive survey that even assorted sales managers couldn't come to a consensus about what types of individuals were likely to make outstanding reps. Today, with the diversity and complexity of products and services, the problem of isolating common denominators that unite the broad universe of sales professionals has, if anything, grown more acute. Basic personality differences are reflected in a variety of subtle ways. High-tech salespeople, for example, seem to enjoy working for companies that have regular hours, unlike their freewheeling, devil-may-care counterparts at home-improvement or retail establishments. (Though there is a tautological aspect to this. Few high-tech companies have irregular hours, so you'd be hard pressed to find an exception. It's a bit like saying, "Frogs enjoy being frogs." It's nice to know, but what choice do they have?)

The business community is replete with whole categories of exceptions to the "general rules" about salespeople's personalities. Bob Swartz, who trains telephone-sales reps for Colonial Corporation, a nationwide ad specialty firm, theorizes that many of his charges are living proof of that old prophecy about the meek inheriting the earth.

"Lots of them are overcompensators," says Swartz, "gentle souls, shy people, and other assorted misfits" for whom the telephone is a shield of anonymity, "an opportunity to express pent-up emotions they wouldn't dare vent in public." Swartz goes on to say that if there were such a thing as a Confidence Quotient (CQ), similar to the IQ, he might arbitrarily call the number 100 normal for ordinary people, and 125 normal for the general sales population. Telephone solicitors might have a CQ of just 75 in person, but hand them a trimline and that figure zooms to 150 or more. Obviously, these Jekyll-Hyde characters don't fare too well at face-to-face job interviews. They are routinely beaten out for available sales positions by experienced direct salespeople whose CQs hang at a constant 125—salespeople they could have easily outperformed had they been given a chance to strut their stuff. For this reason, Swartz will often grant prospective salespeople a live telephone audition as an adjunct to, or in lieu of, the standard interview. There really isn't much product knowledge involved in Swartz's line of work, after all; how much do you need to know about ballpoint pens imprinted with someone's name and phone number?

The truth is that most of us have within ourselves the power to sell. But most of us, for better or worse, are never exposed to the vehicle, the catalyst that shifts those latent skills into high gear.

The effort to uncover that catalyst has sent many major sales organizations to the doorsteps of the growing number of research firms who perform sophisticated sales-aptitude testing. The services of such companies are deemed indispensible by some sales executives. (It's also nice to have a scapegoat; if you hire a guy on your own expertise, and he turns out to be a loser, it's your fault; whereas if you hired him on the advice of a consulting firm employed by someone at a higher level of management, then you don't look so bad.)

"People razzle-dazzle me in an interview," L. "Fritz" Covillo, senior vice-president at Denver's United Foods, told *Inc.* Voicing a genuine and probably universal concern, Covillo added, "Good vibes are okay, but how do I get inside a guy's head?"

Like others in his position, Covillo turned to Personality Dynamics Inc. of Princeton, New Jersey. PDI's sales-profile exams sprang forth from a series of surveys performed during the sixties by the firm's president, Herbert Greenberg, and his wife, Jeanne. The Greenberg surveys revealed that the road to sales success was not paved with deficient DNA. While they were at it, the Greenbergs laid waste to all of the industry's most revered hiring criteria, including age, expeience, sex, and educational background.

A more recent study conducted by Xerox's XLS subsidiary seemingly corroborated most of the Greenbergs' findings, although here the interpretation of the data was a bit different. XLS preferred to concentrate on the (seemingly self-evident?) fact that a person's performance during the sales call was the only true factor in his success or failure at selling. The XLS study went on to pose that the better equipped the salespeople were going into the sales call, the better they'd perform. Not a shocking conclusion, when you consider that Xerox is in the business of teaching salesmanship. It wouldn't do to have people come away thinking that sales talent was something you either had or you didn't.

Getting back to PDI, Greenberg took the results of his studies and formulated a series of questions that would function as a litmus test for sales ability. Every effort was made to ensure the test's 181 questions against transparency. The test's approach to the subject is oblique, in an effort to weed out those who are simply trying to land a job and will lie about themselves in order to do it. (Which is why Greenberg says he will not ask a candidate, "Do you want to be a salesperson or a forest ranger?") The test costs $125, and is evaluated and reported to the client company within one working day.

The tests have yielded some intriguing, felicitous results. Typical was the case of the career accountant for a large insurance company who suddenly decided he wanted to be a salesman. Management scoffed. Accountant types are considered your least likely prospects for becoming top-flight salespeople. Still, the accountant persisted, and was eventually given Greenberg's test. To the astonishment of all, he tested among the top of the class in sales aptitude. He was relieved of his number-crunching duties, handed a briefcase (and, perhaps, a plaid suit?), and dispatched into the field, where he revealed himself to be a top producer.

So much for the stereotypes.

•   •   •

Based on the above, and a good body of additional evidence, the fathers of TNS threw out most of the old notions and started anew. Recognizing that salespeople were not necessarily "born that way," but could indeed be trained to follow a new set of instructions, TNS theorists set out to synthesize the attributes they had discovered in themselves. Their avowed goal was to equip salespeople who lacked such qualities as "niceness," "rapport," or "helpfulness" with adequate amounts of same.

It wasn't a matter of teaching their charges to fake it. Rather, the idea was to provide salespeople with a method for overcoming innate deficiencies by actually assimilating the desired qualities from without. In the end, the properly trained salespeople would feel perfectly comfortable with their new-found behavior, not as though it were something they'd learned, but as though it were something they'd *become*. A new way of life they'd discovered. A brand new regimen for interacting with people. A religion.

It's not really as contrived as it sounds. In fact, there's a perfectly good precedent from the realm of modern medicine. One of the hottest movements in contemporary science has researchers striving to simulate naturally occurring chemicals for use in people who lack required amounts of substances like insulin, or the clotting factor, or hormones, or what-have-you. The beneficiaries of these medical breakthroughs can't tell the difference between the ersatz and the real thing. A diabetic on synthetic insulin, for example, feels the same as the person whose pancreas is putting out the proper amount to begin with. Subjectively, it's as if there's nothing wrong with him.

In the same way, the goal was not to get the new salesman to feign niceness, but to actually become nicer; not to get him to pretend to a cooperative spirit, but to induce him to become cooperative; not to get him to suppress his desire to push people, but to believe that pushing is not only ethically wrong, but financially counterproductive. And what would be the salesman's motivation for adopting this new, wonderfully philanthropic approach to life? Why, the best motivation(s) in the world! Money! Power! Esteem! *Success!* Reduced to a single pregnant sentence, the philosophy behind TNS is this:

The most effective way to achieve your selfish aims is simply to help other people achieve theirs.

Before any of this could happen, however, TNS theologians had to wean the sales population from its dependence on the multitude of bad habits that were so deeply ingrained—the ruses and abuses and Hobbesian assumptions that had long pervaded the world of sales.

The next chapter will give you some small idea of what they were up against.

Sales Miscellany

World's Greatest Car Salesman, according to Guinness:
*Carmen Koosa, who once sold 3,892 cars and trucks
in a single year. Not surprisingly,
the vehicles were Japanese imports (Datsuns).*

2

Shticks and Stones

"The Bad Old Days"

Though the tendency is to associate selling's most egregious abuses with the lower levels of the trade, until quite recently no branch of sales was truly exempt. Not that the large firms trained their sales reps to be dishonest. It's just that those in charge of recruiting invariably looked for people with A Track Record. The typical salesman in heavy industry did not begin his career as a sales trainee in that field, but rather worked his way up through the ranks to the "major leagues," dabbling in shtick-ridden realms like encyclopedias and kitchen cabinets along the way. (This is far less true today; in recognition of how things used to be, many major companies prefer to hire novices—people who don't have scores of bad habits to unlearn.)

As a salesman made his steady ascent up the professional ladder, he took along his assortment of perfidious ploys—and his bad attitude. Like herpes in a singles condo, malfeasance quickly spread throughout the ranks, infecting everybody. Especially since the most abrasive salespeople were usually the ones who exuded that heavy, if specious, aura of success.

You must remember, too, that twenty years ago the walls of sexism had yet to crumble, and masculine/feminine stereotypes were still very much in evidence throughout the business world. An aloof, quasi-belligerent attitude toward the customer was considered masculine, and thus admirable, by the largely male national sales force. The salesman who openly courted his customers' favor—who actually admitted that he considered people's feelings!—was considered something of a "wimp." Hard-driving, hard-drinking, give-'em-hell types were the ones men emulated, the ones women lusted after, and—ironically—the ones America's largely male buying audience wanted to do business with. The perception of the world in general was a rugged, almost atavistic one. Nice guys finished last. Real men didn't even know what the hell quiche was, let alone eat it. Abstemious, bookish types—the kind who ordered seltzer at the typical three-martini lunch—were viewed with suspicion by their peers (as they still are, in some quarters). The customers, therefore, were at least indirectly reinforcing the image and behavior of the salespeople with whom they dealt.

So in a very real sense, the old-style salesman was not altogether to blame for his transgressions. He was a reflection of the biases and perceptions of his customer base. The same is true today. To the extent that salespeople have changed, it is largely because the world has changed.

Then again, some things never change. When California financial-planning impresario Charles Morse was arrested not long ago for selling bogus tax shelters, several of his compatriots observed, quite correctly, that people like Morse would never get very far were it not for the avarice of their customers. Greed, egos, and excessive insecurities (which most of us are ever ready to indulge) not only play into the hands of shady salesmen, but make it possible for them to exist in the first place.

Of course, the dramatic change in selling that forms the premise of this book has made much of this argument academic. Today's customers want sincerity, and so they get sincerity. It may be, in many cases, a kind of fast-food sincerity: mass-produced, portion-controlled, shaped, flaked, and reformed. But it seems to satisfy, all the same.

Nonetheless, an understanding of the present is difficult to achieve without an understanding of the past. Some sort of look backward is called for, at this point, to set the stage for what follows.

There are myriad ways of approaching the subject of what, exactly, constituted The Old Salesmanship. We could talk at some length about a whole insidious catalog of ideas and shticks. We could talk about:

• *The Overage System.* This was a popular payment schedule in which the salesman's commission rate was pegged to the amount he was able to charge above the arbitrary "book price" of his product. The bonus rate on these premium amounts was often two or three times the regular commission rate, and not uncommonly ran up to 50 percent. So, hypothetically, a salesman who sold you a piece of office furniture for its regular price of $500 might earn a 10 percent commission, or $50. But another salesman who sold your friend the same piece of furniture for $600 would earn 10 percent of the base price, plus half of the "overage," for a total commission of $100—fully double what the first salesman earned. The overage system, incidentally, was a compelling rebuttal against the argument, often put forth by sales apologists, that disdain for the customer was specific to certain salespeople, rather than an institutionalized phenomenon.

The overage commission system spawned a variety of price-gouging tactics, including

• *The Jack It Up, Back It Down* approach. In essence, this was simply the practice of promoting a discount that wasn't a discount. The salesman artificially inflated the price beforehand to compensate for any reduction he may have found it convenient to offer as an inducement to buy. Sometimes the discount would be mentioned up front. More often, it was offered as a concession if the customer balked at the price. The salesman's hope, of course, was that the customer wouldn't balk, thus affording the salesman the opportunity of pocketing a goodly portion of the overage.

This is one tactic we really shouldn't discuss in the past tense. Even as we speak, manufacturers knowingly keep the ruse alive by providing their merchandise with list prices whose sole use, in the real world, seems to be as a starting point from which to offer illusory discounts.

Take the case of a sweater marked "Original list $85, now

just $69.95." The boutique, after all, pays only a fraction of the manufacturer's list price. Probably half, or less. So to whom was the sweater "originally" $85? And it doesn't only happen with sweaters. Two years ago in California an auto dealer was accused of advertising "fabulous" discounts on cars that were, in fact, being sold for *more* than the manufacturer's sticker price. So whether you're in the market for a wardrobe or for wheels, you'd best be wary.

• *Kiting.* If you're going to rip off the customer, why not your boss as well? Such was the rationale behind kiting, in which the salesman supplemented his income with deposit money and other funds collected on his employer's behalf.

Although kiting didn't start out being anticustomer, it was likely to evolve in that direction for a very simple reason. Sooner or later—usually sooner—the missing funds had to be accounted for, and there were basically only two methods of doing it:

Method #1: As in a con man's Ponzi scheme, the salesman could use the money collected on his next order to replace monies expropriated from his last orders. But this solution obviously had its drawbacks. Eventually the salesman's indebtedness to his company would exceed the amounts being collected in dribs and drabs from new customers, and the Day of Reckoning would be at hand. Thus was born

Method #2: The salesman could "lose" the borrowed amounts by recording them as discounts off the price, rather than as true deposits. A job meant to sell for $5,500 could be sold for $6,000. The salesman would take a $500 deposit, record the order in his log at its correct price, and Presto! A fast half grand of underground income . . . or, alternatively, enough to cover the shortfall in deposits from Method #1. Provided that the customer didn't cancel and demand his money back (and remember, in the bad old days companies were obliged neither to accept cancellations nor to refund deposits, though the larger firms usually did so voluntarily), the customer end of the transaction would probably never come to light. I knew one salesman who proudly claimed that his income from Method #2 kiting surpassed his income from legitimate sources.

• *The 'Look, I Came All This Way' Close, and related forms of coercion.* Hard as it may be to imagine today, it's possible that in the history of professional selling, more sales were closed with variations on the following theme than in any other manner:

Salesman looks at procrastinating customer with mixture of exasperation and disgust and says, "Look, I came all this way just to see you, and now I've spent the past hour showing you my product. Tell ya what. If you take it today, I'll give it to you for a special price. But this is good today only. If I have to make a second trip back here next week or next month or even tomorrow, all bets are off."

Why customers knuckled under to such blatantly self-serving argumentation is hard to say. But for decades—perhaps centuries—this particular line was a mainstay at all levels of the sales universe. It was a hallmark of the "strong closer" that customers grudgingly admired and competing firms would bend over backward to hire. It was also, in its own obnoxious way, an eloquent statement of the mentality Willy Loman concealed behind his saccharin smile.

We could talk in depth about all of these things. We could talk about how kiting field reps drove more than one small sales outfit to bankruptcy. We could talk about how salespeople struggling to meet quotas took it upon themselves to order mass quantities of product on behalf of their clients.

But in the end, nothing so defined the spirit and slant of the old salesmanship as the trade's crafty response to the momentous piece of consumer legislation known as the Federal Truth-in-Lending Act.

This response—the blithe perversion of a federal law—was the ultimate transgression. More than that, it was an apt barometer of just how far the street salesman, who had always set the tone for the industry, was willing to go before finally giving up his wicked, wicked ways.

•   •   •

Fun and Games with the Federal Truth-in-Lending Act

In July of 1968, the federal government enacted a landmark piece of legislation most notable for its inclusion of the now-familiar "cooling-off period": an interim, lasting three business days from the date of an order, during which that order would be fully cancelable, provided that certain conditions had been met.

The efficacy of the new law hinged on something called a recision notice. The recision notice was designed primarily to thwart the diabolical ingenuity of door-to-door peddlers, who at the time were concentrating their efforts in nouveau-riche ghetto areas, selling everything from monogrammed crumb sweepers to color-enhanced posters of frame 313 of the Zapruder film.*

Basically, the recision notice set forth a pair of main stipulations. First, that no order placed in one's home becomes legally binding until midnight of the third business day after the signing of the invoice; and secondly, that during this cooling-off period, the customer's deposit is always refundable in full, provided the customer agrees to return, *in its original condition,* any property that may have been given him by the sales rep at the time of purchase.

Truth-in-Lending specified that each and every customer must be given a recision notice. The law did not, however, specify that the customer must be aware he had been given the notice. From this subtle loophole sprang an earnest competition among sales pros aimed at devising the most clever and colorful way of secretly slipping the customer his recision notice. This may have been one of the few instances in recorded history when businessmen chose to comply with the letter, rather than the spirit, of a new consumer law.

Through the sales grapevine came the idea of writing a short note of personal thanks to each customer on the blank side of the notice. The notice would then be stapled to the last page of the customer's copy of the invoice, so that the salesman's little tribute faced up, and the preprinted side did not. Thus affixed, the warning would live out its three days of import in silent repose, camouflaged by the salesman's warm sentiments.

Of course, as time went by, and salespeople had a chance to really address the task at hand, this primitive system was im-

*Abraham Zapruder was the amateur photographer who happened to be standing by, with movie camera rolling, as President John F. Kennedy was assassinated in Dallas. Frame 313 shows the fatal head shot in graphic detail.

proved upon. One fellow at a Manhattan cabinet firm is credited with suggesting that the salesman fold the notice into a tiny, neat square, staple it to the customer's guarantee forms (which, in home-improvement circles of that era, typically didn't guarantee anything except that the customer would wind up footing the bill if anything went wrong), and drop both into an envelope. Sealing the envelope, he would admonish the buyer:

"Now put this with your important papers right away . . . don't leave it around because you'll hate yourself if [whatever it was] needs service someday and you can't find your guarantee."

This approach couldn't be used with everybody. Sharp buyers immediately became suspicious at such behavior. But sharp buyers knew their rights, anyway, without being told. It was your less sophisticated, more trusting types—the kinds of people for whom T-in-L was designed—who made the mistake of assuming that the salesperson was simply looking out for their own best interests, and wound up getting snookered.

Credit buyers had always been especially vulnerable to chicanery, owing, probably, to the capricious outlook of people who customarily use credit for major (and many minor) purchases. Salespeople will tell you that the inveterate credit buyer is someone who believes tomorrow will never come.

It may have been put best by Stan Slaughter, a salesman at the company where I worked. Reflecting on his wife's cavalier spending habits, Stan said, "I've come to the conclusion she honestly thinks if she can charge it, it's free."

Because credit allows people like Stan's wife to playact— because it allows them to "borrow" a life-style they couldn't possibly have afforded in those Pleistocene days before plastic— most of them take their credit ratings very seriously.

And therein lies their Achilles' heel.

Granted, the last ten or fifteen years have been a banner time for consumers. Between Truth-in-Lending, Fair Credit Billing, Fair Credit Reporting, and the flood of other legislation passed in their wake, credit users acquired a boxcar full of brand-new rights. They were given access to their once-secret credit files; they were given an orderly procedure for the removal of outdated or incorrect information from that file; they could now place in said file their own version of the story in cases where disputes over credit data could not be resolved to their satisfaction.

Yet, what all these new laws, and the publicity attendant to their passage, did best of all was heighten public awareness —and fear—of the credit bureau: that faceless, microprocessor-laden repository of data on people's life-styles, bill-paying histories, and, some believe, use of the missionary position. (This isn't as far-fetched as it sounds. One salesman I interviewed had some trouble early in his career because of a sodomy arrest that appeared in his file. What had actually occurred was that during his late teens he was caught in a motel having sexual intercourse with a hooker who happened to be above and astride him. Since any variation on the basic, man-on-top position was considered a crime against nature, he was booked not only on the prostitution-related offense, but on a sodomy count as well. The case was eventually dismissed, he would later joke, "for lack of hard evidence.")

If people begin to twitch at the mention of federal law, they absolutely have seizures when the conversation turns to credit ratings. Over the years, salespeople have cultivated the fear of credit bureaus in anticipation of having to use that fear one day as a weapon. Witness the phenomenal success of routines like the one known as the Jersey Shuffle.

This little piece of business, named for the state in which TRW, the electronics conglomerate, once maintained its eastern regional headquarters, was taught to me some years back by a sage old veteran of the kitchen-cabinet wars. He was standing in the phone booth adjacent to mine on Central Park West, scribbling in an address book while I thrashed things out with an obviously disenchanted customer.

As the intensity of my telephone debate increased, I noticed this fellow leaning closer to the glass partition, as though vicariously absorbed in the action, like an onlooker at a heavyweight title fight. At first, when it was clear the battle was going my way, he smiled and nodded rapidly, urging me on. But as the momentum shifted and defeat became inevitable, my sponsor was resigned, impassive, a tight-lipped ring war-horse watching his prized protégé go down for the count. Afterward, as I stood there glassy-eyed and despondent, he introduced himself and shared the benefit of his reprobate know-how.

"Cancellation, huh?" he began.

"Yup," I replied with a shrug.

"Tell me something—what kind of deposit did she give?"

"Two hundred fifty bucks."

"No, I mean what *kind* of deposit—was it cash, check, charge, what?"

When I told him she'd used her VISA (then Bankameri-card), his face lit up.

"Listen to me," he said slowly, his voice and manner projecting all the wisdom of the ages, "here's what you do. You call this lady back—what was her name—?"

"Romano, Frances Romano."

"Italiano? Good.* You call this Romano back and tell her she can cancel if she wants, but you're gonna have to make a report to the credit bureau."

I gulped. "I'm gonna do what?"

"The credit bureau. You're gonna report her to the credit bureau. You're gonna put a derog"—common shorthand for a derogatory remark—"in her TRW."

"But we can't do that." I was nonplussed.

"Of course you can't. But she doesn't know that. Or at least, she's probably not sure whether you can or not. And even if she does know that you got no legal right to do that, she also knows she's gonna have one helluva time clearing something like that up if your company goes ahead and makes a negative report anyway."

"But suppose she goes to her lawyer?"

He exhaled deeply, impatiently, shook his head, and fixed me with his best "Have you got a lot to learn, shmuck" look.

"When did she place the order?" he finally snorted.

"Tuesday."

"Okay, now it's three o'clock Friday, right? She's on her last business day, right? And tomorrow's the weekend, so she knows

*According to stereotypes perpetuated by outside salespeople, Italians were one of the easiest ethnic groups to hoodwink—just a notch above blacks, and about on a par with West Indians. Ranked at the top of scale—hardest to screw—supposedly were Jews, Asian Indians, and people of Japanese descent, not necessarily in that order.

she hasn't got time to run to a lawyer, right? She's got to make a decision, and fast." Very theatrically, he withdrew a gold cigarette case from his jacket—the symbolism was not lost on me—lit a cigarette, took a long, confident drag. "Just do like I tell you," he lectured. "You put the onus on her. Let her worry about it. If she's got even the slightest bit of desire for what you're selling, she'll give in. She'll convince herself. They always do, nine times out of ten."

He began to walk off, then turned around to see me just standing there, rather lamely.

"Go ahead, kid, do it," he yelled. "Take it from me, it works. Nine times outta ten. Scares the shit out of 'em."

Now it so happens that contrary to ethnic stereotypes, Frances Romano was a sharp cookie. She called my bluff, and I had to acquiesce. But I must admit to using the routine many times after, with at least a fifty-fifty success rate. More recently, in the course of preparing this book, I asked old sales friends about the ruse, and their experiences corroborated my own.

"If there's a universal lesson to be learned from this," says Murray Klein, a West Coast sales trainer, "it's that you can almost never go wrong having balls." Given the constraints of polite society, Klein adds, the worst that can usually happen to the speaker of brash words is that he'll be forced to eat them.

The Strange Case of the Vanishing Annual Percentage Rate

Salespeople of all generations are united by the knowledge that the filling out of credit papers is the most treacherous moment in selling. An experienced salesman tries everything he can think of to defuse the situation by taking the customer's mind off what is about to occur. It's difficult because they typically become engrossed in the cold details of the preparatory paper work. They sit there, hands folded in their laps, witnesses to the unsettling spectacle of dire calculations. They catch glimpses of columns of numbers in the ominous little rate booklet, and they envision their paychecks being sucked from their wallets. They picture a six-foot-nine-inch hulk with a broken nose and a two-by-four menacing their children in the schoolyard because "your daddy didn't pay up yet for October, kid!" A catalog of all previous credit purchases that failed to live up to expectations flashes before them. When it comes time for them to approve the agreement, the husband looks at the wife, the wife looks at the husband, and through eye contact alone, they devise some ad hoc pretext for not going ahead with the sale. The word on the street is that the ordinary salesman probably loses between 10 and 15 percent of his sales as a direct consequence of uncertainties that crop up at this point.

The flurry of consumer legislation in the early seventies compounded this problem by decreeing that all retail installment contracts must present a painstakingly thorough numerical description of the contemplated purchase, including two items in particular: the Annual Percentage Rate (APR) and the Deferred Payment Price (DPP).

The former, of course, refers to the rate at which the customer's purchase is being financed. The latter is simply an aggregate statement of cost, counting principal, interest, issuer's fees, and insurance charges—i.e., the Bottom Line. Credit papers printed in the wake of Truth-in-Lending and its companion laws contained highlighted blank boxes for the insertion of these and several other important numbers.

And blank those boxes would stay until after unsuspecting customers had been induced to affix their signature to the bottom of the document. Credit buyers may not be financial wizards, but one needn't be Milton Friedman to know that a 26 percent APR is awfully high.

How did salespeople get away with inducing people to sign half-blank contracts? Says one: "I relied on my gut feeling that nobody ever went broke underestimating the backbone or the intelligence of the average American consumer. Seven times out of ten, I wasn't even challenged."

Occasionally, when someone would surprise this salesman by asking about those suspicious little omissions, he'd say, quite casually, "Our bank"—he always said "bank," despite the fact that much of his financing went through credit sources like Household Finance—"is in the process of revising its rates downward [ha!], and I wouldn't want you to commit to a higher rate than what you'd be entitled to by the time this reaches my office." Seldom did anyone push the issue.

Actually, comparatively few companies had *official* policies that sanctioned shady procedures like those just outlined. Most sales outfits maintained at least a superficial conformity with the various consumer laws, which put sales reps in the unenviable position of carrying on their little games without management's formal consent (if not, strictly speaking, without management's knowledge). I suppose it's similar to what your average CIA operative is up against. The Unwritten Code said, Do it if you think you can get away with it, but if you get caught, we never heard of you. Thus, retail installment contracts needed to arrive at one's office completely filled in, and free of apparent hanky-panky.

Take the case of the shop-at-home salesman who has been ordered by his unflappable consumer to fill in all the blanks. Unaccustomed as he is to such truculence on the part of the clientele, this salesman might become so flustered that he accidentally scans the wrong column and, say, writes down an APR that is five or six points lower than what his company actually offers. He must then rectify the problem before the contract reaches the accounting department. Because erasures and overstrikes on credit papers are not legally acceptable, careless salespeople—and how very careless they seemed to be in days of yore—were often forced to redo entire contracts. Obviously, this would also entail redoing the customer's signature, otherwise known as forgery.

Outside the motion-picture industry, forgery is generally thought of as a pretty serious crime, but there's a lighter side to it as well. One of the cutest true stories concerns the bedraggled home-improvement rep who returns home well past midnight after writing two large orders in a single Tuesday evening. Both required financing. Despite his exhaustion and the lateness of the hour, he sits down at his kitchen table to fill in all the blanks. Naturally, he screws up both contracts and has to rewrite and re-sign them, after which he lumbers to the corner mailbox and sends them on their merry way.

Several days later, his telephone rings. It is a representative of the finance company, eager to know how Mr. Smith's signature managed to get at the bottom of Mr. Jones's contract, and vice versa. Thinking quickly—for he is sloppy, not feebleminded—the salesman says that both Smith and Jones had been given an estimate previously; each sale was supposedly closed during the course of a follow-up phone call, at which time arrangements were made to finalize the deals in person on that fateful Tuesday. To expedite things, the salesman continues, he had prepared the contracts beforehand on his kitchen table (a half-truth, anyway) but inadvertently switched them when he got back into the respective buyers' homes. The deal having already been firmed up over the phone, neither customer bothered to read the contracts carefully; they just signed on the dotted line without looking to see whose name was up top.

The loan officer is skeptical, but he decides not to pursue it. (Probably a case of "Let him who is without sin," etc.) The salesman promises to straighten things out—which he does, once again on his kitchen table, later that afternoon.

A salesman I knew once used a similar story to explain to one of our bookkeepers how he came to charge one customer $128 in tax on a $550 order, and another customer just $44 tax on a $1,600 order. He later confided that he had transposed the amounts while attempting to rewrite the invoices in his car, on the shoulder of Long Island's Southern State Parkway.

Certainly one of the cutest Truth-in-Lending–inspired gimmicks was the Showroom Special. The Showroom Special packed a double barreled whallop, in that it not only dissuaded people from canceling, but it was a marvelous tool for getting them to buy in the first place. Such was its popularity by the waning days of 1975 that then attorney general Louie Lefkowitz is said to have personally petitioned Congress for an amendment to the law.

You see, the Showroom Special evolved from careless wording in Truth-in-Lending, wording that implied that the three-day hold was inapplicable to orders placed outside the buyer's home. If you went to a showroom to buy the product, then you were denied all Truth-in-Lending protections, including the recision notice. This was thought to be true regardless of whether or not a given business derived most of its revenues from its shop-at-home activities. (I'm not trying to be cagey with *my* wording, either. As recently as press time, I still couldn't get a straight answer from assorted government spokespeople regarding the law's final interpretation.)

Thus, a sharp salesman would tell his in-home customer, Mr. Dippo, that there was this fantabulous sale going on at the showroom, and Dippo—the lucky sonofabitch!—was entitled to participate, if he wished, right there in the comfort of his own living room. "It's a one-day special," the salesman would add matter-of-factly, so Dippo would have to make his decision to-day, of course. Of course.

Needless to say, the company was having no such sale. If only because, in many cases, the company had no such show-room. But people fell for it in droves. Factories were awash in orders covered with the phrase SHOWROOM SPECIAL!!

When the customer had his inevitable second thoughts, he'd be curtly informed that since he'd made his purchase under "showroom conditions," he did not enjoy standard cancellation privileges. Should an argument ensue, with the customer hinting at legal recourse, the salesman would threaten to claim under oath that the order had, indeed, been placed at the showroom. Not infrequently, his sales manager would get on the line to back him up. Meantime, as the antagonists continued their my-word-against-yours debate, seventy-two hours ticked away, and the issue became academic.

Fortunately for today's general public, the showroom special is all but extinct. Its primary exponents, the smaller home-im-provement firms, perished in the wake of late-seventies con-sumerism and early eighties belt tightening. The surviving organizations had always adhered pretty much to the letter of the law in the first place. Whether this was so because of any intrinsic moral convictions, or because these larger companies were simply too visible to get away with much, is a moot ques-tion.

One Truth-in-Lending Shtick That Even the Showroom Special Couldn't Rival (Complete with Annotations)

The following ruse was told to me by one of my acquain-tances in the New York custom-drapery trade during the early seventies. It is preserved here as close to verbatim as my mem-ory permits, because it is a masterpiece of misleading rhetoric that serves to underscore the devious methods of selling in that era.

Let us suppose that your name is Irma Vasquez, and that you've awakened the Monday after the Friday of the salesman's visit with a severe case of buyer's remorse. Apparently, you have also taken the trouble to open your envelope and unfold the square. I've numbered the salesman's replies so that we can analyze them afterward.

> IRMA: Mr. Smith, I got to thinking over the weekend, and I'm really sorry for bringing you out here and all, but I just don't know if I can spend that much money for drapes.
> SALESMAN: Aw gee, that's a shame, Mrs. Vasquez, but there's really not a whole lot I can do about it now.[1]
> IRMA (*taken aback*): But Mr. Smith, it says right here on this paper—
> SALESMAN: Yes, I know, that's where the problem comes in. According to the Federal Truth-in-Lending Act, I can't give you more time than you're entitled to, and you've already used that up. It's too late to cancel.[2]
> IRMA (*confused*): But it says "business days"—
> SALESMAN: That's true, and as you know, we're open for business both Saturday and Sunday, so those are business days for our purposes. It's completely legal.[3]
> IRMA: All right, but even so, that's only two days—
> SALESMAN (*very patiently*): Okay, I could see where there'd be some confusion here. The notice says that you have *until midnight* of the third business day to cancel. What they really mean is that you have two full business days, and then only until the very beginning of the third business day. So your time actually expired as of midnight *Sunday,* last night. It's terrible, the tricky way they word these federal laws, isn't it? [*Shifting gears:*] So, would you like to put this on Master Charge, or will you still be paying cash?[4]

The storyteller claimed that after a bit more obfuscatory sparring, the customer finally relented. She put the drapes on Master Charge, and they were delivered the end of that same week. (No sense risking any further changes of heart.) Ironically, the salesman who relayed this story claims that some months later he received a nice little note from the customer, in which she told him how much she loved the drapes, and thanked him for not allowing her to cancel. (Salespeople insist this happens with surprising frequency.) But that, of course, is beside the point. What *is* the point is the manipulation that got the woman to unchange her mind; let us, then, take a look at what may be one of the more misleading arguments ever put forward by a salesman.

[1] The familiar "it's out of my hands" approach. By meeting the customer's initial protest with a quick, straightforward dismissal of her case, the salesman has attempted to thwart her before she develops momentum, to cut her off at the pass, so to speak. The reasoning is based on the grade-school scenario in which you'd return to your seat after getting a second milk only to find the school bully ensconced in your chair. As soon as you'd ever so politely start to say something, he'd stand up and growl, "You wanna make somethin' of it?" You wouldn't, of course. He'd sit back down, while you skulked off to enjoy your milk with the rest of the losers.

[2] The salesman has cleverly inverted the emphasis of Truth-in-Lending—"I can't give you more time than you're entitled to"—as if to imply the bill was conceived for the businessman's benefit. Most old-school salespeople admit that it was great fun using the law as a bludgeon against the very people it was drafted to protect. Says Tim, an elder statesman who claims to have since reformed, "I wish I had a nickel for every time I myself looked a customer in the eye and said, 'I'd love to give you your money back, but *the law ties my hands.*'"

Furthermore, he explains, the very notion of federal law has heavy subliminal overtones to it. A good many customers will feel intimidated and just take the salesman at his word. After all, the few federal laws with which your average citizen must contend—tax laws, for example—are not held in high esteem.

"It's something to see," says Tim. "Just mention the Federal Truth-in-Lending Act"—he lets his voice drift down to an ominous baritone that brings to mind Ernie Anderson, the throat behind ABC's promos for *The Luuuuuvvvvv Boat*—"to most people, and they say to themselves, Shit, that's where I get off."

While we're on the subject of putting federal consumer legislation to perverse use, I should add that apart from the casual anticonsumer activities of individual salespeople, there was also an industry-wide backlash against Truth-in-Lending at the corporate level. Prior to the bill's passage, many major sales organizations had cancellation policies that gave new meaning to the word lenient. Great Eastern Home Improvements, a large general-contracting firm headquartered in Nassau County, Long Island, accepted an occasional cancellation from customers even as the company's work crew stood perched on the customer's roof, ready to do the job. (Great Eastern's own roof eventually fell in; the company went belly up in the mid-seventies.) All this changed with the implementation of Truth-in-Lending. Driven by a visceral, what's-good-for-the-goose fury, top brass at countless firms began abiding stringently by the new law's three-day language. In view of this retributive anger, many salespeople remain in serious disagreement about whether T-in-L actually helped or hurt the American consumer.

[3] A bold-faced lie. It wouldn't matter if the company were open twenty-four hours a day, 365 days a year. Saturdays, Sundays, and recognized holidays are never counted in the three-day hold.

[4] This little piece of verbal legerdemain deserves an explanation. To the best of anyone's knowledge, it was invented by Manny X., a hulk of a fellow who worked for a number of shop-at-home concerns during the mid- to late seventies.

Shortly before Truth-in-Lending was enacted, Manny had received a cancellation notice from his auto-insurance company. It read, give or take, "Your insurance is hereby terminated as of 12:01 A.M. on Tuesday, March 12." The notice went on to say that Manny could keep his policy in force by settling up before the stated date and time.

Like scores of others who've read such notices in cursory fashion, Manny assumed he had all day until midnight Tuesday to pay. So when he casually sauntered into his local Allstate office at 4:55 on the afternoon of the twelfth, he discovered that he'd missed the boat. He was not seven hours and six minutes early, but rather sixteen hours and fifty-four minutes too late, since 12:01 A.M. on the twelfth actually occurs the moment after midnight on the eleventh.

Like all good salespeople, Manny regarded the cancellation of his auto insurance as a learning experience. When the format of the recision notice was shown to him, he quickly saw a practical application for his misfortune, to the dismay of Irma Vasquez and thousands of other shop-at-home customers. Even though Congress clearly intended to give consumers three full business days, right up to the moment between the third and fourth days, an amazing number of people can be convinced otherwise. Bart Conlan, a salesman with Electrolux, often made use of the following analogy in his efforts to help customers get the wrong idea: He'd compare the phrase on the notice, "midnight of the third business day," with the popular cliché, "dawn of a new day."

If you argue the point long enough, the two phrases start to sound alike. At the very least, the one from the recision notice starts to sound hopelessly ambiguous.

• • •

When a customer proved to be of sterner stuff than Mrs. Vasquez, the salesman might have resorted to a second Truth-in-Lending scam. This one involved the aforementioned provision of law requiring cancellation-minded customers to return company property in its original condition.

The law is quite vague about what, exactly, constitutes company property, but it does state that whatever that property may be, it does not officially belong to the customer until after the transaction has been finalized—i.e., after the three-day hold. Therefore, from the salesman's perspective, the obvious solution was to give the customer something that *could not possibly* be returned in its original condition.

Every now and then I used to lunch with a fellow we'll call Dan. Dan sold aluminum siding for a mid-sized home-improvement firm in Richmond Hill, Queens. When Truth-in-Lending was passed, Dan's company chose to focus its Machiavellian counterattack on kids, an approach that eliminated very few families, and thus very few potential customers, in Dan's middle-class, blue-collar territory. The company went on a safari for unusual, irreplaceable gift items to be given out to the kids of people who'd purchased. Finally they found the perfect choice.

They bought out the entire remaining inventory of a model airplane that had just been discontinued by Ravell. That took care of the boys. Finding no suitable off-the-shelf item to satisfy the girls, they ordered something special from a smallish toy wholesaler in downtown Brooklyn: several hundred glue-together dolls. Dan placed his company's total investment at around $750. Not much more than the profit from a single, modest siding job. In other words, all they needed to do was prevent one cancellation, and they'd essentially recouped.

As Dan saw it, it was a brilliant plan. No sooner had a sale been closed than Dan would reach into his sample case, very ceremoniously, and produce the appropriate gift, plus a tube of model cement. With the dramatic, darkly prophetic words, "It's among the last of its kind, a genuine collector's item," he'd hand the toy to the wide-eyed child. The parents would be asked to initial a form saying they'd received one of the items—"just a formality for record-keeping purposes, so we know we didn't overlook anybody who was entitled to one." Dan then winked at the kid, thanked the parents for their order, and left. Should that customer call to cancel, the company would say, Fine, no problem, just give us back the toy in its original condition—unassembled, unblemished by glue, and so on.

Now, the siding company knew damned well that somebody had put the thing together that first night, probably before Dan's seat at the kitchen table had even cooled. It was physically impossible for the customer to comply with the request, and literally impossible for anyone to replace the particular toy with an identical store-bought one. So the company refused to accept the cancellation, citing—what else?—federal law.

Which is not to imply that the ruse always worked. Some customers smelled a rat and threatened to go to consumer affairs, whereupon Dan's company quickly relented. (Vagueness in the law notwithstanding, the company's procedures would have sounded fluky to almost any judge.) But if Dan can be believed there's more than one family in central Queens who wound up having their house aluminum-sided because of a two-dollar plastic toy.

What's interesting is that the surprise-gift plan paid unexpected dividends. Many customers, touched by the salesman's largesse, began telling their friends about this wonderful home-improvement company they'd had the pleasure of doing business with. The referrals poured in. Dan's personal productivity, which had loitered at the same mediocre level for years, suddenly went through the roof. He claimed that at the height of it all, his draw—the amount the company paid him in anticipation of future commissions—shot from $550 a week to almost $1,000!

Ironically, cancellations, the impetus for the whole scheme, dropped off markedly of their own accord. As time went by, fewer and fewer people had to be bulldozed with the ruse's kicker; customers simply stopped trying to cancel in the first place. Dan's theory is that building his presentation around the surprise gift had imbued his whole spiel with a certain kind of innocence; knowing that he would climax his pitch with this charming philanthropic gesture, he had unconsciously adopted a persona that said tacitly, "I am not here to screw you; I'm here as your friend."

Such casual introspection has wide-ranging implications—implications that were ostensibly confirmed by a recent study done by Herbert and Jeanne Greenberg, the husband-and-wife team who formerly gave us the sales-personality tests used by many corporations in evaluating the sales potential of new hires. The gist of the couple's research, which involved 207 salespeople and 200 sales managers nationwide, was that the sniveling shyster "simply cannot succeed in today's market."

Which, taken together with Dan's experience, suggests that a little consideration goes a long way. Even if it's artificial. Or if its motives are less than benign.

Sales Miscellany

Average cost of training a salesperson: $41,990.

3

A Crash Course in TNS, Part One: The Concepts

Its boosters portray it as a glorious amalgam of humanitarian insights that allow both salesperson and customer to proceed symbiotically down the road to wisdom and wealth. Its critics call it sophistry, hype, and worse. But stripped for the moment of its issues and intricacies, The New Salesmanship—whatever else it may or may not be—is clearly the product of three basic assumptions about selling:

(1) SELLING IS NOT AN ADVERSARY PROCESS; THE CUSTOMER IS NOT YOUR ENEMY.

(2) YOU DON'T *TELL* THE CUSTOMER WHAT HE NEEDS TO KNOW TO MAKE A DECISION; RATHER, YOU *ASK* HIM.

(3) BELIEVE IN SUCCESS, AND IT WILL HAPPEN.

At first blush, this may sound less than awe-inspiring. Point One may not ring true, given all these years of uneasy coexistence between salesman and customer. Point Two may not sound very logical—how, after all, would the customer *know* enough to make a decision unless the salesman has first told him all about whatever it is he's selling? Three, meanwhile, probably strikes you as banal or clichéd, and in any case, as philosophically incompatible with Two: Doubtless, most of the confident, authoritative types you've known up to now—having been steeped in the cerebral audacity of Herb Cohen, and other apostles of high-powered "negotiation"—were "tellers," not "askers."

The best way to attempt to make sense of all this is to begin at the beginning.

The advancement of The New Salesmanship, as depicted by its principals, is a quasi-religious crusade aimed at purging the sales trade of not just its connotations, but its sordid practices as well. Less is usually said about the role of the profit motive in all this, but there's no denying its strong twofold impact. While it's nice to think that companies began embracing TNS strategies out of the goodness of their corporate hearts, the facts speak differently. The movement didn't really gather steam until computers, combined with a more sophisticated purchasing audience, had underscored the woeful inefficiency of old-school tactics. Nor were its commercial possibilities lost on those entrepreneurial types who were trying to make a career out of selling selling.

Anyway, when I first joined the arcane world of sales in 1972, my employer's "star" performer was a surly bear of a man whom we'll call Mel. To Mel, the world was a master/slave affair in which he occupied the preferred position. Approaching everything as a conflict, Mel was forever seeking to impose his will on whomever he met. He let few opportunities pass. If he happened upon a parking spot that was reserved for someone, he'd insist on parking there in the hopes of forcing a confrontation. He'd intentionally speed up when he passed a police car so that he might have a chance at bulling his way out of a ticket. As a result, Mel's driving privileges dangled perpetually at the precipice of revocation. Mel carried this attitude even into his—you should pardon the expression—love life. One of the women in the office, having tired of his oft-repeated come-ons, told him, "I'm glad you're so physically repulsive, because it gives me something to take my mind off how obnoxious you are."

Mel's personality, however—such as it was—made him one

helluva closer. Unfortunately, his orders tended to be lacking in the longevity department. Each day he'd need to write four or five pieces of new business in order to offset the loss of three or four orders from the previous day via cancellations. When the dust settled, then, he was generating more paperwork than productivity.

The man himself had few illusions about his formula for success. "You throw enough shit up on the wall," said Mel, master of poetic imagery that he was, "and some of it's bound to stick." Nevertheless, for quite some time he remained management's darling because all they knew, and all they cared to know, was that most of the orders that wound up in steaming splendor on the wall each day belonged to that raging bull known as Mel.

But when the company finally went to computers a few years later, the flies in Mel's ointment were quickly revealed. Although his initial close rate dwarfed that of any other salesman, his per-capita productivity was among the lowest in the company. Plus he was chewing up the turf for everyone else. Sharing the number of available prospects with Mel was like being trapped in a fallout shelter with an insatiable gorilla.

Out went Mel. In came two new salespeople plus a part-timer to cover the massive volume of sales calls he'd required just to retain enough business to survive.

More important, in came a heightened sense of the error of Mel's ways. For the first time, management at our company began to rethink its attitude toward the customer. A similar rethinking process had begun to occur at about the same time throughout the nation. For Mel was not unique. Every company at every level of sales, right up to the top blue-chip industrials, had its share of Mels.

Reeducating Willy Loman was no small task. In most sales circles, the customer was indisputably the Enemy. Sales meetings of the era tended to degenerate into rabid bull sessions where each salesperson, in turn, would regale the remainder of the troops with some particularly obscene injustice inflicted upon an unsuspecting customer.

Still, salespeople were human, and so they needed a mechanism for dealing with the guilt their shticks imspired. Some rationalized, as explained earlier. Others projected their own feelings of contempt onto the customer.

"All buyers are liars," was a popular bit of axiomatic verse that stated the (ironic) distrust with which the average salesman viewed his prospect. Customers, posed this jaded attitude, were not the innocents they claimed to be. They misled you; they diddled you over price; they wasted hours of your time, soaking up every ounce of precious product knowledge you had to give, and then took their business elsewhere to save pennies. They deserved to get screwed. *They had it coming.*

But even at best, these defense mechanisms were imperfect. For, as management consultant Michael Wynne once put it, "Salespeople who rely on tricks rather than skills tend to burn out quickly."

As sales managers and others among America's corporate brain trust saw their organizations beginning to founder amid the changing consumer environment, the sales world became ripe for a new way of looking at things. Granted, there had always been Dale Carnegie. But the Carnegie course, though inspirational, was vague in its methodology, giving the salesman no real way of redirecting his persuasive energies.

At about this time—the early seventies—there were two parallel movements unfolding at opposite ends of the nation. In Connecticut, Xerox Learning Systems, subsidiary of the leviathan office-products giant, had launched an ambitious consciousness-raising salvo at America's largest companies. Out West, there was Tom Hopkins, a sales trainer who set his sights a bit lower. Without the multinational clout of a Xerox behind him, he lacked a certain credibility, his nonpareil heroics in the field notwithstanding. Thus he took aim at the realty profession from which he'd emerged, as well as other direct-sales organizations.

But despite differences in size and scope, both Hopkins and Xerox asked essentially the same question of the Mels and their managers, to wit: Why sell ten widgets a week by treating customers with contempt (and go home feeling at least a little bit guilty), when you could sell fifteen or twenty widgets a week by valuing the customer (and go home feeling that you'd changed someone's life for the better)?

Now, it's worth noting for the record that the Mels—the ones who stood to gain the most from heeding such advice—were not among the first to listen. TNS was embraced most eagerly in the beginning by novice salespeople, those who had no ax to grind, and no pre(mis?)conceptions about what selling was supposed to be. Many of the Mels tried to change, but like those first amphibious creatures who walked the earth, they couldn't fully adapt, couldn't resist their vestigial passion for diving back into the slime. They would go on to perish of their own obsolescence, or to become hangers-on, eking out a subsistence living among the 80 percent of salesmen who, statistics say, are responsible for just 20 percent of the production. Many of them are still selling today, still poisoning the rest of the staff with their belligerent, antiquated notions about the salesperson's "proper" role in the scheme of things. Some of them might have wound up at International Paper Products, which had the dubious distinction of being named the company with the worst attitude among a wide variety of sales firms surveyed by *Sales & Marketing Management,* the trade's self-appointed bible. "Arrogant" was the word used most commonly by survey respondents in describing International Paper reps.

Which is why, today, TNS regimens spend as much time stressing attitude as teaching skills. Typical of these enlightened programs is the interpersonal selling course taught by XLS, which teaches reps how to leave clients with the feeling that they, the clients, made all the decisions. According to XLS marketing director Betsy Moser, this promotes mutual trust and understanding, improves the working relationship, and engenders a feeling of peace and brotherhood among men.

"You want to be a partner with them in the decision-making process, not an adversary," says Moser. "That way, buyers don't feel that the decision was forced on them, but that it was something they arrived at on their own. Our course really helps salespeople put their presentation across in that manner."

Sagely, she notes—with a little long-distance laugh—"It also helps to eliminate buyer's remorse."

The War Against the Red-Flag Mentality

As the XLS course (one of a profusion of such offerings available today throughout the nation) suggests, the very first step in updating professional salespeople was changing the way they came across to their customers. This was seen, at least at the outset, as far more critical than preaching technique, for a bad attitude could sabotage even the most brilliant techniques.

Modifying the salesman's basic behavior patterns entailed purging that sales rep of all outlooks, mannerisms, and language habits that were in any way evocative of the old-style sleaze. The new salesman is holistic, in the broadest sense of the word. Everything he says, does, and is has been carefully honed not just to maximize his persuasive potential, but to put distance between him and his predecessors. The smallest subtleties of language are explored; the lexicon of eras past—words like *buy, pay, sign, deal* or *pitch,* and *down payment* are consigned to the scrap heap of selling antiquity, along with all they connote. Their upbeat, ego-stroking replacements are, respectively, *own, invest, authorize* or *approve,* and *offering* or *initial investment. Contract* is a definite no-no; the correct term these days is *paperwork.*

"What pops into a customer's mind when you ask him to *sign* your *contract?*" asks Tom Hopkins, a look of mock horror spreading over his boyish face. "Visions of lawyers . . . court-room scenes . . . wage assignments . . . a catalog of everything he's ever "signed" for and been sorry about later. Why put those kinds of doubts in someone's mind unnecessarily?"

More important than a simple vocabulary face-lift, however, is mental reconditioning. Not only must the salesman stop refer-ring to his presentation as a "pitch"—he must stop thinking of it as one, as well. The difference, after all, between a pitch and an offering is not purely semantic. A pitch is basically one-sided; the salesman is foisting something on you, his unsuspecting prey. An offering, on the other hand, implies that you're being given the opportunity of involvement in something that will ben-efit *you,* the customer. Today's trainers hope that by immersing their charges in a sea of thought that implies reciprocal benefit, the salespeople will come to understand that only through mu-tual benefit can a salesperson truly triumph.

It's not enough to merely say, "I'm here to help you," insist TNS doctrinaires. The salesman must have the kind of genuine conviction evinced by *World Book* encyclopedia rep Frances

Blais when she says she's "on a crusade to help children read well." A thorough, unequivocal belief in what you're doing is essential for success. Theoretically, to be accepted as a bona fide member of the TNS congregation, a salesperson must meet all of the following criteria:

• He must be selling a product that suits his professional demeanor, something at least a quarter of all salespeople are not doing, according to a recent study by the *Harvard Business Review*.

• He must be convinced of that product's worth, and manifest that belief in his own daily affairs. Suffice it to say that the homes of Amway's best sales producers are not awash in Avon products, nor do AT&T's top sales reps do their homework on an IBM PC. Insurance magnate Joe Gandolfo says that only after he'd invested in his first million-dollar insurance policy was he truly able to communicate the value of such a policy to others.

• He must believe in helping customers attain their goals. "When a client profits as a result of my activities, I feel a tremendous sense of personal fulfillment," says Drexel Burnham mergers and acquisitions specialist Mike Brown.

Do all these things, say TNS proponents, and the money will flow like water. In Brown's case, it flowed to the tune of a million-plus in 1984.

Speaking of money, TNS dogma strives to take the issue of commissions—a touchy subject for salespeople as well as buyers—out of the closet. Often, sales reps are inwardly uncomfortable with the amount of money they're banking on a given transaction, and that self-doubt will be communicated to the customer.

"There's nothing wrong with making money by making people happy," says TNS trainer Danielle Kennedy. "When I was in real estate, I was absolutely in love with the idea of finding people their dream house. I made a lot of money, but I also made a lot of people happier than they'd ever imagined they'd be. I showed people how to make their dream houses affordable, and introduced them to fantastic neighborhoods they didn't know about. It was a wonderful way to make a living."

Nonetheless, it is hardly uncommon for resentful home buyers to request that their broker cut his commission in order to make their dream house that much more affordable. Snorts one rep, "People just can't seem to live with the idea that you're making four or six or ten thousand dollars on the transaction. It goes against the grain."

Which is funny, because this is a phenomenon that occurs almost nowhere else in society except direct sales. You don't walk into a candy store, this same rep argued, and ask the counter clerk to forego a nickel of her salary so that you can get that Cadbury's Caramello bar for fifty cents instead of fifty-five. (Do you?) Nor do you resent that clerk for selling you that candy bar. And yet in a sense, that clerk's vested interest in your purchase of a lowly candy bar is as real as the stake any broker has in your purchase of a new two-hundred-thousand-dollar home.

Of course, in another sense, the realtor continued, the candy-store clerk is seen by her customers as just a go-between, a surrogate for the company that's *really* charging you for the candy. The representative from the actual candy company isn't hovering over you while you make your choice, eager to collect the take. If so, your attitude toward the affair might be less casual. The individual making the real profit—Mr. Cadbury, if there is such an individual—is insulated from you by several layers of merchandising bureaucracy. For that matter, even the salesperson who sells the candy store its candy is someone you'll probably never meet.

Not so when you're out clothes shopping, and there's a living, breathing, commissioned rep standing there in front of you, waiting with baited breath to see whether he pockets 8 percent of $250 or 6 percent of $175. This is certainly the main reason why many in our society begrudge the medical profession. Not only are they taking your money—often right there on the spot—but you're helpless to do anything about it. We might begrudge, but we won't bargain. Not with a doctor. The medical profession is considered "above" all that. We simply hold our healers in too high esteem—despite the grating knowledge that their high-flying, free-wheeling life-style is at least to some degree an outgrowth of our kid's stomach flu.

Where salespeople are concerned, the solution, says Tom

Hopkins, is a matter of reeducating the public by example. Like all TNS adherents, he professes the belief that salespeople can someday be as respected as doctors for the contributions they make to our overall quality of life.

Hence, super-salespeople offer no apologies for their material success; none, they feel, are in order. Confronted once about his Rolls-Royce, Hopkins simply told the woman, "Yes, I've been fortunate enough to help many people, and I'm looking forward to helping you, too." How, he reasons, can people get mad at you as long as they prosper from your actions on their behalf?

There's a second factor at work here, which is the perception that when you buy something from a salesman, your decision is not voluntary. He has *sold* you. When you enter a candy store, no one twists your arm to get you to buy that Caramello bar. But the salesman who comes to your home to sell you a pool, you reason, is out to hoodwink you, to con you into making your decision. And since you know he has a stake in it—a very large stake, in the case of a pool purchase—you tend to resist his long-winded efforts at persuasion.

Which brings us to what may well be the most fascinating aspect of The New Salesmanship.

"So," the Prospect Said to the Salesperson, "Why Don't You Sit Down and Ask Me Something About Your Product . . ."

Traditionally, the sales call has been something of a pitched battle, in which the eager salesman seeks to impose his own view of the product, and the customer's need for it, on his prospect. The battle occurs, inevitably, because few people enjoy being told how to feel about something. And probably no one likes to see himself as transparent, easily "read." Feeling violated and disenfranchised, customers rebel when their hopes and dreams are spelled out for them—triumphantly, no less—by someone they've just met.

So strong is this visceral instinct for self-determination that even the individual who may very much want or need what is being sold will suddenly equivocate when confronted with a salesperson who presumes to tell him explicitly about those wants and needs. This is especially true of upper-echelon executives, who prefer to think of themselves as omnipotent, in total command of their destinies.

Then, too, there's the matter of credibility. Because of the sales trade's poor image, there is a tendency to identify sales-people with mendacity and deceit. Therefore, the more a salesman insists on hawking his product, the more we tend to disbelieve what he's telling us.

Enter the champions of TNS, who reasoned that, while a person might take exception to a salesperson's presumption, no one in his right mind is apt to take issue with something *he himself* has said.

"If you say it, they can doubt you," says Tom Hopkins, "but if they say it, it's true."

Ergo, according to this school of thought, the new salesperson's job is to induce the prospect to voice those same points that the old salesperson might have droned on and on about in a traditional presentation. Increasingly, the emphasis among major industrial sales firms is shifting away from informing the customer; as *Sales & Marketing Management* reported recently, most of the factors that distinguish top salespeople nowadays relate to getting information rather than giving it.

But how does a salesman manage to run a successful sales call without informing? More to the point, how does he get customers to tell him everything he needs to know in order to tactfully maneuver those customers into a position of agreement?

He does it through the skillful, unerring use of questions.

Fortune magazine chronicled the emergence of this approach as a national phenomenon in an early 1985 feature entitled, "How To Sell By Listening." In his lead paragraph, editor Jeremy Main wrote, "Today's sales training teaches the salesperson to be a good listener and questioner, sensitive to the needs of others, knowledgeable about his products, more an adviser than a hustler." Main also quoted one of his sources, an instructor for Forum Corporation of Boston, as saying, "the philosophy is to serve the customer as a consultant, not a peddler."

Actually, the *Fortune* article was just a sophisticated reiteration of a saying that had informally guided the TNS movement since its inception: "You have two ears and one mouth, and God intended for you to use them in that proportion." The motto is available, these days, on plaques, posters, blotters, and desk sets, and is offered by at least one stationery company as a pre-printed option on your custom letterhead.

Besides minimizing guesswork, the question-based presentation helps the salesperson eschew the selling of benefits—real though they may be—that are irrelevant to a given prospect's needs. The familiar canned-script presentations had salespeople droning on and on ad nauseum in a glorious monologue that covered every bit of minutiae about the product. However, the level of sophistication—read cynicism—being what it is in today's society, gone forever are the days of successfully arguing that one's product offers both the best quality and the best price. The quality customers want to be reassured about quality. The price customers want to be reassured about price. You need to know which is which before you start.

"Not everybody needs the best," explains management consultant Robert Scherer. "Telling the office manager about your marvelous six-function digital widget is counterproductive if he only needs one or two functions. All you succeed in doing is convincing him that you want him to pay for four or five more features than he needs." Fred Parr, who trains salespeople for Olivetti, echoes Scherer's point a bit more colorfully: "The 'It chops, blends, purees, and mows your lawn' pitch is an outdated form of overkill that usually does more harm than good."

Salespeople who've abandoned canned scripts in favor of the modern, "consultative" approach report glowing results. Myron Howard, one of a handful of top national account managers for Xerox, has built a career on asking prospects questions like "What, ideally, would you want our machine to accomplish?" Howard then sits back and listens while the buyer proceeds to reel off a list of major benefits he expects from Howard's product, leaving Myron in the enviable position of merely nodding and reinforcing the customer's desires where necessary.

"Persuasion," says a sentence in material disseminated by XLS, a wholly owned subsidiary of Howard's employer, "[is] a matter of consistently reinforcing positive customer expressions and minimizing dislikes and objections."

Additionally, by the customer's reply, and his emphasis, Howard learns which benefits are of greatest importance. Just find out what they want, or need, or think they need, and sell them that. What better way to find that out than simply by asking?*

On the other hand, one doesn't want to overdo it, at least if the results of a recent XLS survey can be believed. After observing five hundred sales calls under carefully controlled conditions, XLS concluded that, while salespeople who asked an average of 16.4 key questions (or "probes") were significantly more successful than those who asked just 9.4 questions, they were somewhat *less* successful than their counterparts who asked 13.6 questions. The customers of the most prolific probers often wound up deferring the decision to another day, rather than tying up the deal right then and there. Which would seem to suggest that if you're a salesperson, you should keep track of your questions; when you get about halfway through number 14, you quit in midsentence and hand your prospect an invoice and a pen.

Overall, the biggest single factor in the salesman's ability to close on the spot appeared to be his use of what Xerox calls *closed probes.* These are questions designed either to elicit a simple yes or no, or to limit the customer's response to a field of alternatives set by the salesman. (Few modern sales theorists would take issue with the latter part of the previous sentence, but many of those same theorists grow apoplectic at the use of questions that expose the salesperson to a negative response, for reasons to be explained shortly.) Using *open-ended probes*—that is, questions that allowed customers to roam freely over the vast universe of their hopes and dreams—were better than asking nothing at all, but not much.

The Assumptive Salesperson

During the seminar that represented my earliest introduction to TNS, the lecturer offered the following dialogue from an

---

*If, right about now, you're beginning to wonder (a) why it took salespeople so long to realize any of this, and (b) why you paid some obscene amount for this book if TNS is nothing more than a matter of asking people what they want, don't despair. The process has been intentionally oversimplified here in order to make the concept clear. The mechanics of it all—how that concept is applied in day-to-day selling—is hardly self-evident, as we'll see once we get to the next chapter.

apocryphal story about a salesman returning from his first evening in the field.

MANAGER: So how'd it go, Harry?

HARRY: Well, it's hard to say.

MANAGER: What does that mean? Did you make any sales?

HARRY: Nope.

MANAGER: How many people did you see?

HARRY (*haltingly*): Well . . . none, really.

MANAGER (*annoyed*): And why is that?

HARRY: Well, you see, I went to the first house, and just like you told me, I waited until after supper to make sure both the husband and wife were home . . .

MANAGER: Good.

HARRY: . . . and I got myself mentally psyched by rehearsing my opening lines . . .

MANAGER: Good, good.

HARRY: . . . and I walked up the steps and stood in front of the front door, but nobody opened it for the rest of the evening. When I saw all the lights go out at about eleven, I figured they'd gone to bed. It was too late to see anyone else, so I went home.

MANAGER (*now incredulous*): Let me get this straight. Are you telling me you didn't even knock on the door or ring the bell or anything? You just *waited* there for somebody to come out and find you?

HARRY (*sheepishly*): Well, it was my first customer and I didn't want to assume too much . . .

The seminar speaker used this anecdote to define the perfect *antithesis* of the modern, assumptive salesman, who should err on the side of presumption, not diffidence.

At first blush, this may sound to you—as it did to me—more than vaguely reminiscent of the Mel syndrome, the kind of look-out-everybody-here-I-come defiance brandished by salespeople who've yet to be enlightened. But TNS boosters assure you that there are profound differences between the kind of assertiveness

73

we're talking about here, and the kind of carnivorous adamancy personified by Mel et al. In fact, they tend not to like the word *assertive*. It has too many hard-sell connotations.

One sales manager used the example of a top tennis pro playing against an unranked amateur. The tennis pro knows he can beat the amateur handily. He doesn't need to stalk around the court, beating his chest. He simply *knows,* in a quiet inner way, that he's going to win. In the same way, said this sales manager, a good salesman *knows* he's going to succeed with every customer—even though, factually speaking, he isn't going to succeed with every customer (and in truth, insofar as most products are concerned, he's going to fail more often than not).

A second salesman, unhappy with the competitive overtones of his colleague's example, preferred to illustrate with the case of an adopted child who has been brought up since birth to believe that his adoptive parents are really his biological parents. If you ask that child, now a teenager, who his parents are, he'll respond without a moment's hesitation; there is no doubt in his mind about who his parents are. Why would there be? And yet you and I know he's mistaken, just as we know that the salesman in the first scenario is not going to sell every customer.

The assumptive salesman, however, knows no such thing. The notion of failure is as foreign to his world view as the concept of adoption is to the teenager who has never known any parents other than the ones who raised him. The salesman believes in himself and in his product, in a manner described by the TNS cognoscenti as being more akin to self-knowledge than brashness or bravado. The salesman simply thinks, speaks, and acts as though there's no doubt that you are about to become the deliriously happy owner of whatever he's selling. There's nothing hostile or pushy about it; it's just *the way things are,* as far as he's concerned. Does Ronald Reagan like to nap? Has Julio Iglesias recorded a song with every other known singer, living or dead? Is the pope Catholic? Are you going to purchase the salesman's product? To the salesman's way of thinking, the answer is equally yes to all questions.

A tremendous amount of time is invested in the mental conditioning required to bring about this kind of self-awareness, for the theory is that the salesman's positive vibes will be absorbed, and acted upon, by the customer. In the world of TNS, the best way to get someone to buy something is to make him believe it's a *fait accompli*. First, though, the salesman must make himself believe it's a *fait accompli*. Otherwise, despite his veneer of confidence, his inner uncertainty will undo him; he will radiate subliminal clues to the customer that plant doubts about the wisdom of the offering.

Tom Hopkins takes it even a step further. "A lot of salespeople worry about a particular deficiency their product has—and let's face it, every product has some deficiencies, in one way or another. Anyway, the salesperson is so worried about being hit with a particular objection that they unwittingly do and say things that cause the customer to raise that very objection! It becomes a self-fulfilling prophecy."

Fortunately for the salesperson, this appears to be a self-fulfilling prophecy that works both ways. Superior sales pros are unanimous in the conviction that the more you believe in the odds of making a sale, the higher those odds go in your favor. The belief, however, should be genuine and all-consuming—not just a little pep talk you give yourself before you ring each doorbell.

While most of the more sincere trainers dismiss as a dangerous oversimplification the old saw that the best way to become successful is to act successful ("Salesmanship isn't about acting," said one, speaking for the majority, "it's about a genuine commitment"), the fact is that a superficial layer of sincerity and conviction probably never hurt anybody, even if his heart wasn't really in it.

"It's like painting the outside of an older house you're trying to sell," admits Danielle Kennedy, who had many of her clients doing just that in her days as a nonpareil real estate salesperson. "You'd be surprised. It makes everything inside look better somehow."

And sometimes, she adds pointedly, painting the outside will motivate the homeowner to fix things up through and through.

• • •

For the salesperson with the proper assumptive attitude, the glass is always half full.

Consider the case of Glenn Turner. Turner would eventually

run afoul of several state's attorneys' offices as a result of the multilevel marketing scheme he called Koscot Interplanetary—a psuedo firm that turned out to be less a cosmetics company than an exalted chain letter. It was determined that Turner was not as interested in selling facial cream as he was in selling franchises to sell franchises to sell facial cream, a pyramidlike form of business architecture that, in the absence of sufficient quantities of an honest-to-goodness product, has been deemed illegal.

But technicalities aside, you couldn't fault the assumptiveness of his thinking. Business writer Andrew Tobias once wrote of the man's lecture before an audience of Tobias's classmates at Harvard Business School. Turner spoke of his early days as a door-to-door salesman, and how his harelip often elicited expressions of discomfort from the housewives who greeted his knock. As recounted by Tobias, the unflappable Turner would explain away his handicap as follows:

"I notice you're looking at my lip, madam. Well, in truth, it's not a harelip, but something I put on every morning so people notice me. I can let you have one for a hundred dollars."

Turner thus turned a liability into an asset, while letting his customers know—in a facetious way—that he was someone to be reckoned with. He assumed his self-worth.

To an assumptive salesman like Turner, inaction is an implied yes. As is indecision. As—in many cases—is silence. It is common for a customer who has been asked a closing question to just sit there silently for a few moments, mulling over his options. Several of the more successful salespeople for one New York mirror company have a standard policy, to be observed at all times: If they feel the customer is basically leaning in the company's favor, but is just being held back by some minor reservation and needs a little "nudge," they rise from the table and simply start drawing their plumb lines across the customer's wall in pen. (Plumb lines are vertical and horizontal lines, drawn with a carpenter's level, to determine where a wall's perimeter is "out of square," or measures unevenly.) Drawing those lines usually resolves the issue.

In the same vein: Some years ago the Boy Scouts of America published a book on salesmanship. "We Are All Salesmen," proclaimed the opening chapter of the handbook-sized treatise, which purported to introduce scouts to the fundamental selling skills they would one day need as adults. Somehow, though, you got the impression B.S.A. had hopes of putting those skills to use a bit sooner—like maybe during the next candy drive?

At one point, the book told its young doers of good deeds how to avoid having doors slammed in their cherubic faces. "Hand them whatever it is you're selling as soon as they open the door," suggested the text, which went on to observe that "nobody is going to slam the door on you when they're holding your merchandise."

Defenders of TNS insist that such tactics are warranted. And if the truth be known, there is a not inconsiderable body of psychological data supporting such claims.

In a recent book entitled *Overcoming Indecisiveness,* Dr. Theodore Isaac Rubin explained how most of us, in the absence of powerful external stimuli, tend to preserve the status quo, even when it is of questionable wisdom or even genuinely harmful to do so. We are not by nature risk-takers, says Dr. Rubin; we'd rather do nothing than submit ourselves to the threat of the unknown.

Using the term *abdicators* to describe people who prefer not to make decisions, Rubin told one interviewer, "I think most people are abdicators and don't know it. They simply abdicate the whole process. . . . They do things on a rote level," he went on to say, because "they've been trained to do them."

Or because they've been conditioned. Olivetti's Fred Parr has often spoken of the difficulty of getting prospects "over the IBM hump." Parr believes, and many industry observers agree, that Olivetti's "smart" typewriters are superior—certainly in a technological sense—to the good old IBM Selectric, which has been the staple of the business office for lo the past two decades. Nonetheless, customers continue to buy the IBMs anyway, presumably because they've always bought IBMs, which, again presumably, is because the acronym *IBM* has become synonymous with office typewriters in the same way that Kleenex and Frigidaire had eventually become generic terms. In fact, in IBM's case, the product identification may be far stronger. Parr:

"People will certainly buy different brands of tissues, if they have a certain preference, or if there's a sale, or if they have coupons. And Frigidaire has hardly cornered the market on refrigerator sales. But when an office manager neeeds a typewriter, he'll just automatically ring up the local IBM distributor—*and even pay extra*—just because it's an IBM."

Given that mentality, who wants to break the chain? Who dares to be the first office manager who's actually gonna send out for one of those newfangled jobs with the strange, overseas-sounding name?

IBM, of course, couldn't be more overjoyed at the situation, a joy expressed in the assumptiveness of its own sales force. This kind of thing has its own self-perpetuating momentum: IBM reps make the sale because they know they work for IBM, and IBM *always* makes the sale.

TNS trainers feel strongly that, faced with such a marketing dilemma, powerful tactics are not only justified, but necessary to break the spell. "It's not that we're hypnotizing people," says a manager for yet another victim of the IBM mystique, "but that we're trying to combat the mentality of those who've already been hypnotized by IBM." He likens the role of his small sales force to that of the free-lance deprogrammers who were running around the country rescuing kids from cults during the mid-seventies. "We're not trying to seduce anyone," he claims. "We're just trying to restore their minds to some semblance of open-mindedness, so that our products can be considered fairly and objectively."

Still another salesperson: "You owe it to the customer to expand his horizons to include alternatives he might not be considering. If you have a product or service that's going to do him some good, it's your obligation to do what you can to get him to take your offering seriously."

Before we deify the modern salesman on the strength of his pristine motives, however, we might do well to realize that such sentiments are not quite universal. In fact, to assess the ethical underpinnings of The New Salesmanship is to submerge yourself in a morass of impassioned, often contradictory, arguments.

Not all behavioral analysts agree with Tom Hopkins's avowed belief that you have to "honestly love" people in order to be successful at selling. Depicting the manner in which salespeople maneuver their customers through the use of "sheer animal dominance," respected industrial psychologist Donald Moine has written, "the best sellers seldom care deeply whether people like them." Moreover, Moine writes, while good salespeople are concerned about the worth of their products, they are not, by nature, "rigidly moralistic; experience has taught them to accept the imperfections . . . of the real world." They are, in other words, sufficiently jaded to do what needs to be done in order to close the sale. So much, Moine would seem to be saying, for loving your customers.

Then, too, there are many definitions of love. Under questioning by LAPD deputies about the rationale behind her 1969 savaging of actress Sharon Tate, who was more than eight months' pregnant, Manson follower Susan Atkins is said to have smiled and cooed, "You have to have a real love in your heart to do this for people." The deputies said Atkins seemed grotesquely sincere.

Actually—and this is not to imply any relationship between modern salespeople and Susan Atkins—sincerity does happen to be of the essence, for otherwise the assumptiveness comes across too harsh, strident.

Ten years ago, when salesmanship was in a state of flux—an odd middle ground between the coerciveness that was its past and the empathy that would be its future— many sales presentations featured coercive material couched in the warmest, most sympathetic language, resulting in a peculiar disjunction between form and content. Though salespeople were beginning to get indoctrinated in the ways of niceness, they had yet to free themselves completely of the antipathy of yore.

Rodney Queen (of the nervous tic), who bills himself as a devout exponent of the straight sell (no b.s., no mind games), would take leave of procrastinating customers as follows: He would walk slowly to the door, turn, survey the home, zero in on the man's wife and kids, return his gaze to the husband, smile benignly, and say, "Here's mah card. Give me a call if you decide you'd like ta pro-tect your family." The line was delivered with warmth and feeling, and was, presumably, an honest manifestation of Queen's concern for the safety of his customers.

But let's face it, it wasn't a terribly sweet thing to say. Queen might as well have told the man, "Give me a call if you decide you'd like to prevent your wife and kids from being dismembered by a drug-crazed prison escapee."

And Queen usually got away with it—indeed, he made a killing (pardon the expression) because he impressed his customers as being sincere. No doubt, they ascribed the uncharacteristic bite of some of Rodney's remarks to his intense commitment to their security.

In short, they trusted him.

And the fact is, many did go on to buy Queen's security systems, and they did pro-tect their families, and they did live happily ever after, in comfort and in safety.

So who's to judge?

Nothing Succeeds Like Failure

One of The New Salesmanship's most stunning features is its redefinition—negation, actually—of the concept of failure. This lovely piece of positive thinking, often credited to Larry Wilson (of *One Minute Sales Person* fame), rationalizes failure so that it comes out sounding like success.

Say your past performance indicates that you need to knock on five doors in order to come up with a single sale. Say each sale is worth one hundred dollars. Assuming that the one-out-of-five track record is statistically valid—that it represents an accurate picture of your sales abilities—then it is possible to attach a value to every door on which you knocked, successfully or not. By this logic, each door is worth twenty dollars, regardless of whether you sold anything. Therefore, each time you fail, you have, in a sense, earned twenty dollars. Wilson goes so far as to exhort the members of his seminar audiences to say "Thanks for the twenty!" as they take leave of a customer who hasn't bought. (Presumably, he means for them to say this to themselves, not aloud.)

Sophistry? Maybe. But if you think about it, much of life works this way, with our successes and failures being spread out—amortized, as it were—over the whole of our activity. What, after all, is a batting average? A .300 average means a player has a 30 percent chance of getting a hit on any given trip to the plate. That .300-hitting ballplayer is sent in to pinch-hit for a .250 hitter in the ninth inning of a close game because the manager believes he is more likely to hit safely, based on past performance. And statistically speaking, that .300 hitter is a full 20 percent more likely to get a rally going. Now obviously, the manager doesn't expect his .300 hitter to get 30 percent of a hit when he sends him up to pinch-hit for a weaker hitter. He is simply acting in accordance with the only viable formula he has for deciding whom to play, a formula that takes all of the player's successes and averages them out over the sum total of his attempts. This, basically, is the same thing Wilson's doing.

To belabor the baseball metaphor for just another moment: Ballplayers say of a teammate who's been mired in a bad slump, "The guy's due for a hit." Why is he due? Because as he continues to defy the law of averages by performing beneath his ability, the chances that his dismal performance will go on for much longer become increasingly remote. With each successive failure at the plate, success gets that much closer. The little 30 percents are adding up and getting ready to produce a full hit.

Same thing with life insurance. Your rates go up when you hit thirty-five not because the actuaries expect you to do a swoon into your birthday cake, but because the members of your group—white males between the ages of thirty-five and thirty-nine, say—show a higher overall mortality than white males aged thirty to thirty-four. Remember the old saying "Each day I die a little"? Well, actuarially speaking, it's true.

The good news, if you're thirty-five years old, is that you shouldn't worry so much when you get sick. No matter how lousy you feel, you can draw comfort from the fact that the odds of dying at your age are still exceedingly slim (even though they're higher than they were a few years back). You're not reassured? You say you have a friend who died at age thirty-five? So much the better. He took the statistical fall for the group. The strong probability is it won't happen to you, or anyone else you know.

And so it is with selling, at least in the world according to Larry Wilson. If your history indicates you're a capable salesperson, then be happy, says Larry, when you go through a bit of a cold streak. It'll all even out in the end. Meanwhile, those little twenties are accruing, and a hot streak is just around the corner.

What Does the Word No Really Mean?

Still, everybody wants to improve his batting average. It's nice to know that every "no" is actually a full fifth of a "yes," but wouldn't it be nicer, salespeople muse, if they didn't have to wait so long? If they could cut the ratio down to one of four, or one of three, or as close to *all* yeses as possible?

Better still, they argue, wouldn't it be nice if we redefined the word *no* so that it meant *yes*?

In their admirable efforts to do just that, the high priests of TNS usually begin by tracing the etymology of the word *no*—not its Latin roots, or its linguistic development, but its profound role in our development as human beings.

A passage from *How to Master the Art of Selling* by Tom Hopkins:

> . . . Mom has told you not to touch the saucepan. When she walks into the kitchen, there you are, you little rascal, straining to reach the saucepan. What happens next?
>
> Our mother could've said, "Sweetheart, come here and sit on Mommy's lap. I love you, honey. Because I love you, I don't want you to hurt your body. If you reach up and pull the saucepan off, you'll scald yourself. Now, since I haven't been able to effectively communicate with you, darling, I'll inflict a degree of pain on your backside to help you understand.

Besides learning to hate and fear the word *no*, the argument goes, you also learn from this Pavlovian conditioning not to make decisions. Or to make them very cautiously. After a while, this knowledge becomes subconscious, ingrained in your psyche, where it gets reinforced by a variety of bad decisions you make as a youngster. You decide to play with a strange dog and get bitten for your efforts. You decide to cross the street on your bike and the latter gets demolished by a car (and you very nearly with it). You decide to put a water balloon down Mary Jo McCarthy's blouse in Psychology I and you end up explaining your motivation to the principal. So, as an adult, when someone presents you with a matter requiring a decision, your intuitive reflex is to say no. Even in cases where you really need or want to have something changed, your subconscious predisposes you toward sustaining the status quo. (Just ask Dr. Theodore Isaac Rubin. Or executives at the Wrigley chewing gum company, who learned a graphic lesson in people's affinity for the status quo when they tried changing the packaging on one of the company's popular brands. People stopped buying it, despite an aggressive awareness campaign and the fact that the contents were identical to those in the old package. Rather than try to swim upstream, Wrigley quickly reverted to the original packaging.)

But what, ask Hopkins et al., are we *really* saying when we say no?

For the answer to that, TNS masters would have us go back into the earlier scenario and take a closer look. Mommy is not really telling the child *never* to touch the stove. Someday, after all, the child will grow up. There will come a day when that child is twenty-three years old and wishes to make a Denver omelette. At that point, it will be okay for the "child" to touch the saucepan (albeit with trepidation, left over from those early lectures). So what the mother was in fact saying—even though all the child heard was a simple and emphatic "no"—was "You don't yet know enough about this situation to come to an informed decision of your own, and I'm probably not capable of making you understand, so for the time being, at least, don't mess with it."

As you grow up, ever mindful of your dog bites and broken bones, you instinctively learn to use the word the same way. *I don't know enough about this new situation, and I'm afraid it would be ill-advised to just leap right in, so I'll say no instead.* It's easier, you reason. And safer.

Hence, an updated definition of the word *no,* courtesy of The New Salesmanship:

Coming out of the customer's mouth, the word *no* is nothing but a signal that additional information is needed before a genuine decision can be reached. Or, as Hopkins simply puts it, "The word *no* is the customer's way of saying, 'Tell me more.'" Not exactly a *yes,* perhaps, but damned close.

Xerox Learning Systems takes an equally flexible approach to the concept of rejection, as embodied in *no* and similar words. In Xerox's world, any sales call that terminates in the prospect's saying no can still be considered a success so long as the salesman is able to exact from said prospect an agreement to keep in touch. In other words, as long as the lines of communication remain open, the prospect is still perceived to be saying, "Tell me more," and the salesman can consider himself not to have failed.

How many nos must a salesman hear before he concludes that a given customer does not wish to be told one iota more? Before he accepts the fact that a genuine decision has been arrived at and it's futile to go on?

Well, consider the evidence presented during several sales seminars I attended recently. Most outside representatives said they closed the majority of their sales on the *fifth* or *sixth* try. It was unclear how many individual visits those attempts spanned—whether it was five tries during the course of a single four-hour pitch, or distributed more or less evenly over the course of five visits. But *Forbes* estimated not long ago that most sales in an industrial setting were not finalized until the salesperson's fourth visit. And at the real upper strata, sales of corporate jets, major capital equipment, and the like, it's not at all unusual for salespeople to have to endure literally dozens of temporary rejections—nos—before they get that one, all-important yes. Although there's no way of knowing for sure, the modern-day record for corporate indecision may be held by IBM. Perhaps in oblique retaliation for some of the stalling tactics used against its own salespeople on a daily basis, Big Blue put representatives of Trammel Crow's Infomart (a kind of high-tech swap meet) through their paces *forty* separate times before agreeing to join the roster of Infomart presenters.

The coup de grâce in taking a creative approach to the word *no* may have been authored by Roy Chitwood of Max Sacks International, a thriving sales-training venture with offices in Los Angeles and Minnesota. Chitwood has actually restructured the interrogative technique for his trainees, so that a no will serve as the functional equivalent of a yes:

"If we can have this [whatever product it is] by [a certain date], can you think of any reason why we shouldn't set it up for you then?"

If you're the salesperson, you hold your breath and hope for a no.

If You Want It, Write It Down

In no respect is TNS closer to the much-maligned pop-psychology movement than in its approach to career goals. Nonetheless, top trainers take goal setting very seriously, and TNS dogma as a whole has a very specific perspective on how the matter should be handled.

If you don't write them down, the rules say, they're not goals at all. They're just ideas. Hopes. Dreams. Nor does a salesperson merely write them down and file them away somewhere. Goals must be reviewed every morning and every night. Or else they won't "take."

You won't get an argument from Ted Fisher. Seven or eight years ago, he was eking out a mediocre living selling men's haberdashery in that sui generis part of New York known as the Garment District. Ted's frustration was twofold: In addition to being ever short of funds, he found himself among all these beautiful model types, yet unable to get his love life moving. Water, water, everywhere, so to speak.

So Ted began writing down his goals, personal as well as professional. Under the former column (and borrowing heavily from Larry Wilson's treatise on failure/rejection) Ted wrote, "If I ask five women out, it's reasonable that at least one will accept. Therefore, my success rate is one out of five. Therefore, each time I ask, it brings me that much closer to success. Therefore, my goal is to ask at least ten women a week for dates." Ted figured he'd wind up with at least two good candidates out of the initial ten, and thus have his weekends subscribed. To give himself a head start, he also wrote, "I am irresistible to women."

Ted began asking like crazy, and he discovered something. He discovered that yeses beget more yeses. The more he asked, the higher his success rate. He later said, "I guess I got smoother, better able to handle the reflex objections." Reflex objections, in sales parlance, are the nos people give you unthinkingly—not because they don't like you or your product, but because they haven't really had a chance to give it much thought, and in such circumstances, the natural answer—as we've already explored in some detail—is no. "At one point," Ted recalled, "I could've dated three women a night if I wanted to. When I first started doing this, I was lucky to get a date a week. It was incredible."

Tom Hopkins believes it all has to do with making goals real, palpable, and psychologically omnipresent. This is why the goals must be written down, and reviewed constantly. "The more your mind deals with it—confronts it—the more sophisticated you get about handling it, achieving it, making it happen," says Tom.

There are three things a salesperson's goals must be in order for this to work: specific, active, and written in the present tense. For example, a salesperson would not write, "I'm gonna be rich someday." Instead, the sentence might be "I am working toward my goal of having two million dollars in a money-market by 1990." Or "I am rapidly accumulating cash for a red Ferrari Mondial." (It's not enough just to say you're saving for a car, Hopkins cautions; ideally, you want to pick the make, model, color, interior upholstery, and options. The realer the better.)

TNS philosophy is careful to hedge on the matter of whether or not all those who follow the rules will realize their goals. They'll get it, the logic stipulates, if they really want it badly enough. How do you know if you really want it badly enough? Well, one way to tell is by whether or not you finally get it. If you do, you must have wanted it badly enough.

In a case where a salesperson writes down a goal which is not, strictly speaking, true*—Ted was eminently resistible to women when he first began his regimen, the language of his goal notwithstanding—one of two things will happen, according to TNS tacticians. The individual will either begin to realize the goal, or be unable to say the words any longer.

---

*By definition, all goals are at least partially untrue at the moment they're first conceived. Otherwise, they'd be realities, not goals. But there are different levels of untruth. For example, the salesman whose goal is to improve productivity by 20 percent is already producing something—he's not starting from scratch, so his goal is not nearly so impractical as that of the piss-poor drifter whose goal is to be a millionaire. Although in both cases the goals would be worded in the present tense, one would be considered a goal, whereas the other would probably fall more into the category of a pipe dream.

A salesman whose goal is to treat every customer with consideration and respect will not be able to face himself in the mirror after going through a month of blatantly violating the pledge he repeats each morning as he shaves.

"This happens frequently with people who want to give up smoking," says Hopkins. "After three weeks of saying 'I am free of this disgusting habit; my lungs are fresh and clear,' they're either going to have to quit smoking, or they're not going to be able to say the goals anymore because they can't keep lying to themselves." He says the guilt that you might expect to accumulate like the tar in a smoker's lungs is actually helpful to the cause. "If you're not what you want to be, you have to goad yourself into action. Sometimes painfully. But progress—change in general—is almost always hard, isn't it?" No pain, no gain, and all that.

You may be interested to know that Ted's goal-writing bore professional fruit, as well. Last I heard, the ex-haberdashery salesman was wearing a different hat as the owner of a thriving computer peripheral venture in Dallas, Texas. After three years of steady six-figure compensation as a sales rep for the firm, he had goaled his way to the top.

No salesperson, of course, survives strictly on writing down and repeating pithy little phrases over the morning coffee. Nor, for that matter, will any concepts-in-the-raw—no matter how brilliant or revolutionary—have much of an effect on the lifestyles of too many salespeople.

What makes the difference for Ted Fisher, and his thousands (soon to be millions) of TNS cohorts nationally, is the diligent translation of the outlooks sketched over the past few dozen pages into highly specific *techniques*. Techniques that have been scrupulously crafted, and have proven themselves time and again in the unforgiving crucible of industrial selling.

Sales Miscellany

*Average number of attempts at closing
that must be made before customer says yes: five.*

4

A Crash Course in TNS,
Part Two: The Techniques

The techniques described in this chapter will unfold as part of
what those in the trade have labeled the Inductive Presentation.
(Those not in the trade are inclined to be less kind; "dialectic
entrapment" was one industrial psychologist's way of describing
the logic on which much of the Inductive Presentation rests.)

Regardless of what you call it or where your sympathies lie,
inductive selling is an umbrella term for a whole category of
sophisticated strategies that rely for their efficacy on questions,
as opposed to statements. The familiar canned pitch—at least in
its recognizable form—is abandoned. The salesman's function
consists, in a very literal sense, of getting the customer to make
the sales presentation for him. When it's handled properly, the
customer sells himself.

It's hard to fully appreciate the impact of inductive selling
without first studying its component parts; described in thumb-
nail fashion, the overall concept has a tendency to sound faddish
and sophomoric. On the other hand, the component parts lack
authority if one does not first have a cursory understanding of
the big picture—the long term objective of inductive selling, and
the context in which its various tactics are likely to be applied.

The scenarios below were the product of a conversation with

one of Minolta's more successful salespeople in the western region; they juxtapose two different ways of selling the same copying machine to the same customer. Salesman #1 is a partisan of the old school, whereas Salesman #2 is a card-carrying TNS disciple. Though both scenarios are grievously simplistic, they should suffice for giving you a reasonable overview of today's brand of selling, and how remarkably it differs from its precursors.

SALESMAN #1 (*who has vigorously grabbed the hand of his quarry, over whom he now hovers, resplendent in his Day-Glo plaid jacket*): Mr. Jones, I'm here to show you the XYZ Special. It's our newest, most versatile model. It can print up to a hundred copies a minute on both sides of the page. It's been factory tested to withstand as much as a thousand hours' continuous usage between servicing and it's got color capabilities and it's just the most wonderful thing you have ever seen. It'll mow your lawn and rotate your tires and make perfect toast every time so-whaddya-say-there-Mr.-Jones-can-I-put-you-down-for-five-of-these-babies, huh?

MR. JONES (*who, in fact, really does need a copying machine, but like most of us, just hates to make on-the-spot decisions*): Well, I'm not really sure I can use all those features, although the bit about the toast does sound pretty good. Tell ya what, though. Why don't you leave me your card and I'll think about it. . . ?

(*Salesman proceeds by threatening to pour a bottle of toner into Mr. Jones's fish tank unless Jones relents. But Jones will not be cowed. Sales call ends unsuccessfully, with both parties agitated.*)

SALESMAN #2 (*who did not go for Mr. Jones's hand until it was proffered by Jones himself, and is now seated opposite the man, his gray pinstripe sleeves resting earnestly in his lap*): Mr. Jones, what aspects of your office copying capabilities do you feel could use the most improvement?

JONES: Uh, well, that Pitney Bowes in the corner over

there is getting on in years. It takes forever to get a document done.

SALESMAN: Slow, is it?

JONES: God, yeah! You should see how the work backlogs when we're really busy.

SALESMAN: Roughly speaking, about how much faster would it have to be in order to meet your needs?

JONES: Hmmm. That's hard to say.

SALESMAN: Well, I'd guess, judging by that model, that it does about thirty copies per minute. Do you think you'd need the ideal machine to be twice as fast—or would three times as fast be better—or even more?

JONES: Oh, I guess *ideally* we'd need something that could do at least three times the work.

SALESMAN: At least three times the output, you say?

JONES: Well, ideally.

SALESMAN: So if my math is correct, you'd like something to run at about a hundred copies per minute, is that right?

JONES: Yeah, that's about right.

SALESMAN: And I notice you've got a lot of documents here printed on both sides of the page. Did you do that in-house or do you have to send out to the printer?

JONES: In-house? Are you serious? On that old war-horse? Nah, we have to send out every time we need something like that done.

SALESMAN: So do you suppose it would be advantageous to you to have a machine that could print on both sides simultaneously?

JONES: Jesus, it sure would. (*Pensive*): If nothing else, it'd probably save us a fortune in printing costs.

SALESMAN: Wouldn't it, though?

JONES: But would the copies look as good as they do when they come back from the printer?

SALESMAN: That's important to you, is it?

JONES: It sure is. A lot of these things are direct-mail proposals. It's the first time our clients hear about us. We need it to look professional.

SALESMAN: By the way, do you ever send anything out in color?

JONES (*sighing*): It's one of the things we've always wanted to do, but other than our letterhead, which we have pre-printed in great quantity, of course, it's just not economical to have things done in color.

SALESMAN: But if it were economical—if you could have that feature on a copying machine without having it cost you much more than black-and-white—would it be desirable?

JONES: Of course it would. Color always helps a proposal stand out above the crowd.

SALESMAN (*recapping*): So if you had a copier that could give that 'professional look' to your mailers, and could print both sides of a page, in color, and could do all this at the speed you said you needed—that was a hundred copies a minute, right—?

JONES: Right.

SALESMAN: —then you'd have the perfect copying machine for meeting the needs you've just outlined for me, is that correct?

JONES: Well . . . yeah. I suppose, in a nutshell, it is.

SALESMAN: Mr. Jones, I believe you'll agree that the XYZ Special is the perfect solution to the problems you've indicated . . .

JONES: Not so fast now—does it make perfect toast every time?

Okay, I threw the last line in for kicks. The fact is where else can Jones go but to his checkbook? Under the sales rep's skillful guidance, he has painted himself into a corner. What can he now say he wants to think about? The copier the rep is about to demonstrate conforms to Jones's every wish, as delineated by none other than Jones himself just a moment before.

Contrast this with the case of Salesman #1, who simply rattled off a brochure full of specifications without any advance knowledge of the reception those specs would be likely to get from his customer. As a result, Jones had a whole list of convenient stalls at his disposal: He could've said the machine was faster than necessary, and thus probably more expensive than necessary; he could've said that he had no use for a machine that printed on both sides of a page; he could've said, "Color? Who needs color?" But Jones can't say that to Salesman #2, because those are the exact qualities that our man Jones *himself* said he'd like to see in his next copier. (And the salesman's careful phrasing constantly reminded Jones whose mouth those needs had, indeed, come from: ". . . do you think you'd need the ideal machine . . ." ". . . if my math is correct, you'd like something . . ." "do you suppose it would be advantageous to you . . ." and so on.) So, aside from getting prospects to set the very ground rules to which they'll later be asked to adhere, inductive selling also tends to eliminate spurious objections.

Then, too, there was always the chance that Jones could've perceived some of the machine's features as genuine negatives. Suppose he'd once heard that two-sided copiers are much more unreliable, prone to frequent breakdown—not generally true, I'm told, but suppose, anyway, that he'd heard it, and resolved never to buy a copier that printed on both sides of a page. All the while Salesman #1 was extolling the virtues of his wonderful machine, Jones would be thinking, *You're trying to sell me something I know I don't want; you're trying to sell me something that's inferior. I don't like that. You're not on my side.* He might not be thinking it quite that lucidly, but at some gut level, no doubt, he'd begin to suspect the salesman's integrity. In any case, it certainly wouldn't help the salesman's cause.

Salesman #2 has no such problems. If one or more of Jones's answers force a detour, he'll go wherever the presentation takes him. He can be flexible. He's not committed to any particular course of action. If Jones's replies indicate he's not a good candidate for the XYZ Special, Salesman #2 can always fall back on an alternative product. That's harder for Salesman #1 to do as gracefully, after he's invested so much time and enthusiasm in a glowing dissertation on the wonders of the first machine.

Which is not to imply by scenario #2 that selling in the age of TNS is a piece of cake, exactly. For one thing, price is a hurdle that remains to be cleared. But the ground on which Salesman #2 stands is substantially more solid than that occupied by his predecessor. Jones is merely being asked to pay for things he has admitted he wants, not for things the salesman had no way of knowing Jones wanted. There's a profound difference.

Not just that, but the customer is paying for things he now *realizes* he wants. The salesman's probing interrogation has unearthed and reinforced needs that often remain untapped in the traditional, lecture-type presentation. For example, until Salesman #2 adroitly raised the corollary issue of sending stuff out to the printer, Jones may not have been that interested in two-sided copying. Therefore, being told that a machine had that particular ability would've left him unimpressed.

Remember, this is just an overview. Remember, too, that the beauty of TNS (to its adherents) is its simplicity, its unselfconsciousness. "The object," says sales trainer Ken Clifford, "is to get the customer to commit without leaving him with the feeling that he's been *sold.*"

Together, the strategies that follow—gleaned from the most fertile minds among the TNS elite—compose what many sales managers consider to be the most powerful motivational tract yet devised by man.

Assumptive Language

Simply put, assumptive language is the manifestation of the assumptive attitude described in Chapter 3. In practice, it is the sprinkling of subtle, almost subliminal hints throughout one's presentation. When the man from IBM greets you, his prospect, by asking, "Where in the office will we be putting the computer?" the presumption of the question may register at some preconscious level, but you're only vaguely aware of it, and you don't feel at all threatened. Besides, what kind of niggling curmudgeon would actually take issue with that kind of question? It seems, after all, like such a natural, spontaneous thing for any salesman to ask . . . *maybe,* you think, *he wasn't even aware of the way he phrased the sentence.* Surely there was no offense intended. Why spoil what promises to be an informative sales call by reminding the salesman that *he's* not putting anything *anywhere,* at least not yet. After all, you do need the computer.

Left unchallenged, however, such a remark lays the ground-word for a series of escalating assumptions.

- "What features do you think you'd like to see in our machine?"
- "Who, besides yourself, will be using the IBM XT?"
- "When do you need for us to make delivery?"

Notice that each question takes greater liberties than the one before. (Also notice, once again, that they *are* questions, not statements.) Such ostensibly innocent remarks create a powerful forward momentum. By the time the salesperson gets to the last question, you're well on your way to owning a new computer, often without quite realizing how you got there.

One of the reasons assumptive language is so effective is that most buyers—even once they wake up to what's going on—feel squeamish about stopping the salesman. The linguistic assault has been gradual. You let him get away with everything else he said, didn't you? How do you justify stopping him now?

It's a similar situation to when children are making a lot of noise. People who don't have kids find it hard to fathom how parents can read, watch TV, even carry on reasonably intelligent conversation, while the kids' noise crescendos to a deafening roar in the background.

But the kids didn't pop out of the womb raising that kind of ruckus. They started out by testing the limits, making a little bit of noise and waiting to see what would happen. When indulgent parents didn't bother correcting them, they graduated to the next noise level. The parents become inured to the regular cacophony of family life and, by the time the kids really come into their own vocally, it is too late. The parents reason, Well, we never corrected them before, so if they're now screaming loud enough to drown out the civil-defense sirens, we've got no one to blame but ourselves.

Customers use the same rationalization when dealing with an assumptive salesman. You let him get away with it because you've let him get away with everything else. The pattern has been established—by the end of the sales presentation, almost institutionalized—and you feel awkward about suddenly putting your foot down.

As the presentation moves along, assumptive language usually blossoms into assumptive behavior. The salesman will begin to take charge physically. Joe Girard, former "World's Greatest Salesman" (in the eyes of the *Guiness Book of World Records*, anyway), says that a good portion of the 1,425 cars and trucks he put on the street in 1973 were sold just by assuming the test drive. Girard didn't even ask his customers if they wanted to go—he merely pulled the car out of the lot and motioned for them to get behind the wheel.

Later, if that same customer waffled and said he'd like to go have a drink someplace to mull over Girard's offer, Joe'd ask what he drank, then obligingly whip out a glass and the appropriate liquor from the fully stocked bar he kept in his office. Not exactly protocol for the average car salesman, but then Girard was hardly average. How many car salesmen—*domestic* car salesmen—were taking home nearly four thousand dollars a week at the height of the Arab oil embargo? How many are doing it even today? Very, *very* few.

Girard was keenly aware that such tactics create a sense of obligation in his customers. In addition to liquor, he kept an inventory of cigarettes (all brands, which he would dispense by the full pack to customers who asked if he had a light), balloons, and sundry other items for the kids. In the kids' case, he was not above getting down on all fours and riding the tots over to his goody drawer, horsey style.

While Girard's approach, at least with regard to the balloons and such, might be viewed in some milieus as fawning and transparent, his thinking on the subject fostered an entire school of thought that remains a hot topic today. Wherever home-improvement reps are found, the theory of "the unrelieved debt" is discussed frequently and fervently. The argument goes that a salesperson should never, *ever* accept the small courtesies offered by the customer—a cup of coffee, a drink, whatever —because that acceptance assuages the customer's feeling of indebtedness to the sales rep for showing up and spending his time. If you leave that sense of debt "unrelieved," the theory goes, the customer is more likely to feel obliged to buy your product, since he can't let you leave the house without doing *something* for you.

Not all salespeople agree, of course, and shop-at-home reps have been known to accept a wide variety of favors—not necessarily limited to coffee and cookies—from their hosts.

A compelling variation on assumptive reasoning is known as "assumptive martyrdom." San Francisco consultant Robert Scherer offers a classic illustration of its nature and efficacy:

"Say you come home from work one night, and you're exhausted, and your young son comes over and says, 'Daddy, can we play Monopoly?' You sigh, and you say, 'Maybe tomorrow, son, okay?' You tell him you're awfully tired. He makes a face, but he leaves you alone.

"On the other hand, suppose that instead of coming right over and asking you, he went downstairs, all by himself, and struggled up the stairs with the card table. And then he went hunting all over the house looking for a pad and pencil. And then he went and got the cards, and he came over—lugging the table and the pencil and everything—and he asked you which playing piece you wanted to be?

"How many parents are going to have the heart to turn him down, after he went through all this?"

In the same way, how many people have the heart (or nerve) to turn down a salesman who went ahead and broke his back for them while apparently under the illusion that they were committed to doing business with him? Real estate agents, especially, seem fond of this tactic. Are you really going to be "unfaithful" to that sweet young guy who spent his last three weekends driving all over the country in search of your dream house?

Not likely.

In the final analysis, the thrust of assumptive behavior might be best expressed by a dictum attributed to Joseph Faltermeier, a well-known sales executive with a realty-investment firm in ultra-affluent Newport Beach, California.

"It's easier," Faltermeier is said to have remarked to a colleague during a sales luncheon, "to ask for forgiveness than to ask for permission."

The Tie-Down

A personal favorite of the late, great J. Douglas Edwards (the sales theorist on whose embryonic concepts many of today's more involved strategies are patterned), the *tie-down* is an innocuous-sounding little semantic device for exacting a modicum of agreement from—and establishing more than a modicum of control over—the customer. A textbook example of the tie-down, as used inadvertently in everyday life, is the sentence "It's a lovely day, *isn't it*? The last two words, changing the thought from a statement to a question, compose the tie-down.

Professionally, tie-downs come in a variety of forms. There are the standard tie-down (such as "You can really make a killing using linguistic tools to get people to do what you want them to do, can't you?"), the internal tie-down ("You can really make a killing, can't you, using linguistic tools to get people to do what you want them to do?"), the inverted tie-down ("Can't you really make a killing using linguistic tools to get people to do what you want them to do?"), which is always asked with rhetorical certitude, and—last but certainly not least—the tag-on tie-down (FIRST SALESMAN: You can really make a killing using linguistic tools to get people to do what you want them to do; SECOND SALESMAN (*gleefully*): Can't you?) TNS masters find the last version particularly useful for reinforcing constructive remarks that may have been uttered by the prospect on impulse, in an unguarded moment.

> CUSTOMER: Wow, this house has a lot of cabinet space.
> SALESMAN: Doesn't it, now?
> CUSTOMER: It sure does.

Edwards felt that by using tie-downs, the salesman achieves several things. First of all, rephrasing statements as questions softens the impact of thoughts that might otherwise seem a bit presumptuous. A salesman who uses a tie-down is not telling his prospect what to think; rather, he is leaving it up to the customer to decide the merits of the thought preceding the tie-down. This may sound chancy, but in practice, a sales rep would never use a tie-down unless the statement were obviously true, or the answer obviously yes.

Sales trainer John Thompson uses a facetious illustration that has the salesman saying to his customer, "A reputation for integrity is important, isn't it?" Now assuming the role of the customer, Thompson replies, as though outraged, "Integrity! You mean to tell me you have . . . integrity!?"—his intonation makes integrity sound like herpes—"Why, get out of here!" The point is that you can't go wrong tying down questions of that genre. No rational person is going to take issue with the importance of integrity, or professionalism ("No," jibes Thompson, once more the devil's advocate, "I'd rather buy from someone who doesn't know what he's doing . . ."), or other similar attributes.

A second benefit of the tie-down is that it gets people nodding along with you. Spend more than five minutes with motivational guru Zig Ziglar and you find yourself nodding and smiling, smiling and nodding, like one of those spring-loaded puppets in the back window of a car. That's because Ziglar's repartee makes liberal (and, to the uninitiated, at least, inobtrusive) use of tie-downs. Here it works to establish and strengthen a subliminal bond between trainer and audience. Later on, the people in attendance, having learned from their mentor's example, will go forth and use those same tie-downs to establish and strengthen the bond between salesperson and prospect.

Zig, not usually one to overintellectualize things, calls this "building agreement." But most of his peers prefer to come up with more pedantic labels. Joseph Todd, a West Coast sales trainer with a penchant for trade jargon, calls it "establishing a positive-psychological-yes-set." (Last year, in a single five-hundred-word article for a regional magazine, Todd used all of the terms, *prioritize, quantifies, needs-verification,* and *needs-fulfillment.* He used *prioritize* twice.)

Though no salesperson can survive strictly by adding terse phrases like "aren't we?", "don't they?", "won't it?" to the end of every sentence, tie-downs are an integral part of the mental conditioning on which most of TNS relies. As Martin Shafiroff, stockbroker to the stars, once told author Robert Shook, "It's very difficult for an individual to say yes four or five times, and then say no when you request the order."

Even in instances where the customer has not been mesmerized by the salesperson's calculated questions—cases where the positive-psychological-yes-set has not quite taken hold—the salesperson still has a strong logical argument to make. When a customer who has said yes every step of the way suddenly hesitates at the close, a salesperson can reasonably challenge the customer with a quick, polite recap of all those yeses. "But Mr. Smith—just to get my thinking clear—didn't we agree that this forklift would help you do [such-and-such], and that it would also help you do [what-not, and so forth]. . . ?" In other words, how can all these yeses add up to a no? Nobody wants to seem like a liar or a flake; if you recant all your yeses, then either (a) you were lying when you affirmed the salesman's tie-downs, and therefore wasting his valuable time, or (b) you're a hopeless nerd who doesn't even know his own mind. In such circumstances—confronted with his own past agreement about the worth or utility of the product—the average customer will simply yield to the momentum of the sale.

Above all, say the TNS pundits, tie-downs help the customer clarify his own thinking. Many people are reluctant to buy for reasons that have nothing to do with any deficiencies in the product under consideration. They may want it and/or need it, but they don't buy it simply because of the universal proclivity for deferring decisions that involve money. Often, with the knowledge that one has affirmed every feature of the product or service being presented, comes the realization that there is no logical reason for hesitating any further.

Myron Howard, a leading national account manager with Xerox, says the company's "consultative" method of selling, which uses questions that get the customer to probe his true feelings toward the product, often produces sales in which Howard has to make little or no effort at closing. Introspectively, the customer becomes aware of his overwhelming need for the product and indicates his readiness to buy.

"The actual request for the order," concludes Howard, in a whimsical tone of voice that suggests he still doesn't quite believe what he's about to say, "is made not by me, the salesperson—but by the client himself."

The Hot-Potato Parry

Pretend for a moment that you're a salesperson. (Aw, come on, now—what's one lousy moment?)

Say you're in life insurance, and you're talking with a brand-new prospect. During the early going, before you've had much of a chance to get a fix on his thinking, he asks if you sell a lot of endowment policies.

Now, the endowment policy is to insurance what booze is to restaurants. Sensing a big commission in the offing, you impulsively blurt, "Why, we sure do!" You segue into a glowing five-minute soliloquy on the wondrous endowment options offered by your company. You then add that an endowment policy was the very first thing you looked for after emerging from the womb, that you personally happen to believe they're the greatest thing since foreplay and Häagen-Dazs ice cream. For good measure, you add that you sell them to at least half your customers.

Whereupon your prospect looks you straight in the eye and snorts, "Well *I* think they're the biggest goddamn rip-off in history, and I defy you to try and sell one to me!"

In the hope of salvaging something, you spend the next ten minutes trying to smooth over the tension caused by your goof. But it's no use. You blew it. Your credibility is gone, your empathy is down the tubes. You alienated your customer; instead of establishing common ground, you set yourself up as an adversary. You might as well remove your shoe from your mouth, write this one off as a total loss, and hope for better luck elsewhere.

Reading this, your initial inclination is probably to think that you should've limited your answer to a simple yes and let it go at that. But in this case, that wouldn't have helped much. To a buyer with such extreme prejudices, even an unadorned yes might have triggered doubts about the salesman's integrity. And in any case, a yes answer gives the salesman not a clue as to what's really going on inside the prospect's mind. The buyer will have found out something important about the seller, but the seller is no further along in his knowledge of the buyer. In today's brand of selling, that is not the way the flow of information is supposed to go.

The Hot-Potato Parry provides the salesman with an effective alternative to committing such gaffes. Rather than answer the prospect's query, and risk admitting to a certain point of view before knowing the customer's feelings on the subject, the rep simply bides time by asking a counter-question designed to extract the mental context in which the prospect's question has been asked. Simply put, he tosses the hot potato right back.

The revised scenario, then, would go something like this:

> CUSTOMER: Do you sell a lot of those endowment policies?
> SALESMAN: Do you think an endowment policy best suits your family's insurance needs?

Now the burden of divulging salient information has been shifted back to the customer—which, in the minds of the TNS brain trust, is where it belongs.

Incidentally, this is not to imply that if, as happened in our example above, the customer comes up with an extremely negative response, the insurance agent would automatically abandon the notion of selling that customer an endowment policy. But he'd be alerted to the fact that this is treacherous territory to be approached with utmost caution; he does not, after all, want to trample blithely over one of his prospect's pet peeves.

It's worth noting that, depending on the customer's answer, this particular strategy provides the salesman with a wonderful opportunity to establish a positive-psychological-yes-set, as Joe Todd would put it.

> CUSTOMER: Do you sell a lot of those endowment policies?
> SALESMAN: Do you think an endowment policy best suits your insurance needs?
> CUSTOMER: Well, yes, I've done some research and it sounds like it might be a wonderful way to build for the future.
> SALESMAN: Doesn't it, though?
> CUSTOMER: It sure does.

It's also worth noting that Tom Hopkins refers to the Hot-

Potato Parry as the "porcupine technique," for reasons that are probably inscrutable to all but Tom himself.

"Well," he says, trying to explain, "what would you do if someone threw a porcupine to you? You'd throw it right back to them, right?" Sure, Tom. Happens all the time.

Dialectic Entrapment

So far as I've been able to determine, this term was coined by industrial psychologist Donald J. Moine in characterizing the overall thrust of inductive selling. However, it is now being used to refer to a specific closing strategy in which the sales rep, having already deduced from certain signals that resistance is inevitable, goes about influencing the customer to commit to the most insignificant objection: i.e., one for which the salesman feels he has a near-perfect rejoinder. Thus, the seller can be said to have "entrapped" the unwary customer with his own objection.

This particular technique feeds on the dislike most people have of taking responsibility for their decisions, or indecisions. When was the last time you told a salesperson flat out, *"Your product stinks and it's overpriced, too"*? We don't, most of us, do things like that. We prefer to ascribe our indecision to factors having nothing to do with the salesperson's product. New-breed salespeople capitalize on this foible, and the archetypal example, offered by at least three or four of the people interviewed for this chapter, would have to be selling to a woman at home.

Let's say a housewife has certain vague reservations about a product a salesman has come to show her. Chances are that instead of presenting her doubts forthrightly, she'll pawn off her indecision by claiming the need to talk to her husband. (Men use the same tactic, by the way, when looking at cars. Hoping to defuse the closing efforts of a determined salesperson, they'll typically insist they must consult their wives about color or interior selection.)

Knowing this, the salesman will seize upon the housewife's excuse and undertake what aficionados call "isolating the objection." He'll confirm that the absence of the woman's husband is the only thing that's preventing her from going ahead with the sale. Through a painstaking process of question-and-answer, he will specifically rule out all the other conceivable objections, one or more of which may be the woman's actual objection.' ("Okay, just to clarify my thoughts then, you're saying that the price is acceptable?" "Oh, the price is fine." "And you're sure it's not the color?" "No, I adore the color." "And you don't doubt my integrity, do you?" "*God,* no, I think you're the most wonderful human being who ever walked the face of the earth. . . ." And so on.)

Usually, the sales rep will throw in a couple of reasons why it would've made sense to buy today—if only she could—and get her to agree to those as well. The woman will probably go along with everything the salesman says at this point, because she feels she's already crippled his pitch. There's no sense compounding the pain of rejection by rubbing salt in the wound. She's thinking, *I'll be rid of this guy in a few minutes—why make him miserable by telling him I'm not really that crazy about his product to begin with?*

The kicker comes when the salesman reaches the end of his list, having now gotten the customer essentially to agree that she thinks it's a great product and she'd certainly buy it in a minute *if it were only up to her, but alas . . .*

Ta-daaa! He whips out something called a conditional order and slaps it on the table. "Now, Mrs. Jones, we've already agreed that you can't finalize the agreement today. But at the same time you did say you'd like to take advantage of the [sale, special offer, whatever] if you possibly could, isn't that true?"

Although she's no doubt regretting all those effusive yeses she authored a moment ago, Mrs. Jones almost *has* to nod here or else reveal herself as a liar.

"Well," the salesman continues, on a roll, "here's a way of accomplishing both objectives at once."

Bingo. The salesman has the woman authorize a conditional order, which gives her the right to cancel if her husband disapproves. He also takes "a nominal binder" so that the order can be activated without any bookkeeping delays once the husband rubber-stamps the sale.

She can't very well argue. After all, just thirty seconds ago she "admitted" that for her part, anyway, she was sold on the product. The salesman also makes an appointment to come back as soon as possible to talk it over with the husband and wife together, "since I realize how much this means to you, and I'd hate to see you lose out because you might have forgotten one or two of the product's most important features. I just want to be able to explain things to your husband if he has a question or two that you may be unable to answer. Fair enough?"

How can she say no?

Surprisingly, this technique works just as well in high-powered industrial circles. Top executives who find themselves cornered with a real sales pro will often—despite their sophistication and imperial demeanor—still look for convenient pretexts for their unwillingness to commit: "It's not fast enough," "It's not big enough," "It's not cost-effective," "We've been dealing with your prime competitor for a thousand years and we're not about to disturb what's been an excellent business relationship for us"—you wouldn't think high-level decision makers would be shy about telling a salesperson these things, but they are, insist those who would know best. Instead, they'll mumble something like "Well, it sounds pretty good, but we don't finalize our budget projections until next month and I have to see how everything shapes up before I commit."

The salesperson goes about isolating the objection just as with a recalcitrant housewife, then has the executive authorize a postdated purchase order:

"Of course it's contingent on your budget figures, but since we both agreed that you do need this product, won't it be nice to know that the order is already in the works the minute the fifteenth comes around? After all—provided there's room in the budget—you're going to have to buy this thing from someone, right? And you said you liked what we had to offer, didn't you?"

Bingo again. Half the time the executive forgets that there's a conditional PO floating around out there somewhere, and when the fateful day arrives, it becomes quietly valid. The vendor submits the bill, the client's accounting department pays it, and the transaction becomes history. Interestingly, many customers—having taken that first tentative step and committed to a conditional order—will suddenly be seized by an "oh, what the hell" attitude, which prompts them to tell the salesperson to write it up sans conditions and deliver as soon as possible. Which only serves to underscore what top salespeople say about the necessity of getting people "over the hump" of unfounded sales resistance.

Sometimes the entrapment strategy will force the executive to produce the Real Reason he's not buying. And this is good, say the experts, for it gives the salesperson an opportunity to relieve the client's genuine reservations and shoot for a bona fide sale. Top producers are unanimous in the belief that the biggest hurdle is not so much overcoming the objection as getting the prospect to confess the real objection in the first place. "If I only knew in every case exactly what was holding them back," says California real estate broker Phyllis West, "my income would double."

Certain Real Reasons lend themselves to entrapment better than others. One of the most convincing rebuttals is that designed by salespeople to overcome the objection *I've been dealing with your competitor for years.* Salespeople who are fearful of being hit with more substantive criticism—criticism that focuses on the shortcomings of the product itself—will often maneuver the prospect into the position of voicing this objection, and this objection alone, as the primary reason for not buying. They can then entrap as follows:

SALESMAN: So you're saying you're quite happy with our competitor?

CUSTOMER: Quite.

SALESMAN: And you've never had any problem with them?

CUSTOMER: Never. We've been thrilled with the service they've given us ever since the first day we started with them, five years ago. *(The customer will say this even if it isn't strictly true, to give his objection more weight—not realizing that he's playing right into the hands of the salesman's next line of questioning.)*

SALESMAN: So then I guess you'd say it was a good decision when you switched from the company you'd been using earlier to our competitor.

CUSTOMER: I certainly would.

SALESMAN: Well, don't you think it's possible the same thing might happen if you switched from our competitor to us? Isn't it at least possible that we might open your eyes to a whole new level of service, just as our competitor opened your eyes five years ago?

The key thing to bear in mind is that with dialectic entrapment, the salesman can win whether or not the Real Reason ever surfaces. The customer who has been maneuvered in this manner is totally hamstrung; he can't fight the salesman's logic without confessing the real objection, and he can't confess the real objection without first contradicting a slew of things he said a few moments earlier.

Faced with a decision between buying something that they do in fact need, and revealing themselves as liars, most buyers take the easy way out.

The Alternative Choice Question

There's a scene in a movie I once saw where the film's central character, who has just been convicted of a capital offense, is given a choice between being shot and being hanged. It isn't much of a choice, of course, but it's the only one he's offered. He can choose to play it one way, or he can choose to play it another—but he can't choose not to play at all.

. Such, from the salesperson's perspective, at least, is the understated beauty of the Alternative Choice Question. Used informally for decades, then popularized through Dale Carnegie and refined by countless sales theorists since, the ACQ has evolved into one of the most revered underpinnings of The New Salesmanship.

In fact, such is its unobtrusiveness that customers seldom realize it's being used. Yet it is devastatingly effective, especially when being employed to overcome surface resistance—the hesitation we have to commit for no reason other than that we're hesitant to commit. It isn't that we don't need or want the product, it's just that we're fearful of making the all-important decision.

This is why the man from Chemlawn who's desirous of dropping by to give you your special-no-obligation lawn survey quickly follows the observation that he'll be right in your neighborhood this afternoon with the question "Should I come at two, or would four be better?" He doesn't ask if you want him to come by at all—he knows the odds are you'd sooner check into the hospital for a sigmoidoscope than voluntarily entertain a sales rep in your home. Instead, he plants an assumptive seed with his opening remark about being in the area, then leaves you with a choice of *when* you'll see him, not *whether*. Joe Gandolfo, who in 1975 became perhaps the first salesperson to write a documented *billion* dollars' worth of insurance, embellished the technique by asking for appointments at very specific times on separate days. ("Can I see you at four on Tuesday or would one-thirty next Monday be better?") That way, Gandolfo explained, the customer would not only have a choice, but come away thinking, Jesus, this guy has some tight schedule—he must be a real pro.

This won't work with everybody, of course, and then there are times when neither of the alternatives will be suitable. You are not, after all, going to cancel a lunch date in order to watch the Chemlawn technician crawl through your crabgrass looking for chinch bugs. But one thing is certain, claim TNS soothsayers: His odds of getting into your thatch are far better if he broaches the subject with an ACQ than if he simply asks if you're interested in having him survey your property.

"Women instinctively do this to their husbands all the time," says sales trainer Zig Ziglar. "They don't ask, 'Should I get a new pocketbook today?' They ask, 'Should I get the red one or the blue one, honey?'"

Stores do their best to cater to this natural phenomenon. They carry sixteen lines of everyday china not because they love stocking inventory, but because they want your decision to come down to a choice among options, not a choice of whether or not to buy. They have already determined through careful analysis that the cost of the added inventory—some of which (usually the upper and lower extremes) is never intended to be purchased by anyone—is easily offset by the "which one should I pick" mentality it engenders in the shopper.

Many sales organizations have tiers of prices designed specifically to allow their salespeople to use this technique in closing. The rule of thumb at shop-at-home companies is, try to get at least three items on the table, representing three distinct levels of "financial involvement" (cost). That way, the customer will be hard pressed to reject your entire offering. Similarly, the insurance salesman—having led you through his wonderfully inductive, masterful piece of persuasion on why you need to be indemnified against crazed wombats—is not about to have the entire sale hinge on a simple yes or no question: "So, whaddya say, fellah, ya want some insurance?"

Rather, he'll bring it down to a question of which line you think "best suits the personal security objectives you've outlined" for him.

In major industrial settings, this approach is seldom feasible, at least in its textbook form. It's doubtful in the extreme that an aircraft salesman would ever have the leeway of asking his customer a closing question like "You want to go for a coupla 747s, or should I just put you down for a dozen of the rebuilt Cessnas for now?" The product most likely to be purchased was identified and analyzed to the nth degree by the prospect's buying committee relatively early in the selling process, and the salesman knows it; more often than not, he participated. Nonetheless, chances are the salesman will try to incorporate some type of nominal decision into his close: "Would you prefer delivery on the first, or would the fifteenth best coincide with your bookkeeping?" Even if the choice the customer is given is banal and contrived—"Would you like me to include your company logo on the side of the copiers, or should we leave them blank?"—it's better than giving no decision at all, say the forefathers of TNS. Salespeople who channel the customer's thinking into a choice between two options that are both favorable to their goal of making a sale improve dramatically the odds of that happening.

There are, as you might expect, ACQs for all occasions. Closing on the Minor Point usually involves a choice between two anticlimactic options—as when the Volvo salesperson wraps up the purchase of a twenty-thousand dollar car by asking whether you'd prefer the whitewalls or the blackwalls.

But if any particular adaptation stands out above the myriad others, it is the tactic that one leading trainer calls Changing Their Base. This strategy is employed with customers who have unaccountably begun to waver, or have gotten so overwhelmed with options that they seem to have lost sight of the original objectives on which everyone agreed their decision was to be predicated. This is actually a common defense mechanism, according to super-salespeople; customers begin introducing new considerations as a way of confusing the issue, and thus relieve themselves of the responsibility of having to go through with the purchase.

Fervently dedicated to eliminating confusion (and removing impediments to the forward progress of the sale), the modern sales rep will use this special kind of ACQ to get things back on the right track, to remind customers of the "base" from which they started. He'll ask a question that juxtaposes one of the original bedrock criteria with this latest one in a way that makes the newer objection sound trivial and ridiculous.

Should an automobile salesman return from the men's room to find his customers quibbling about the stingy rear leg-room of the economy car they'd both loved until two minutes ago, he might reasonably ask, "Mr. and Mrs. Smith, will your final decision be based on the fact that a car gets forty-five miles to a gallon of gas, or the fact that it *might* be a bit short on rear leg-room?" Smith has already told the salesman that he intends to use the car for commuting, a sixty-mile daily round trip. In that context, the complaint about rear leg-room—given that the car is going to be driven principally by Smith alone, and presumably from the front seat—is almost silly.

Smith buys the car.

Leading Questions and Their Good Friends, Ownership Questions

Although the thrust of these two tactics differ, they are closely related in the sense that they're not really questions. Not in the true sense of the word, anyway. Rather, they are statements or admonitions rephrased in question form so as to soften their impact, as a prelude to jogging the customer's thinking, or raising potentially sensitive issues, or planting a certain notion the customer might not have thought of on his own.

From an informational standpoint, it wasn't really necessary for Copier Salesman #2 to ask Mr. Jones whether or not the company had its proposals done in-house. He already knew damned well those slick-looking brochures hadn't come off that superannuated contraption in the corner.

But from a selling standpoint it *was* necessary. The sales rep wanted to remind Jones of another important benefit of doing business with him; it was his way of saying, Hey, you know, if you owned a state-of-the-art machine, you could probably save a fortune on outside printing costs without sacrificing quality. For maximum effect, according to the rules of TNS, the words had to come from the buyer's mouth. Yet in order for Jones to say it, he first had to think it. So the salesman asked the appropriate Leading Question.

Similarly, when the insurance salesman admires your family portrait, pats your little daughter on the head, smiles warmly, and asks you to tell him "a little bit about your plans for her continuing education," he's not just making small talk, nor is he really asking you a question at all. He's reminding you of something. He's reminding you that, although your daughter may be just a tyke now, careening merrily around on her new three-wheeler, someday soon she might want to trade her tricycle for a lawbook or a scalpel or an accountant's PC. And guess who's gonna have to pay for all that? *Do you have a financial plan that provides for that contingency, Mom and Dad?*

Even less of a true query is the Ownership Question, which is intended to fast-forward the customer's thinking to a time when he already owns the item being tendered. Essentially, an Ownership Question is a rhetorical device to get the prospective buyer thinking thoughts he would normally think only after he'd bought the product. The answer is almost irrelevant. What matters is planting the right thoughts or associations in the prospect's mind, the rationale being that the closer the buyer gets to feeling that he owns the product mentally, the closer he gets to owning it factually.

A favorite among real estate agents: "Can't you almost smell the steaks cooking?", asked when they show customers back-yards outfitted with elaborate patios that have gas barbecues as their centerpieces.

Obviously, the customers can't smell anything cooking, except possibly the broker reckoning his 7 percent commission. But it doesn't matter. The agent has accomplished his objective, to wit, flooding their minds with the heady imagery of backyard barbecues, sizzling ribs, burgers with all the toppings, good times, good friends, good beer, good cheer, the whole en-chilada.

"I sold a lot of barbecues in my day," muses one broker: "The houses just happened to come along with it."

And Now for Some Questions The New Salesperson Does not Ask

Remember Max and Mavis and the dress shop on Park Avenue South? You will recall that Michelle, the saleswoman in the anecdote, dispensed with the classic retail salutation "Can I help you?" Instead, she just told the couple to look around, and to come find her when they needed her.

The reason she did so might be clear from your own experience with retail salespeople; what, as a rule, do people say when salespeople strut over and ask, "Can I help you?" They say—all together now—"No, I'm just looking." Given the premium placed by TNS theorists on establishing a bond of progressive affirmation, it's only logical that today's sales workers would want at all costs to avoid being greeted with a no in reply to their very first sentence.

Accordingly, they don't ask questions that leave the buyer the option of saying no (except when a no is a functional yes, as in the case of questions like "You wouldn't want to do business with a company that offered a lesser guarantee, would you?").

"Notice," says California trainer Ken Clifford, "that when Johnny Carson interviews somebody on his show, he seldom asks questions that call for a simple answer. He asks delving questions—unless it's a put-on, an intentional dead-end conversation like the type of routine he does now and then with Robert Blake [of *Baretta* fame, known for his sullen, incommunicative press posture]. Johnny doesn't ask you if you enjoyed your trip to Montego Bay—he asks you to 'tell us about your trip to Montego Bay.' That way he's almost assured of getting a halfway decent response out of the person he's interviewing." Clifford singles out Barbara Walters, too, as one who has mastered the art of asking questions that elicit important information.

Clifford also says that the modern salesperson should "learn from Paul Newman's mistakes." The reference, Clifford explains, is not to Newman's spaghetti sauce, but rather to a scene in the actor's critically acclaimed film *The Verdict*.

Newman, a lawyer seeking damages on behalf of a comatose patient, is trying to wrest from the doctor he's cross-examining an admission of negligence. Newman's character demands to know why it took the surgical team a full ten minutes to restore the woman's heartbeat, the implication being that she would not have emerged from the operation so tragically impaired had her heartbeat been reestablished sooner. The surgeon replies in his superior manner that it wouldn't have taken ten minutes for the woman's disability to occur; in her particular case, the massive damage could have happened in just three minutes.

Newman is clearly nonplussed. "Three minutes?" he asks. "And why is that?"

The doctor smirks triumphantly. "It's right there on her chart. She was anemic. Her brain was getting less blood anyway. Less blood, less oxygen."

The chagrined Newman sighs and retreats to lick his wounds. Soon after, he is admonished by his partner, Jack Warden: "You broke the first rule I ever taught you in law school, Frankie. *Never ask a question you don't know the answer to [italics mine]*."

A cardinal assumption of TNS is that the salesperson must know what the prospect needs. As Joe Carter, national sales training director for AT&T, puts it, "The salesman, today, is a prime resource to his customer. You're there to solve his problems. If all that you can offer him is information he already knows, then what does he need you for?" As the presentation moves toward its conclusion, the salesman must somehow lead the customer to a position of concurrence about that need. He must, in short, already know the answers to the questions he is asking. A surprise response during the closing phases of a sales call presents a major tactical dilemma that requires a substantial amount of backtracking, and may even kill the deal. Ergo, as he reaches the end of his presentation, the salesman has to be sure—before he asks—what answers he is going to get.

But this puts the contemporary salesman in a catch-22 quandary. On the one hand, he's got to make decisions about what's in the customer's best interest. On the other hand, he's not supposed to lecture the customer. How do you communicate —or subconsciously implant—a buying decision without sermonizing, without falling back on the old crutch of a canned presentation?

The solution is for the salesman to focus the customer's thinking through the use of carefully devised test questions. The test questions themselves are based on information that might have been available to the salesman initially, before the sales call began. As the interview progresses, the salesman refines his analysis of the customer's needs in accordance with the feedback he receives from those test questions. Gradually the salesman can fashion a framework in which no answers other than those he wants to hear will suggest themselves to the customer. His queries become more and more focused, leaving the customer with fewer and fewer options, until his final questions are phrased in a manner that will inexorably extract the one, ultimate answer he wants to hear.

This ain't easy. It requires an exquisite sensitivity to clues that may be either subtle or tacit. And for many salespeople, it represents an ethical, as well as a tactical, stumbling block.

A young IBM rep: "I know all about the line that goes, I've got to walk in there and solve the client's problems for him; it's in his best interests for me to take things into my own hands and make positive decisions on his behalf; it's for his own good. But that's a platitude. You can justify everything that way. When you come down to it, you're still manipulating people to get them to do things you want them to do."

Another fellow, formerly with a top insurance company known for its good hands, put it even less flatteringly: "You always hear rapists say, 'You know you want it, baby. Lemme give you what you need.' That's what we used to do. It was an abuse of persuasion, plain and simple."

Needless to say, most TNS apostles do not share such skepticism. They are possessed by the belief that no matter how much a customer objects, the right-thinking salesman must persevere in his philanthropic quest to enrich his customer's life:

"Every day, my prospects and customers beat me and scratch me and kick me and claw me," Pat Knowles, a tax-shelter purveyor, told *Psychology Today,* "but I persist, and I help them solve their tax problems." The kind of benign (if not terribly humble) conviction embodied in Knowles's remark is what enables the new salesman to feel justified about the process he uses to attain compliance.

The best illustration of the process itself is a card trick used by top trainers to show how unselfconscious true suggestion can be. I first saw the trick performed with hypnotic effect by one Lonnie Joe Kindred, a fast-talking Texan with an eclectic style fashioned from the teachings of Zig Ziglar, Abraham Maslow, and half a dozen others. (Not that it's relevant, but Kindred would later be the principal figure in an investment scam in which scores of hopeful security franchise owners were bilked of amounts varying between four thousand and sixty thousand dollars. As of this writing, the San Diego lawsuit remains unresolved.)

Kindred told us he could pick a card from a deck and get anyone in the audience to name his choice—without his telling us anything about the card itself—simply by asking us a brief series of questions. He then picked his card, the three of diamonds, as we would subsequently learn, and went about the task of selecting someone "at random" from the audience. I put the phrase in quotations because it later came out that the person he'd picked at random was actually on his payroll—a shill—but that had no material bearing on the success or failure of the card trick, only that old Lonnie Joe had misrepresented things to the audience.

Anyway, the person came up to the head of the class, and Kindred proceeded with his questions:

> LONNIE JOE: Now, would you agree that every regular deck has fifty-two cards?
> SHILL: Yes.
> LJ: And would you agree that each deck is composed of two colors?
> S: Yes.
> LJ: And what are those colors?
> S: Red and Black.
> LJ: Would you pick one for us?

s: Black.

LJ: And that leaves. . . ?

s: Red.

LJ: Fine, and would you agree that among the red cards, there are two suits?

s: Yup.

LJ: Would you pick one for us?

s: Diamonds.

LJ: Great, and would you also agree that in diamonds, there are picture cards and number cards?

s: Sure.

LJ: Which would you prefer?

s: Picture cards.

LJ: Okay, and that leaves. . . ?

s: Number cards.

LJ: Fantastic, now is it true that among number cards, you have even and odd numbers?

s: It sure is.

LJ: Would you select one?

s: Odd.

LJ: Good, and if we examine all the odd-numbered cards, would you agree that there are high cards and low cards?

s: Seems fair enough.

LJ: And which would you choose?

s: Low cards.

LJ: Now, that would be three and five, wouldn't it?

s: Uh-huh.

LJ: Would you choose one of those, please?

s: I'll take the three.

LJ: Fantastic! You've selected my card—the three of diamonds!

In reality, of course, the subject didn't "choose" anything. The choice was completely controlled by Kindred's savvy interrogation. But most everybody in the audience was duly awed—until Kindred went through it again, slowly, revealing his own tactics, whereupon we all felt kind of dumb for not having seen through it at once. It's like a magic trick; as long as it remains unexplained—as long as it's done professionally, and not handled in a manner that tends to focus attention on the methodology—the person on the receiving end is left with the feeling that *he* made all the critical decisions.

As we've said, this can't work in real life unless the salesman knows what answers he wants in the first place, which is the principal reason why all new-salesmanship doctrines stress the importance of what Xerox calls "preapproach planning." The more a salesman can find out about his prospect in advance, the closer he gets to knowing ahead of time where his presentation is going to wind up. He can't get the customer to say "three of diamonds" unless he himself already knows that's his hole card.

It should be obvious, however, that in practice, a salesman can't entirely avoid asking questions for which he doesn't already have the answer. No matter how good a salesman's advance info, or "intelligence"—industry is increasingly borrowing this phrase from the realm of espionage and diplomacy—there will always be things he needs to ascertain during the course of the sales interview. He's got to garner enough honest data in the early going to come to his momentous decision.

But once the preliminary discovery process has been accomplished, the contemporary salesman begins to confine the field of possible responses to conform with his developing sense of ultimate purpose. The seventy-five thousand or so reps trained by Xerox Learning Systems last year were particularly well schooled in this; an article in *Fortune* described them as quickest to close among three of America's top industrial-sales-training firms (not surprising, given the firm's theories about the counterproductivity of prolonged open-ended questioning; see Chapter 6).

Thus, closing, in the age of TNS, becomes less a matter of coercion, or even persuasion, than simply reminding the customer of his own insights. Or, as one manager euphemistically defined it—I was present when the man actually said this to his small staff of office-products salespeople—"concretizing customer objectives." The sales rep asks his questions, then, based on feedback, asks more focused questions (really statements in disguise).

And if he's done everything right, the customer—his objectives having been duly concretized—will authorize the paper-work.

Easy as one, two, three of diamonds.

• • •

The day I attended Lonnie Joe Kindred's seminar at the Sheraton-Anaheim was the first time I'd seen the card trick done. I would go on to see it performed many times after, as I became more deeply immersed in the subject of contemporary selling. The trick is regarded in the trade as though it were an epiphany, a revelation handed down on the mount. It is the showstopper in many a sales trainer's presentation.

No one, however, has eclipsed the performance of the fellow I would see in Cherry Hill, New Jersey, a year or so after I'd been introduced to the trick by Lonnie Joe Kindred.

Kindred's delivery had been good, but this other guy was . . . indescribable. The routine, after all, has an inherent redun-dancy. If your subject keeps coming up with the wrong choice—as happened that day in New Jersey—you're put in the position of asking "And that leaves. . . ?" half a dozen times or more. Alert listeners catch on.

This fellow never used quite the same inflection twice, though. And his pacing was extraordinary. He was clearly the consummate professional. He had it all *down*. Yet his words never seemed pat, stiff, rehearsed to death. Slick? He was slick as a backwoods road in Green Bay during a January hailstorm. Yet surprisingly empathetic, so much so that the room at times seemed suffused with a warm, transcendental glow. Smooth? As smooth as . . . as the burled rosewood dashboard of his new Rolls-Royce. And yet not so smooth that you'd be moved to wonder about his sincerity.

Overall, he struck that perfect, fragile, improbable balance between icy precision and radiant humanity.

As I stood outside the banquet hall before the seminar be-gan, I heard a young man wonder what the delay was in getting under way. A female voice answered, "I don't think Tom has arrived yet."

She couldn't have been more wrong. Tom Hopkins had ar-rived a long time before, bringing with him not just the ideology of TNS, but a brand new approach to merchandising it. Simply put, Tom augured a revolution in sales training. The selling of selling was elevated from an entrepreneurial exercise to an international phenomenon, and an art form.

Let us move on to meet the man to whom all practitioners of TNS, for better or worse, for richer or poorer—almost certainly richer—are largely indebted.

Sales Miscellany

Number of books by leading TNS trainers
that made The New York Times *best-seller list in 1984:*
*two (*Zig Ziglar's Secrets of Closing the Sale, *by Zig Ziglar,*
and The One Minute Sales Person *by Larry Wilson).*

5

The Selling of Selling, Part One: Tom Hopkins

Lights. Camera. Action.

The short man with the blue suit and the baby face struts to the podium. Much applause. A woman toward the rear of the assembly yells, "We love you, Tom!" The audience erupts, then settles into an expectant hush. The electricity in the huge room is palpable.

The savior has come.

He surveys his flock with a warm, toothy grin. His dark eyes flash, and then widen. "How we doin' this morning, Champions?"—the line is delivered in an odd, singsong drawl. It seems to hang in the air, gaining intensity. More applause, and this time, cheers.

I sit in the rear of the audience, near a sign that says capacity is 550. In the aisle beside me, and in a similar aisle on the far side of the hall, there are dozens of people standing. To my right, an attractive young woman wearing a two-piece suit taps her legal pad with the eraser end of her pen. She is impatient for things to begin. But she is also smiling, because up at the podium, Tom is smiling. *I* am smiling. You can't help it; it's contagious. To my left, one of the standees has struck up a conversation with the fellow next to him.

"Ever been to one of these before?" he asks.

The second man shakes his head.

"It's unreal," says the first man, with zealous animation that suggests he might have burst had he gone another five seconds without venting his enthusiasm. "Last time, on Long Island, Tom had everybody completely mesmerized. You had to be there. I think after the first hour or so, we all would've gone out and done just about anything he told us to."

Intrigued, the listener begins to ask a question, but his new-found acquaintance raises an admonishing finger in the air between them. For up at the front of the room, Tom has begun to speak, and one does not speak while the master is speaking. . . .

• • •

From the street, the corporate headquarters of Tom Hopkins International is no threat to the Taj Mahal. It is an unimpressive, low-lying building in the middle of an unimpressive, low-lying industrial park in Scottsdale, Arizona. The unimpressiveness ends at the door, however. Once inside, one is overcome by a kind of mass jubilation that borders on cultism. Inspirational axioms are everywhere. (Example: "The number of times I succeed is in direct proportion to the number of times I can fail and keep on trying.") Everyone is up, everyone is alert, optimism reigns supreme. Which is as it should be for any firm that has as its sole purpose the training and motivation of professional salespeople.

Nor is the enthusiasm forced or affected. The on-site employees of THI have every reason to be cheerful, for their mentor has somehow managed to attract as large an audience as the very largest corporate training firms, including Xerox and the various Dale Carnegie incarnations. Tom Hopkins held almost two hundred training seminars in 1984—personally. On any given morning you may find him in Duluth or Dublin, Jacksonville or Johannesburg. His itinerary looks for all the world like something spit out by a travel agent's computer gone berserk. Over the past five years—a time when his would-be competition grew in geometric fashion—Tom single-handedly imparted his wisdom to about three quarters of a million salespeople (most of whom paid upward of forty dollars each to attend open seminars like the one I went to). In so doing, he established himself as the premier individual in a line of work projected by some analysts to blossom into a ten-billion-dollar-a-year industry in its own right by 1990. Along the way, he watched his W-2 stretch first to six, then seven figures (plus investments), wrote a quartet of strong-selling books, recorded and sold a few million cassette tapes. He had already grasped the enormous potential of video back in 1979, before terms like "beta" and "VHS" had found their way into the national vocabulary; he says he had "a few thousand" such tapes in circulation by 1981, when *Thriller* was just a gleam in Michael Jackson's wallet.

"Tom's energy is phenomenal," says one of his outclassed competitors, not without a trace of pique. "You know the old saw that goes 'Work fills all space'? Well, Tom fills all space with work, and when he runs out of space, he adjusts his schedule so he can cram still more work in. He defines the word *ambition*."

Somewhat less ambitious is the size of Tom's office in the Scottsdale facility. However, this, too, is misleading. One must take into account that up until quite recently, there was no such thing as Tom Hopkins International. The whole operation sprang up virtually overnight (as these things go). The rows of partitioned cubicles, each with a cluttered desk and pleasantly traumatized employee, are an apt barometer of just how far the enterprise has come since Hopkins first hung out a shingle and began calling himself Champions Unlimited.

"The old name was fine for a grass-roots, local-yokel kind of thing," says Tom, not without affection, "but it had to go when we took aim at the big guys, a couple years ago. We needed something more decorous. Champions Unlimited would've sounded a bit hokey to a company like IBM."

These days, few people consider Hopkins hokey.* His list of testimonials, featured on all company literature, reads like the proverbial *Who's Who,* comprising the biggest and best of America's industrial giants. Also represented are a respectable and ever-increasing number of foreign firms—hence, the "In-

---

*Among that few, however, is Joe Carter, director of sales training for AT&T. See Chapter 7.

ternational." Even Xerox's name appears, which is both peculiar (to most insiders, since the leviathan manufacturer of office products maintains a perfectly good sales-training division in-house) and amusing (to Hopkins, who enjoys the ironic implications of having penetrated one of his foremost competitors). On minimal provocation, Tom will produce a Xerox-sponsored pamphlet entitled "Selling the Xerox System." The publication, which Hopkins insists "was not solicited for by us in any way," counsels fledgling Xerox salespeople that Hopkins's books and tapes are of inestimable value to the serious-minded sales pro. The pamphlet thereby snubs Xerox's own XLS (Xerox Learning Systems) subsidiary, which boasts, among other things, of having itself enlightened the sales staffs of 407 out of *Fortune*'s current 500. Stranger still is that XLS's marketing maven Betsy Moser professed no knowledge of the man whose name was so glowingly featured on training material circulated by her own parent company.

"They may not always know my name," says Hopkins, grinning sardonically, "but they sure seem to know my material."

• • •

Truer words were never spoken. Hopkins-inspired strategies—whether paid for, borrowed, or informally absorbed through others—have been popping up in the sales presentations and marketing plans of countless firms across America, from the smallest retailer of sporting goods, to the largest distributor of heavy machinery. ("We don't try to *sell* you a car," says the ad copy of a West Coast car dealer, "we help you *own* one.") *The porcupine technique. Closing on the minor point. Changing their base.* All key pieces of jargon from a concerted sales philosophy that postulates: (a) you don't win by bullying people, at least not overtly, and (b) there is no such thing as failure, at least in its traditional sense.

The Hopkins-trained salesman is a *holistic* salesman; that is, everything he says and does, from the most obvious uses of body language to the subtlest nuances of the spoken word, is carefully honed to maximize his credibility.

Strictly speaking, these were not Hopkins innovations. He

admits that he owes much to the early training received at the hands of J. Douglas Edwards, the so-called father of modern selling. (Fittingly, Edwards wrote the foreword to Hopkins's first book on salesmanship.) But the alert young Hopkins did what no one had really done before. He took Edwards's general theories and reformulated them into a subliminal blitzkrieg, an organized system of specific stimuli and responses that allows any given salesperson to maintain unerring control, to keep the presentation always on the path leading to a sale. Hopkins teaches his charges to listen more than they speak, and to quickly process the information for immediate use. They become the computers in a game of computer chess, expertly programmed to make the right move at every turn, to play a different game each time, but with the same inevitable result.

"But you know," Tom protests, as we chat before a seminar, "when you put it in those terms, it makes it sound sinister, and it isn't. I once was sitting next to an elderly woman on an airplane, and I noticed she was sizing me up pretty good. Finally she asked me what I did for a living. When I told her I trained salespeople, she actually gasped, as though I'd told her I trained child molesters or something.

"People with that kind of an attitude don't have any idea what good selling's about. Good selling is based on the customer's needs. If the customer has a need for your product—and in most cases, you wouldn't be there if they weren't—then you have a genuine obligation to make sure they wind up owning it. You should feel guilty if they leave your store without it, because you've let them down. You've deprived them of something that would make their lives better, simpler, more fun."

Without forewarning me, Hopkins decides to illustrate. "Let me ask you something," he begins, innocently enough. "We all have problems, don't we? I have problems, you have problems. At least some minor ones, and maybe a couple major ones—isn't that right?"

I nod, not quite sure what he's driving at.

"Well suppose you knew somebody—somebody with a proven track record—who said they could eliminate some or all of those problems for twelve dollars. Twelve bucks! Somebody who said they could remove some of the obstacles standing between you and a more fulfilling, successful life. Wouldn't it be well worth it to you? For twelve bucks? Even if it just eliminated one nagging problem?"

"Sure," I reply casually, whereupon he reaches behind him and hands me a copy of one of his books, *The Official Guide To Success*. The cover price is $11.95.

"There you go!" he says with a broad, triumphant grin. "And you get a nickel change." He turns earnest. "Now, I'm not actually gonna make you pay for it. I had intended on giving you the book anyway, as a souvenir. But I'm just proving a point. If I'd gone ahead and taken your money, some people watching the whole thing unfold might've said I tricked you, I sucked you in. But I didn't at all! All I did was make it possible for you to own something that will help you be a happier person. Something that'll help you get rid of the problems you yourself said you had.

"What could be wrong with that?" he concludes. Yet for just the briefest instant, something in his eyes says the question is not entirely rhetorical.

"Never," says an executive I know, "trust anyone who tries to give you a lecture about spiritual health from behind the wheel of a Rolls-Royce."

• • •

Nonetheless, for most people who have met the man—listened to him talk—it is hard not to come away convinced that such admonitions are inapplicable in Tom's case. Hopkins has a folksiness that belies his stature, fancy rings and flaunty cars notwithstanding. And he has a rationale for all the glitter: "How," he asks, "can you teach people success if you don't have it yourself?"

To attempt to answer that question is to get hopelessly bogged down in the realms of philosophy and ethics. What, after all, is success? How do you define it, whose criteria do you use, and so forth. Far less speculative, however, is Hopkins's ability to take people and turn them into true believers. Somehow, jaded as you are, he will probably convince you that success—whatever it is—can be yours if you just follow his lead.

It is a fact, for example, that exposé-hungry reporters who've gone in expecting to find a jet-setting, self-indulgent, chew-'em-up-and-spit-'em-out super-capitalist, have come out feeling like members of the flock, friends, even confidants. "He has a wonderful way of putting himself across," says a former aide. "Even when you do something wrong, Tom makes you believe you're the most important, capable person in the world. He just tells you that by doing it in such and such a way instead, you can let your true abilities stand out for all to see." With a laugh, she adds, "You really have to sit down and think about it to realize he was criticizing you for something you messed up!"

Nor, seemingly, does this talent wear thin with continual exposure. Witness the thirty-five or forty full-time Hopkins employees, who float up and down the halls, in and out of Tom's office—he is Tom to everyone—in various stages of bliss. Tom's special brand of magnetism has a narcotic effect, an effect felt at our first meeting, when his hectic schedule limited our conversation to a dozen uninspiring words.

"Welcome to Scottsdale," he said. "I'm Tom. Sorry about the delay."

The outstretched hand was attached to a body that, despite a certain corpulence, looked far too slight to have accorded its owner such dominance over so many. The face was warm and sweetly handsome (like the faces of the guys who sing and dance for Lawrence Welk), the smile relaxed and unthreatening, the hair in an updated, Hyannis Port bob. Physically, he did not cut a very imposing figure.

Still, there was the magnetism, that incredible *presence,* which imbued his greeting with some special, indefinable meaning. In Richard Burton's heyday, people joked that he could make the phone book sound compelling. Tom does the same with routine salutations.

Maybe you've had the experience of meeting someone you don't trust right off the bat. You have no evidence whatever to support your intuition, it's just a *feeling,* an unformed sense of wariness or foreboding. With Tom, it's just the opposite. His words have the ring of gospel truth. Intellectually, you know enough to remain aloof, to retain your journalist's skepticism. Emotionally, though, you just *want* to believe him. Which, I suppose, is to be expected of a man who began his career not just by breaking, but by obliterating all the single-year sales records in the volatile Southern California real estate market of the late sixties.

"And then," quips Tom's partner and business manager, Tom Murphy, "he decided to apply himself."

• • •

We are back, live, in Cherry Hill, New Jersey, where about 549 people besides myself are expected to attend a Hopkins real estate seminar. Unlike its ancestral forms, today's brand of sales training is anything but cut and dry. It is an event, a ritualized assault on the mind and senses. To no small degree, Hopkins has been responsible for the metamorphosis.

The indoctrination is well under way before Tom even makes his appearance. While the members of the audience are getting settled in their seats, seminar coordinator Ron Marks plays something called "The Champions Song." It is a Glen Campbellesque country-and-western ditty, penned, we are told, by none other than Hopkins himself. The lyrics confirm that the tune was not written by Cole Porter.

On a hi-fi with the tinny fidelity of a child's toy, Marks plays the song not once, but twice. Audience reaction varies from genuine excitement to oh-Christ, what-kind-of-bullshit-did-I-let-myself-in-for cynicism. But those in the latter category are a decided minority.

In fact, if there is any doubt about Hopkins's status in the minds of those who've showed up at 8 A.M. on this lovely October morning, it dissipates when the man himself is introduced. That honor falls to a black realtor named Gordon Parks, who refers to a Hopkins seminar he attended some years back as "the three days that made the difference in my life." The audience goes berserk on cue. So intense are the revival-meeting overtones as Parks surrenders the mike to his mentor that the building seems in jeopardy of being shaken to its very foundations by a chorus of "hallelujahs."

The room is full, and getting fuller all the time. Earlier, Tim Hopkins, Tom's son and road manager, had told me that dad had already trained 1,600 people in two days in Jersey. "The room size may vary, but it's always full," he said with a certain smugness. Interestingly, though Tim possesses the same imperial bearing as his famous father, he seems to lack the compensatory sincerity that helps to soften Tom's overall effect. Tom comes across as reassuringly competent. Tim came across to me as mildly cagey—someone I'd want to watch—an ironic testament to his father's theory that salesmen are made, not born.

Typically, Hopkins starts a seminar off with his law-school anecdote, and today is no exception: "In nineteen sixty-three, I quit college and broke my father's heart." In wistful afterthought, he adds the word "literally," though the full significance of the remark is lost on people who lack familiarity with Tom's personal affairs. The fact is, the elder Hopkins's heart troubles are traced by Tom back to that episode, which insiders say began an estrangement that took a great while to heal. Careful listeners might wonder whether it has ever healed, for Tom. He mentions the falling out often, even if most of the allusions are couched in his characteristic sardonic humor.

"Your mother and I will always love you," he recalls his father's words, "even though you're a loser and you'll never amount to anything."

From here he segues into the celebrated Hopkins saga, telling this audience, as he does each and every audience, how he floundered about for a while before finally taking a job as a steelworker.

"You ever see those long iron girders that are always laying around construction sites?" he asks. "Well, what I did was carry those things, over my shoulder, ten hours a day." Whimsically, he says, "I used to be six-two before I took that job." The audience eats it up.

Not surprisingly, it wasn't long before Hopkins, at five feet eight inches and "maybe 150 pounds," decided that he had not exactly found his ideal calling.

"So," he says, "I did what millions of red-blooded Americans do every year. I said to myself—"Hey!"—here he contorts his face into a Red Skeltonesque mask of idiocy, and in one of his seemingly innumerable funny dialects, says, "whah don't ah trah say-els?" He allows his face to resume its usual boyish intensity, as the audience regains its composure.

"Now let me ask you something," he continues, suddenly deadpan. "How many people do you know who wake up one morning and say, 'Hmmmm. I need a change in my life. I think I'll *try* brain surgery'?" A wave of giggles rolls through the room. "And how many surgeons do you know who start off by saying, 'Oh well, I really don't know what I'm doing, but I guess I'll learn as I go along. Somebody hand me a scalpel'?" The laughter swells, but Tom drowns them out in order to make his point.

"And yet," he says, in a near-yell, "how many of us still do what I did then? How many of us start off by saying, I think I'll *try* sales? Well, it don't work that way, my friends"—he is now at his evangelical best—"this is a *pro-feh-shun,* a specialty, every bit as complex in its own way as medicine. You need a commitment. And you need the *knowledge.*"

Lacking that knowledge, the young Tom Hopkins spent his first six months in real estate floundering about uncertainly. "We had a training program that went more or less like this," he often says, imitating one person giving another person an encouraging pat on the shoulder, "'Hang in there.'" At the end of six months, he'd netted forty-two dollars. Luckily, he explains, a salesperson who happened to walk into the office one day sold him on the idea of attending a J. Douglas Edwards seminar. And the rest, to coin a phrase, is history.

• • •

By this time in the seminar, there are people crammed everywhere—and I mean everywhere. If you were somehow able to gingerly lift away the walls, the people left behind would form a human casting of the room depicting every nook and cranny as precisely as a chocolate Santa reflects the mold used to make it.

In fact, the persistent milling about of the standees has begun to irritate Tom. "Those of you who are standing in the back so you can be with the people you came with, I'd like you to split up now and find a seat. You can see your friends later." When his words are interpreted by some as humor, he stiffens and pans the back of the room with the closest thing he has to a fixed glare.

"You know, I don't do this for money anymore," says the man who took home a million-plus for his seminar efforts in 1984. "I do this for commitment. You can't concentrate if you're not comfortable, and you certainly can't take notes if you're standing there with your hands at your sides. There's enough seats here for all of you, and I'm not going to continue until all of you find a seat." He tells everyone who has an empty chair next to him to raise his right hand, and instructs each of the standees to head for the nearest raised hand. He waits silently for his orders to be carried out. My intuition, after several interviews with Tom, is that he dislikes standees because he feels, at some subconscious level, that they represent a threat to his supremacy in the room. This is, perhaps, one of Tom's few stylistic throwbacks to the old school of selling, wherein the salesman was supposed to maintain control by towering over his seated— and presumably cowering—customers.

All but half a dozen do manage to find seats before the supply of raised hands is exhausted. At which point, Tom instructs his son and Ron Marks to go outside and lock the doors.

"If they're not here by now," he says, checking his watch, "then they missed the boat." Nonetheless, a dozen additional people file in when Marks reappears a few moments later with chairs for the original remaining standees, and stragglers continue to show up throughout the course of the morning.

By now, I'd have to say we've eclipsed Tim Hopkins's crowd guesstimate by at least a hundred or more.

Just before lunch, Tom launches into a protracted pitch for his products: his books, cassettes, and videotapes on all facets of modern salesmanship. Tom devotes a not inconsiderable amount of time to hawking these ancillary goods (he is hardly unique in this regard) apparently on the theory that if you bothered to show up at all, you're already half sold on Tom Hopkins—so you therefore represent the perfect, prequalified target market.

But the folks in Cherry Hill this day seem uncomfortable with Tom's sudden efforts at selling them. This despite his ingenious way of backing into the subject. He had begun by raffling off various items to people who'd put their business cards in a large bowl prior to the seminar. As he called the name of each winner he'd give a glowing description of the book, tape, or other product they'd won, sounding just as though he were Don Pardo telling us what's behind Door Number Three. Then, feeling that the audience's appetite was sufficiently whetted, he began his spiel.

Nonetheless, the appeal is not going over well, and the perception that the giveaway was just an enthusiasm-building gimmick for promoting the stuff descends on the room like baked turbo-diesel emissions on Rodeo Drive in mid-August. Up at the podium, however, Tom the vibemaster is unperturbed. He extricates himself from this tricky terrain with supreme grace, and even manages to leave them laughing.

"Now I know that some of you are thinking, You're trying to sell us, Tom," he correctly proposes. "You got us here where you want us, and now you're trying to sell us."

He pauses and pans the audience, smiling his contagious, choirboy grin. "Well," he says, "let me tell you this: You should never expect to learn anything from someone who can't *do* what he's trying to teach you."

The line sinks in. When I leave the room, carried out in a yellow sea of Century 21 humanity, the product tables are abuzz, with Tim Hopkins, Ron Marks, and a couple of other THI personnel scarcely able to keep up with the customers. Meanwhile, behind me, I hear Tom's final admonition to the group: "Remember, if you're not back here on time you're going to have to get up in front of the room and tell the class why you were late."

• • •

Every so often—not too often, but just now and then—Tom will say something to me in an aside, or in answer to a question, that makes me wonder if he really understands what I'm doing back there taking all those notes. It happens again when I corner him as he leaves the stage and ask about the wisdom of his trying such an intense, clearly commercial pitch so early in the day. Wouldn't it have been better to wait until later? Wasn't Tom worried about alienating his audience before they were thoroughly taken with the Hopkins mystique?

He shrugs. "We try a lot of different formats for presenting the products, and we see which works best. But you know, the people down here"—he grimaces, shakes his head—"you gotta wake 'em up early if you're gonna get 'em to spend anything at all.

"I mean, they are really *cheap*."

• • •

There are two interesting developments during lunch in Cherry Hill, which, at Tom's invitation, I spend with him and a quartet of regional Champions. The foursome is affiliated with the brokerage firm of Bailey and Bailey of Wildwood, New Jersey. Wildwood is a smallish seaside resort community that used to give Atlantic City a run for its money in the days before casino gambling came along to suck all the coins from the pockets of vacationers from Maine to Miami. Since then, the Wildwood real estate market has flattened out, grown bitterly competitive, and LaVerne Frantz, one of the Bailey and Bailey salespeople, has noticed something.

It seems that the increased competition has driven more and more local reps to invest in Tom's sales-training courses. While some people, particularly among the larger corporate training firms, will give you an argument about Tom's standing in the sales-training field generally, his status as America's premier real-estate sales trainer is unchallenged. As a result, says La-Verne, "We're all starting to sound alike. I've had people tell me, when I respond to a certain question, that somebody else with another brokerage gave them the same exact answer yesterday." What, she wants to know, do you do in a case like that?

Without missing a beat—and wielding his fork for emphasis—Tom replies, "You tell them that sales is getting more and more professionalized these days, and the answer you gave them was simply the professional answer to their question. Any pro would have given that same answer."

Once again the Hopkins magic is in evidence. His explanation appears to satisfy Frantz, although in reality it merely begs a series of much deeper questions.

Reduced to its essence, the great selling point of Hopkins's training program is that it will allow the average rep to escape mediocrity and achieve unparalleled sales heroics. But what happens to that promise of a fabulous competitive edge once all the salespeople know all the answers, a phenomenon Tom himself expects to occur sometime within "the next decade or so"?

The situation already exists in some milieus; as Burroughs's eastern regional manager Marvin Edelstein puts it, "you don't sell hundred-thousand-dollar information systems the way you sell ties in front of Penn Station." Virtually all high-tech selling nowadays has been professionalized to the nth degree. Essentially, doesn't that put everyone back at square one? If everybody is a star salesperson, is anybody?

More important, perhaps, is the question of consumer response to this kind of uniformity. After attending the seminar, I made it a point to raise the issue with as many people as possible, and the response (at least among Californians and New Yorkers) was nearly unanimous. Most everyone is a little leery of the scenario Hopkins describes, in which every answer to every question is being plucked from a standardized catalog of officially sanctioned choices, neatly indexed and cross-referenced for all occasions. What, one woman wondered, ever happened to the personal touch?

Beyond that, people were troubled by the between-the-lines import of Tom's pithy platitude: *The answer you gave them is simply the professional answer.* Isn't that just a veiled way of saying to the customer, "I said what I said because it's been statistically determined to persuade people like you to *buy*"? Even if that's what all selling is basically about, the participants of my informal survey wanted to know, doesn't such an admission come a bit too close to the heart of the matter?

I suppose only time will tell.

The second intriguing development involved Tom's customary practice of lauding members of the audience for their notable achievements. Shortly before the break he had singled out Edward Bailey, the junior partner of a firm, and credited him with having done "eight million dollars in sales volume last

year." Looking mildly chagrined, Bailey stood up and acknowl-
edged the applause with a quick wave. He now confides, as Tom
slips away to confer with Ron Marks, that it was not he himself,
but *the entire office* that did eight million dollars. Needless
to say, Bailey's co-workers did not appreciate his being given
sole credit for an achievement in which they played a significant role.

I ask Bailey if he made the distinction clear when he gave
Tom his business card during the first intermission.

"It wasn't a case of making anything clear," he replies.
"There was no doubt in the first place. I went up and I told him,
'Our office did eight million dollars last year, and I'm sure your
training program had at least something to do with it.'"
Shrewdly, he adds, "I suppose Tom thought it would make the
testimonial that much more impressive if he attributed it to one
person rather than an entire brokerage."

Perhaps the incident was an honest mistake on Tom's part,
but it also was consistent with Tom's tendency to come up with
facts and figures that seem (often) obscure, (sometimes) arbitrary, and (once in a while) invented. Earlier in the day, Tom
had cautioned people who did a lot of sales work via the telephone, "Never leave a customer on hold for *more than seventeen
seconds.*" (And you always thought it was 16.5 . . .) He also
mentioned—while explaining that he'd long ago set the precedent of riding through tract developments and giving out Halloween pumpkins with business cards attached—that there were
"ten million pumpkins given out by realtors last year." (Now
honestly, how the hell do you keep track of something like
that?) After lunch, Tom would offer the following advice on
how to hold the line on price, and thereby boost commissions, in
the current real estate climate:

"When a prospect who is really interested in a property asks
you to make an offer which is substantially less than the asking
price, tell him two things. First, that if your offer is too low, you
risk offending the seller, and they may refuse to sell it to you for
any price. Second, tell them that even in today's market, the
average house comes down only two-and-a-half percent off the
listing price."

Perhaps feeling that the figure is not credible, given the soft economy of the past few years, someone in the front asks Tom where he got his information.

"Who cares?" Tom replies glibly. "Use it."

• • •

Control—of your environment, your prospect, and so forth—is a key element in Hopkins training, and so not surprisingly, it also ranks quite high on Tom's seminar agenda. But it doesn't just have to do with getting people to find seats. And it's seldom expressed in a severe manner. Actually, if there's one thing that sets Tom apart from the crowd, it is his ability to establish and maintain control of his audience through the kinds of silly-funny little shticks that are normally amusing only after you've had five or six mai tais.

Tom, for example, is big on physical stuff. He is a great believer in getting people actively involved in the seminar, in having them physically participate in the various routines he uses to illustrate his points. By doing this, Tom assumes a natural position of dominance, and people begin to follow his lead mentally, as well.

He breaks in his audiences gently. Early in the seminar, he will begin to establish his hold by making them follow simple commands—"now raise your right hand and repeat after me"—and will not proceed with his presentation until he has secured virtual 100 percent compliance. He might lecture for a while, and then it's back to using our right hands again, this time to trace the emotional cycle of the real estate agent, with its extreme highs and lows. Soon the room is like a huge aerobics class, with all 550 or 600 of us (yes, including yours truly) windmilling our arms up and down and around in a wide arc.

As if almost to test the bond of faith, he graduates later in the day to exercises that carry this physical leadership to increasingly outlandish dimensions. He insists that we all "zip ourselves into our protective shells" to insulate us from the negative thoughts of "people who are even more messed up than *you* are." Complete with sound effects, he performs the actual zipping process with both hands, starting over his head and working downward, as though he were installing himself into an upright body bag. By now totally conditioned, the large majority of the audience zips right along with Tom.

When he feels his authority over the group is being put to the test, he is ever ready for the challenge. Somewhere during each seminar, he leads his acolytes through a monotonous sing-along of the proper responses to a dozen separate customer objections, his theory being that you must internalize the exact words, they must become second nature. Inevitably, though, the crowd's enthusiasm for the undertaking begins to fall off after the first few choruses, and pockets of silent resistance develop here and there throughout the hall.

Tom will simply stop in midline and just stare for a moment, hands on his hips, his brow furrowed, his lips pulled tight about his teeth. The image of a cranky Richard Simmons comes to mind.

"I know some of you are thinking that a salesman shouldn't be a robot," he says, again at his omniscient best. "You're thinking that you shouldn't have to learn these things word for word.

"Let's talk about that for a moment. When you were born, you didn't know any words, did you? You learned them *all* word for word. Isn't that right? You didn't pop out of the womb and say, 'Hey doc, how ya' doin'? Whaddya say we cut this cord here 'cause I got lots of things to do.' No—you learned words gradually, and the way you learned them was you noticed the right things happened when you said them! If you wanted milk, but you said *truck,* you weren't gonna get that milk. You had to learn to say the right thing in order to get the results you wanted." Dramatic pause. "Well, it's no different here, gang."

Invariably, when he resumes his sing-along, not one mouth remains shut.

Another of Tom's momentum-building gimmicks involves the use of hypnotic phrases, most of which are either poetic or highly alliterative in nature. "Imitation is the first step of creation," he is fond of saying. And: "Today's brand of selling is asking, not telling; telling is pushing, asking is pulling." Also: "I am now going to tell you the two most important *f* words you will ever know"—a mischievous chuckle always spreads through the audience at this point—"the two words are *flexible* and *feasible*. . . . If they tell you they want to put down $800 on a $250,000 house, no matter what you're thinking, you tell them, 'Financing is quite flexible.' If a buyer tells you she wants something included in the transaction that the sellers have already told you they're planning to take with them when they go, you say, 'We'll have to see if that's feasible.' Everything—I don't care what it is—is either flexible or feasible."

Granted, once in a while Tom will say something that's just a bit too cute, a tad too clever, a pinch too evocative of pop-psych bullshit. Shortly after the Cherry Hill lunch break, he raises his index finger in the air and says, very pontifically, "The enemy of learning . . . is knowing." A woman four or five seats removed from me sighs disgustedly and says, to no one in particular, "The enemy of learning is knowing"—she regurgitates the sentence with almost unbelievable contempt, as though it were bile rising in her throat—"Oh, that's beautiful. And all of us paid forty dollars to come hear him say that."

Such sporadic cynicism notwithstanding, Tom does exhibit an uncanny grasp of human nature. Here, for example, are his thoughts on why selling has such a poor public image:

"Many people don't like salespeople because (a) they tried it once and couldn't do it, so they harbor a certain subconscious resentment, or (b) they did it as kids or teens and were told to say *a lie* as part of their presentation. As a result, they developed a guilt, which became a distaste, which they carry with them now as adults." (And events on the West Coast suggest that "being told to say a lie" is hardly the worst of it. In early 1985, according to Associated Press, the California Department of Labor was considering banning the use of children in door-to-door sales roles because unscrupulous crew leaders would "gather up children . . . drive them long distances and threaten to leave them far from home if they [did] not sell enough candy." How's that for motivation? In addition to such mind games, AP reported numerous instances of physical abuse and molestation.)

Indeed, Tom's inventory of insights is only slightly less awe-inspiring than his ostensible spontaneity, his proclivity for coming up with unrehearsed witticisms, rebuttals, or rationalizations on demand, although it's hard to tell whether it's truly spontaneous, since he *always* sounds so spontaneous, even when delivering spiels he's obviously given thousands of times before. It's sort of like watching Lucille Ball at the special fetes the Hollywood elite seem to throw in her honor every two weeks. Sure, she looks sincere and utterly lovable sitting there crying in front of all those nice people, but you have to wonder—after all, she looked sincere and utterly lovable sitting there crying in the show with Desi. It's her *job* to look sincere and utterly lovable, for chrissake.

Inasmuch as Tom is forever stressing that a salesperson must prepare for every conceivable situation, it's only reasonable to ask yourself whether *he* does the same thing with his seminars in mind. Maybe he's thought about every conceivable situation in advance and rehearsed his hypothetical response, so that when that situation finally does come up at some seminar in Cherry Hill or Des Moines or Johannesburg, he's ready.

Is it real, Tom, or is it memorized?

•   •   •

Like most seminar speakers, Hopkins makes frequent use of a screen projector, which takes the words he has scribbled on a white card in front of him and throws them up, big as life, on a white screen to his rear.

At one point during the Jersey seminar, Tom is writing the four stages of professional development on the screen. During Stage 1, he writes, you are "unconsciously incompetent" ("you don't know that you don't know what you're doing"); during Stage 2 you are "consciously incompetent" ("you know that you don't know what you're doing, but don't know how to remedy the problem"); Stage 3 finds you "consciously competent" ("you know what to do, but you have to think about it in order to do it right"); and ultimately, through the magic of Tom Hopkins, you get to Stage 4, in which you are "unconsciously competent" ("it's automatic—you don't have to think about it to do it right").

The system is thoughtful and the presentation amusing, but there is a distraction that has some members of the audience abuzz. Each time Tom writes the word *conscious,* he misspells it. C-o-n-c-i-o-u-s is what beams out across the crowd from the large white screen, literal proof of Hopkins's oft-repeated assertion that academia just wasn't his gig.

Up the aisle, two members of the Century 21 contingent, clad in their familiar Dijon-mustard blazers, exchange knowing looks.

"How much faith," says one, "can you have in somebody who doesn't know how to spell the word *conscious*?"

• • •

The seminar is over, and assorted businessmen want Tom. A reporter wants Tom. Tom's aides want Tom. Everybody wants Tom. ("Are there sales groupies?" I asked him once before. Tom replied, "Now and then you get people who follow you around your hotel. It doesn't happen often, but it does happen." He says they never throw underwear up on stage while he's speaking, though.) Indeed, such is the demand for Tom's time that companies who want his undivided attention will pay ten thousand dollars a day for the privilege. Hopkins does not consider his fees exorbitant.

"I understand Paul Harvey [the outspoken talk-show host and touring motivator discussed in Chapter 6] is getting seventeen five, and that's just for a talk. No real instruction. And no customization." Tom stresses his last point because unlike other sales trainers and the broad-based Dale Carnegie derivatives, Hopkins will tailor his material to the individual client footing the bill. When working in a corporate setting, he teaches his audience not merely how to sell, but how to sell the specific product or service offered by the host company.

"What I do is far more personalized than what's generally available," he contends. "I even go out and have a talk with some of their high-level people a few days ahead, so I can pick up on some of the buzz words and inside terminology." An outside consultant, he explains, is often seen as a threat or otherwise regarded skeptically by established sales staffs—especially the managers, because he's usurping their role. The more inside dope he can add to his standard presentation, the greater his rapport and credibility.

"It's like when you watch Bob Hope," he says. "Did you

ever notice, when he does his USO tours, how he sprinkles a half-dozen or more inside jokes throughout his monologue? He uses words and names and phrases that may mean nothing to a general audience, but they mean everything to the military audience he's working in front of. It's the same here. It relaxes people, makes them feel more comfortable, like you're one of the guys."

Whatever Hopkins does, it apparently works. If the general response to his instruction is not universal ecstasy, it is damned close. Not only did his selling insights reportedly up the productivity of Avon's sales workers on the average by 11 percent, but his motivational sermons solved the more immediate problem of employee turnover, cutting it by almost two thirds. Reynolds Aluminum Solar, a subsidiary of Reynolds Metals and purveyor of home-heating products, quotes an overall improvement in sales of nearly a third. Top brass at other companies credit Tom with helping them to stave off bankruptcy, or to turn red ink to black.

Of course, Hopkins himself is ever ready with the sparkling figures. He says his staff "followed" the audience of one particular open seminar a few years back, and discovered that nearly half had achieved a significant jump in performance within six months. "And," adds Tom, "only one tenth said they'd had no improvement at all."

All of which helps to explain *why* everyone wants Tom, and why his working day often extends from 6:30 A.M. to 8:30 P.M. (later on seminar days), six days each week, fifty-one weeks each year.

In the past, he tried to delegate some of the speaking chores to assistants, an arrangement Zig Ziglar has managed with some success. But for Tom it just didn't work out.

"People feel they are paying for Hopkins," says his partner and business manager, Tom Murphy, "and they don't want anything less to show up on that stage. They're not after the Hopkins method, they're after Tom himself." In other words, the man is the message. And a pretty entertaining one.

On any given afternoon Hopkins may include parodies of Falk's Columbo or Brando's Godfather, plus a host of original characters who look and sound as though they arrived, breathless, from the set of one of Joe Sedelmaier's bizarre efforts for Federal Express. Tom is a natural actor, able instantly to assume the persona of any character. A walking anecdote. If he's portraying an old-fashioned shyster, his eyes twinkle malevolently as his voice grows thick and foreboding. "Yeaahhh, baby," he purrs, showing his flock precisely the wrong way to explain your Rolls to a cynical customer, "I bought this little beaut with the commissions I banked from my last sale—and I hope to get my Maserati from you!" If he's portraying a salesman who's had a bad day, his voice actually cracks while his eyes swell with tears. He gets more out of a facial expression than most of us could achieve with a thousand-word essay. I once heard him tell a group of salespeople about how it was impossible to overstate the importance of first impressions. "Like, for example, when people walk into your office, it can't *reek,*" he said, scrunching up his face into a rotten-egg-smelling grimace that drew howls of laughter as he just let it hang there for several seconds. With Tom, the teaching is often less by lecture than by illustration, and the illustration is often comedically oriented. One attendee at a New York seminar may have pretty well summed things up when she leaned over to a companion and said, "You know, this is better than Vegas."

As if that weren't enough, the man is a master of onomato-poeic sound effects, which he sprinkles liberally throughout his oratory to heighten the dramatic effects. His routines are a symphony of gongs, whistles, ricochets, explosions, and assorted other noises he may invent specially for the occasion.

"Hopkins is a genuine entertainer in his own right," says one sales executive who admits to catching Tom's act each time the tour hits California. "Except that in Tom's case, for fifty bucks you not only get entertained, but you learn how to multiply your income."

It is a logic advanced by virtually all who subscribe to the Hopkins road show. Neither surrogates nor imposters need apply. Give us Tom, the clients say, or don't bother.

•   •   •

Giving Tom a hard time is what I seem to be doing on an unusually crisp fall afternoon in Scottsdale. I've just finished telling him that I see something sinister in the notion of sales training for a mass audience.

How so, he asks.

"If your kind of training is so potent," I venture, "then how can you justify administering it to just anybody? Suppose a guy is selling something worthless?"

Tom is impassive. "Then he shouldn't be. One of my first criteria for good selling is a true feeling for people. You have to love people to consider yourself a member of this profession. You know—and I've said this many times before—the very best *pure* salespeople in our society have to be locked up. Those are the con men, and they'll sell anything to anybody without regard to what happens afterward. But if you have that genuine feeling for people, then you won't sell them something that's not going to do them some good."

"But what about those strategies of yours that teach salesmen to sort of imply that their product is 'The Best,' or 'Exactly What the Customer Needs'? How can those strategies be applicable to all comers? There's a lot of well-intentioned salesmen out there who just don't happen to be selling 'the best' whatever-it-is. It's good, but it's not as good as what their competitor is selling, and they know it. How do you justify teaching those salesmen techniques which will convince people to buy their product anyway?"

"Look, Steve," he says, sighing deeply, "this gets into philosophy, and we could debate the subject all day and still not have an answer. But what it basically comes down to is, Who is the judge of what's good and what's less good? If everybody sat around waiting for the ideal, nothing would ever happen."

"Yeah, but there's a difference between my waiting for the ideal and your selling me something *you already know* isn't the ideal."

"But then, not everybody can have the ideal, wouldn't you agree? Maybe it's too expensive or it's too big or too difficult to insure or to garage or fix or whatever. And besides, you get a hundred people together in a room and you'll probably get about ninety-eight different versions of what 'the ideal' is. So the only thing that makes any sense—the only thing that makes it possible for you to go ahead and live your life—is to get away from those kinds of abstractions and simply try to enjoy yourself. And that's what a salesman's primary motivation should be: to help people, as many people as he can, to enjoy the benefits of his product."

"So it doesn't concern you at all that what might wind up happening is that people buy things because the *salesman* was good, rather than the product itself? That consumers wind up buying inferior products just because the company that markets those products has a superior sales force?"

"No, because when that happens, the people in charge at the companies marketing the better products will wake up and smell the coffee. Sooner or later they'll realize—financially, they'll have no choice but to realize—that if they want to compete in the marketplace, they better go out and find somebody to teach their salespeople how to present their product."

And that, one suspects, won't bother him at all.

• • •

It is known in business circles by two different names: *critical mass* (usually applied to products) or *competitive coercion* (usually applied to services). But in either case, it works the same way.

Your rival gets himself a toll-free number, you get yourself a toll-free number. Your rival offers a five-year warranty, you offer a five-year warranty. Your rival goes out and hires an expensive consultant to train his salespeople, you go out and hire an expensive consultant to train your salespeople—preferably the same expensive consultant, so your guys are assured of learning whatever the other guy's guys learned. Then, of course, your other competitors, or those who are just a notch beneath you and want to become your competitors, will want to hire that same consultant, and then *their* competitors will want to, and then . . . you get the picture.

Needless to say, this sort of thing can have a profound impact on the product or service everyone suddenly sees as being essential. These days, at Tom Hopkins International, it keeps the ball rolling quite nicely, thank you.

Interestingly, the demand for Hopkins's offerings mightn't

have existed in the first place were it not for the awesome—and totally unforeseen—success of his 1980 book, *How to Master the Art of Selling.*

"Tacky title," concedes Tom Murphy, who is far more inclined than his celebrated partner to discourse on the hard realities of merchandising, "but then again, tacky sells." True enough, although in the beginning it looked as though selling a book idea to a major publishing house was the one art Hopkins hadn't mastered.

"They wouldn't give us the time of day," Murphy recalls. "Then, when we published it in-house and sold a hundred thousand copies by mail order at twenty dollars each, that got their attention."

Warner Books magnanimously agreed to assume distribution chores at this point, and immediately had the book reprinted in five or six languages. During the following summer, a softbound version of the book lingered in the top fifteen at B. Dalton stores nationwide.

Hopkins was sent on the customary author's whirlwind tour—except that in Tom's case, it was more like a breather. "It sounds really funny to other writers I've talked to," he says, "but the book tour, with all its speaking engagements in different cities, was actually less crazy than my normal working schedule."

Tom got to do his thing on Mike Douglas and a couple of the morning shows. "It was a blast," he adds, sounding genuinely excited, while noting parenthetically that he'd "really love to do *Donahue,* because Phil [orients a lot of his shows toward] women, and we're moving more and more into the women's sales markets now." Indeed, Hopkins sometimes seems to be moving beyond sales into the general audience, a crossover accomplished with notable success by the aforementioned Zig Ziglar.

"Zig has gone into the spiritual end of it. His book, *See You at the Top,* has a tremendous mainstream readership, I hear," says Tom, obviously impressed. Not coincidentally, perhaps, Hopkins's *Official Guide To Success,* now in a second incarnation, is aimed less at the sales professional than at your average-Joe-who's-having-some-trouble-getting-ahead-in-life. Similarly, although the Cherry Hill shindig had been publicized as a real estate seminar, Tom took obvious pains throughout to augment the relevance of his monologue to life in general. Early on, he had asked how many nonsalespeople were with us that day; his query yielded the fact that the audience included, among others, a horse breeder, a psychiatrist, and a disc jockey.

"We're all salesmen," Tom explains. (His friend and protégé Danielle Kennedy puts it a bit more colorfully. "Everybody sells somebody sometime," she says, one of the rare instances in which a pupil has out-Hopkinsed Hopkins.) "Some of us get paid for it professionally, and some of us get paid in other ways, but it's something every one of us does daily. For instance, there's a lot of unemployed people out there who, if they bought my book, could learn how to prospect for a job, how to present themselves to an employer, how to overcome the employer's objections to hiring them, and how to close the sale of themselves to that employer. Then they wouldn't be unemployed anymore. And that benefits society as a whole."

Sometimes, listening to Tom, you get the idea he won't be happy until he has *trained* society as a whole; his output toward that end is as extraordinary for its diversity as for its sheer volume. He has been called the Joyce Carol Oates of sales training. Tom always seems to be where the action is.

Indeed, when we first met, in 1982, his voice was hoarse and barely audible from three solid days' worth of taping a video geared specifically to the sale of computer products.

"That's really what has gotten this whole training thing to take off," he rasped. "With the advent of the microcomputer, you had an entire generation sprouting up composed of people who were basically twenty-two-year-old electronics wizards right out of school. No one was teaching the fundamentals of selling. Nobody knew how to relate. Even today, many computer firms train their sales workers by saying, 'Now here's how the keyboard works, here's how the printer works, here's how . . .' and so on." He sighs. "That's their training program. Plus, you have a lot of companies who prefer to hire engineer types rather than sales types to sell their products, so you have technicians teaching technicians how to sell. But as business got more competitive, with more and more companies looking for a piece of the computer pie, sales training became essential for growth. Even for survival."

Hopkins also cited the downturned economy under the Carter administration as a major factor in the zooming demand for sales training. "A decade or so ago, when we had a real hot economy, you didn't need exceptional salespeople. A good product sold itself. Today, that's no longer true."

Tom Murphy, at his visceral best, gets down to cases. "Why do you think General Motors had us do a new car introduction for them? That never would've happened ten, fifteen years ago when GM owned the automotive world. But now, with the domestic car industry backed against the wall, their outlook is somewhat less cavalier." With a triumphant sneer—the comic-book hero nobody kicks sand at anymore—he adds, "They know damned well they need outside help."

Not that Hopkins was the only one listening when the distress call went up from corporate America. Since he began conducting seminars in 1974, membership in the National Speakers Association has soared from just a dozen to over 1,500. Tom admits that among the hundreds of people who answered the call were more than a few charlatans. It is a painful, if self-serving, admission for him, since he likes to portray selling as a pristine, philanthropic pursuit. ("Without salesmanship, life would stagnate, and self-improvement would virtually stop," he told the thousand or so people who turned out to see him in Pasadena, California. In Pasadena, by the way, about half that many typically turned out for barnstorming candidates during the last election.)

Further, Tom says that many of the frauds actually took their cue from him. "You get some people who attend one of my seminars and they start adding up: A thousand people times fifty dollars each, plus the revenues from the product tables, and they say to themselves, 'My God, Hopkins made seventy-five grand today! I can do that!'" In point of fact, one woman at the Cherry Hill seminar reacted with those exact words. "So," he continues, "they start advertising themselves as trainers, or if they want to be a little less brazen about it, as 'motivational therapists.' Fortunately, they usually don't last too long."

While Tom's legitimate competition has held up far better—several of today's top trainers have been pulling down six-and seven-figure incomes for years—none among the group seem within reach of eclipsing Hopkins, whose sixteen regional directors here and abroad assure the company of a steady flow of new work.

The regional directors, Tom feels, are emblematic of what distinguishes him from others who saw the same opportunities he saw. "We have a systematic, totally professional approach here. Our directors may work for four or five months setting up a single seminar, or qualifying and closing a single corporate prospect. That's grueling, expensive work. But this is a business, not a part-time, moonlighting deal." He pegs his monthly overhead at upwards of three hundred thousand dollars, in stark contrast to the many trainers who work out of their homes, or rent a tiny office condo "with an answering machine for a secretary," as he puts it.

•   •   •

Will success spoil Tom Hopkins?

Certainly, he is an ideal candidate for the swollen-head syndrome, with all its insidious implications. His career to date has been a litany of millions, featuring a major milestone about every five years: sold a million dollars' worth of California turf at age twenty one*; earned his first million in income at age twenty-six; distributed his millionth cassette tape at age thirty-two; and by the time you read this, he will have trained his millionth salesperson. Tom Hopkins wanted to have it all by the time he was forty. He had most of it ten years ahead of schedule. Too often, people in such lofty circumstances tend to self-destruct.

But there is another side of Tom Hopkins, expressed most often in misgivings about his lost family life. "Critics hear that I made a million dollars last year and they say, 'Lordie Lord'"—another one of his famous dialects—"'in a world where people are starving!' They don't realize I live a life most people would not lead for almost any amount of money. I live on an airplane.

*This, mind you, was preinflation California, when homes sold for a small fraction of their value today.

I work constantly." He smiles. "You know, one of my favorite lines used to be that I can never afford the luxury of a day off or an off day, and it's true. This business *consumes* you. There was a time a year or so ago when I only saw my family a couple weekends a year. I've stopped that now, and no matter what my schedule says, it's getting to be where Sunday is always a family day. It was taking too much out of me. I know people get impatient when they hear millionaires complain, but I think what I'm saying is understandable, isn't it?"

It's especially understandable if you've met his wife, Debra. She is absolutely gorgeous—disturbingly so—and about half a head taller than Tom, which would make her a hopeless over-match for any man lacking her husband's awesome presence. In fact, there's a tendency, at first, to consider her part of the Hopkins accoutrements, like the Rolls, and the diamonds, and the custom-tailored suits. This sounds sexist, I know, but the world in which Tom moves is a flamboyant one, a world where, like it or not, people are judged by their trappings. Yet to see Tom and Debbie together, to watch them cavort around the office with their picture-perfect kids, is to know that you are seeing a good, old-fashioned, apple-pie family. There may be some rubies and opals and sapphires mixed in with the apples, but what the hell—you can't condemn a guy just for that, can you?

What's more, when Debbie speaks, she sounds not like the long-on-lashes, short-on-substance beauty queen you might expect, but like the able administrator she is. Listening to her, you understand her real value to Tom has little to do with the stirrings men may feel when she walks through the door.

Among the others who walk through the door at Tom Hopkins International on any given day are Debbie's dad and various other members of the Hopkins extended family. Together, they compose what is known affectionately as the Entourage. There was a time, though, at the very beginning, when the Entourage might not have included the person you'd expect to be proudest of Tom.

You get the feeling that the early distance between father and son has never really been far from Tom's thoughts—troubling him, and at the same time, stabilizing him. Preventing him from getting too full of himself. More than anything else, perhaps, it is the memory of that twenty-year-old bitterness that keeps Tom from drowning in a sea of adoration.

• • •

I was wrapping up an interview with his partner, Tom Murphy, when Murphy suddenly asked if I knew about Hopkins's dad.

"About his dad?" I replied innocently.

"He passed away yesterday."

I was stunned. Nothing had been said by Hopkins's assistant when I called a day earlier to confirm the interview. Tom himself had given no real indication—although now, in retrospect, it did strike me that some of his musings on his early years had seemed slightly more nostalgic, even sentimental, than what was called for by the questions I'd asked. But it's not something you would have noticed if you hadn't been looking for it.

Moments later, when I ran into him in the main corridor, I fumbled for a suitable expression of sympathy. As almost always happens in such cases, I wound up ad libbing some banality. Sensing my chagrin, he waved me off. His manner was resolute.

"It's okay," he said. "We knew it was coming for a while. A long while now." I knew by the way he said it that he was thinking back, once more, to his fateful decision to give up law, and to his father's reaction to that decision. But in an instant, the wistfulness was gone, and Tom was again the picture of enthusiasm.

"Hey, did you see this?" He thrust a brochure at me. It was done in fiery red and icy gray, and bore the words "Women Who Win" across the top. It represented the firm's campaign for the female sales staff.

"Pretty slick, don't you agree?" he asked, affirming the observation with one of his favorite tie-downs. Then, without waiting for my answer, he nodded quickly and invited me to stay for lunch. All the employees were getting together at noon, he told me. It was going to be one of the company's communal meals (a regular morale-boosting event, according to insiders).

Would I stay?

I said sure, and began to ask another question, but it was too late. Tom was already halfway down the hall, walking briskly, humming softly. "Tom lives in the *now*," I would later be told by Danielle Kennedy, one of the women who won. "The worries of the past don't exist. And the uncertainties of the future don't matter."

Sales Miscellany

Cost of holding a typical sales meeting
(for a staff of four dozen)
in Minneapolis in the summer: eighteen thousand dollars.

6

The Selling of Selling,
Part Two: Motivational Minstrels

Like some mammoth funnel cloud, industry's demand for salesmanship that works has plucked hundreds of top-achieving sales tradesmen from the ranks of everyday people and transformed them, overnight, into professional gurus. Collectively, these gurus epitomize the consulting field's answer to home-delivered pizza: the highly touted inspirational speaker who flies from city to city imparting his wisdom to thousands of eager listeners. The usual venue is a corporate meeting room or a rented hotel auditorium, for, as Tom Hopkins has suggested, many of today's wandering minstrels of motivation have a home base in name only.

Yet the better ones—while not in Hopkins's class—easily outearn most of the top brass at the major United States companies whose sales forces they have been called upon to train.

Also caught up in the sales-training vortex nowadays are subsidiaries of some of America's most visible industrial giants. Sensing the market potential, they have followed Xerox's lead and established sales-training divisions that not only train their own, but welcome "outpatient" candidates as well—not infrequently from firms in their home industry whose salespeople will go on to become their direct competitors in the marketplace. This suggests that companies feel the revenues that can be generated through sales training can more than offset the increased competition engendered by the sharing of powerful sales insights with competitors. Xerox apparently has more to gain by teaching Minolta how to sell copiers than it has to lose by having well-trained Minolta salespeople steal away a certain percentage of Xerox's copier customers.

In other words, sales training has become a viable "product" in its own right—every bit as viable as the millions of more traditional products to which the sales skills themselves were originally intended to be applied.

This rapidly expanding new universe of modern sales training really began at Xerox. The company's stodgy, often incommunicative posture—a Xerox trademark*—has prevented XLS from gaining the notoriety attracted by its more flamboyant rivals. Still, there's little doubt that when members of the *Fortune* 500 need sales-training help, XLS's corporate phone number is the very first one they think of.

Xerox Learning Systems

In 1965, a small market-research firm calling itself Basic Systems released a study that posed that good selling was not an exercise in legerdemain, but rather an honest, interactive process occurring between salesperson and prospect.

Not exactly front-page stuff.

Within twelve months, however, Basic Systems would be in-

You say you've been in sales for twenty years and you've never heard of XLS? It's partly by design. Chances are you won't hear about them unless they decide they want you to. The outfit is part of Xerox's Information Resources Group, but you won't even find a footnote about XLS specifically in the parent company's annual report to shareholders. Xerox is reticent about its sales-training division, primarily because it considers itself one of the originators of the concept that salesmanship can itself be sold as a commodity (like typewriters and copying machines) and management is loath to have its complex marketing strategies—the results of millions of dollars in R and D—fall into competitors' hands for free. Actually, this is nothing new for those who are used to working with Xerox. So intensely secretive is the parent company that my simple attempt to locate their top producer on the West Coast turned into a ludicrous odyssey of unreturned phone calls, referrals to people who simply referred me to other people, and, finally, what I took to be a deliberate effort to confuse the issue. In the end, officials at XLS declined to play an active role in the preparation of this book.

gested by the budding multinational giant, Xerox Corporation. Using information contained in the newly acquired company's study, Xerox formulated an embryonic sales-training regimen to which it gave the unassuming name Professional Selling Skills. Before long, the operation had blossomed into Xerox Learning Systems, and would begin billing itself as "the world's largest" sales-training network.

How large is large? At last count, in 1982, the firm had penetrated some 407 of *Fortune*'s then-500, but marketing director Betsy Moser says that figure has almost certainly been surpassed since then. The company staffs thirty-four sales offices nationwide, plus fifteen more in places like Brazil, Finland, Singapore, and other far-flung locales. And the operation continues to grow, says Moser, at an annual rate of about 30 percent.

Like IBM, Xerox has always been very much a salesman's firm, and this is especially true where the commodity being sold is salesmanship. "Our reps are not only representing the company, but they are in a very real sense the personifications of the product," Moser explains. She attributes no small part of Xerox's success at selling selling to the singular spirit of dedication with which the firm's representatives approach the task at hand. Though Moser declines to specify dollar amounts, she says her "account execs," who earn a combination of salary plus "initiative," are well paid, and adds that the earnings of the cream of the crop have kept pace with the 30 percent annual growth of the company as a whole. "In fact in many cases," she notes, "their incomes have probably gone up a lot more than 30 percent."

Equally rewarding to the Xerox rep, Moser assures me, is the sense of personal fulfillment that comes with knowing that one's recommendations have been acted on by a given customer; often, the XLS input is the beginning of a corporate-wide policy reevaluation that yields great productivity benefits for the client firm. "It's very gratifying to have that kind of impact on a company's productivity," Moser observes.

The number of XLS reps wandering America in various stages of gratification currently runs seven score. They are assigned territories not based on geography alone, but also on market potential. For example, a single rep handles both Dakotas, while there are several reps operating within walking distance of the Dakota co-op in Manhattan.

From its simple beginnings, that first prototype Xerox course spawned an entire generation of more specific courses, counseling fledgling sales reps on everything from how to dress (though a recent XLS study to be discussed below has called the entire dress-for-success issue into question), to account development strategies, to time and territory management, to "a full line of supervisory training programs," as company literature puts it.

But that original course—now in its third generation as PSS-III—remains the spark behind the XLS engine.

"Above all, the course teaches you to think on your feet," says PSS-II alumnus Don Chinery. Chinery's company, Hirsch USA, sells—to use the company's own advertising lingo—"leather bracelets." (I suppose when you're selling them for as much as one hundred dollars, you don't call them watchbands.) Chinery has been one of XLS's most ardent fans, and with good reason. He committed his seven-man staff to Xerox's second-generation program in 1977. Over the next year he watched sales zoom from seven hundred thousand dollars to an estimated three million dollars at the close of fiscal 1978. Of course, that kind of growth is not uncommon in infant industries, but Chinery insists he saw a tremendous subjective difference in the way his staff handled customers.

"Accounts we hadn't been able to crack for months suddenly started ordering," he says. "The income of my least producer suddenly shot up to what my best producer used to be making, and the income of my best producer doubled." Chinery concluded that "it was too much, too soon, to be coincidence."

Don Chinery is not alone in his euphoria. Statistical gains under the first two versions of the course are quoted by Xerox at between 5 and 57 percent. And Moser is quick to point out that repeat business accounts for some 85 percent of the XLS take, so few first-time clients go away unhappy, apparently.

Moser says she expects even better results from the newest version of the Professional Selling Skills concept.

"Compared to earlier versions, it's more streamlined," says

Moser, more focused on the empirical truths that have revealed themselves since TNS first got under way. One rep who'd undergone both PSS-II and PSS-III was even more lavish in her praise; she said the only thing the two courses shared was their duration—three days, a time period that has become the standard for most sales training. One of the newer wrinkles—evidencing the high-tech awareness you'd expect from a Xerox—is that the program is, for the first time, available on laser videodisc. The new technology permits an ersatz interactivity, whereby the flow of the show can go in different directions depending on the responses of the role-playing salesperson.

XLS has always prided itself on the extent to which its marketing reflects the painstaking sophistication of its research, so it should come as no surprise that the company's promotional literature is aglow with tempting lures and important-sounding psychological allusions. In two successive paragraphs, one brochure makes reference to both the "Rogerian" and "Skinnerian" realms of behavioral thought. The same piece of literature says that a salesperson can reasonably expect to emerge from an XLS seminar knowing all of the following:

• "how to *ask questions* [italics theirs] to get prospects, even the silent or uncommunicative type, to share what *you* need to know"

• "how to steer a customer to topics of *your* choice without being pushy or overbearing"

• "how to make hay of even the most mildly encouraging customer remark, observation, opinion or assertion"

• "how to build a *climate of consensus* that makes asking for the order totally natural, untraumatic and logical"

And, last but not least:

• "why 'no' doesn't always mean 'no'"

The price of such knowledge is $750 per participant when the learning is administered during an open seminar. The Xerox open seminar is held in much smaller groups than a comparable Hopkins shindig. Closed seminars, with material customized for a single corporate client, start at around $5,000 (and escalate rapidly if the company is large), but fees are always individually negotiated. Do-it-yourself types can purchase the Xerox program outright for just $250.

Though Xerox seminars are more costly than those run by some of the other trainers profiled in this chapter, Moser defends them on scientific grounds: They're rooted in detailed research under laboratory conditions, not just "somebody's vague ideas of what selling is supposed to be about." She cites the background research often, and is especially high on that recent study, which examined five hundred sales calls as they unfolded. She claims that the inquiry exploded a number of important myths about the selling process.

"We found, for example, that there's no best way to open a call," she says. "As long as you don't get thrown out right off the bat, you can probably recoup from whatever you do." The XLS study also confronts the dress-for-success chimera: What you wear—or at least, what the 500 subjects in the Xerox study wore—is essentially irrelevant. "Obviously, if you walk in wearing a pink suit, it may have some effect. But beyond that . . ."

Actually, Moser draws much encouragement from the fact that, as she puts it, "We didn't find any big secret weapons." She sees the study as an affirmation of what Xerox has been preaching all along—namely, that such highly touted factors as sex, age, experience ("there are no significant differences whether somebody's been selling for two years or twenty years"), and so forth are extraneous to the act of closing a sale.

"Perhaps the biggest mistake the owner or manager of a midvolume business makes," says Moser, "is assuming that because he doesn't hire beginners—because his salespeople have . . . 'track records'—it means they automatically know what they're doing, that they understand the dynamics of a sales call. Often, managers simply go out and hire the pushiest people they can find, and that becomes their sales force.

"A lot of people still believe that all salesmen are born, not made," she continues, approaching the subject from a slightly different perspective. "Our top five salespeople at XLS are all very successful, and they're all very different people. We have one guy who's very cerebral and reserved, not your typical profile at all. We have another guy who *is* very aggressive. We have a girl who's knock-out gorgeous" (this would seem to be more of a refutation of the myth of the dumb blonde than the born salesperson, but. . .). She concludes, "Anybody can be taught to sell, given the right system."

The right system, as defined by Xerox, places a heavy emphasis on a practice known as "confining the field"—that is, limiting the discussion to those aspects of your product or service that you have determined to be of primary interest to your prospect. In marked contrast to the ardent spieling of days gone by, the salesman does not try to overwhelm you by telling you everything about his product. Instead, he focuses only on those factors he's determined you need. And, as is the case with most TNS strategies, he cultivates those primary needs, and expresses the ability of his product or service to meet them, via questions, not statements.

However, confining the field is not universally accepted, even in staunch TNS quarters. Some salespeople in Xerox's own camp confess private doubts about the reliability of this method of plumbing the depths of the customer's soul. They point out that it is not uncommon for a salesman who is trying to confine the field to be undone by the sheer brilliance of his questioning. So powerful are TNS interrogation methods that they raise the potential for having one's entire presentation thrown off course by needs that are not really needs at all, but specious by-products of the can't-say-no artistry of one's questions. Thus, in order to ensure that a customer's responses are valid, a lot of cross-referenced questions must be asked. And yet the use of too many questions can itself be counterproductive, as Xerox demonstrated in the study Betsy Moser is so fond of quoting.

Compounding this problem is the simple fact that it's hard to know beforehand which question is going to strike the customer's hot-button. *Fortune*'s Jeremy Main touched on this dilemma in his discussion of Forum Corporation of Boston, a relatively new entry into the sales-training field:

> Forum instructors talk about the importance of the "high-gain" question—the question that gets the prospect to open up with revealing information about his needs. Unfor-

tunately, Forum can't define a high-gain question except in terms of the answer. So the salesman doesn't know if he has asked a high-gain question until he hears the answer.

Nonetheless, says Moser, "we've got the statistics to back up the strategies we teach. When you're dealing with the human mind, no system is perfect. But what we're doing now is certainly a lot more productive than what was being done in sales before. And more productive than what some others are doing."

Competition from the field's more flamboyant trainers is something of a sore spot for Xerox. Moser will tell you she believes that motivational lecturers "have their place," but you get the feeling she's just being diplomatic. "We don't do those little dog and pony shows," she says, the supercilious sarcasm hanging heavy in her voice. "If a company has a choice of spending money on skills or motivation, we'd say spend the money on skills."

Still, evidence suggests that even staid old Xerox is loosening up a bit these days, perhaps in response to pressure from the market, which seems to like a bit of showmanship tossed in with the strategies. Xerox's new videodisc system can be used to conduct cute little quizzes with, as one newsmagazine reported, "the visual and sound effects of a TV show, including a fanfare for correct answers."

An interesting footnote to all this is that Xerox the office-machine company does not always use Xerox the sales-training company to train its outside reps. Asked about this situation, Moser replies that most large industrials employ a number of outside consultants in the course of training their salespeople, and Xerox is no different. (Indeed, some companies will listen to just about *anybody.* IBM and AT&T are just two of the companies who've consulted Markita Andrews, the pubescent Girl Scout Cookie Queen, for her insights on selling.) While Moser's reply is true enough, it does sort of beg the question: After all, if XLS is really so state-of-the-art, why would Xerox go anywhere else?

Then again, maybe they can't afford it. Moser says there is

no reciprocality between Xerox and its training subsidiary. Xerox would thus pay for XLS training at the regular rate of $750 a person, less a "nominal" in-house discount—just as XLS pays for its Xerox machines.

Basically, Moser believes, it comes down to a question of free choice.

"They have an option to buy whatever suits them. Just like I do," asserts the marketing director for Xerox Learning Systems—who, it just so happens, sends her correspondence out on an IBM Selectric.

Zig Ziglar

If you've ever gotten mail from Zig Ziglar before, the odds of your failing to recognize it when it comes again—and rest assured, it *will* come again—are almost nil. Anyone in the business will tell you the same thing. Maybe it's Zig's distinctive stationery: an enormous blue logo framed by the quarter-inch-thick red line that runs around the page and terminates in a bold, upswept arrow near the top left-hand corner. Maybe it's the celebrated Ziglar sign-off, SEE YOU AT THE TOP!, a phrase that has evolved from being the title of a book to a kind of rallying cry among the Ziglar brethren. Or maybe it's the signature beneath that, a stylish rendering formed, it is clear, with slow, painstaking precision. Or even the name itself, with its consonant, nursery-rhyme cadence.

Then, too, maybe it's Zig's message, which is always so damned . . . *uplifting*. Read the first few paragraphs of a Ziglar work—any Ziglar work—and you feel your troubles being soothed by Zig's special brand of all-God's-chillun-got-wings tranquility.

The man behind all this is the elder statesman of TNS training and at the same time the closest thing selling has to a genuine evangelist. The most interesting thing is that, at forty-eight years of age, slim, bespectacled Zig Ziglar may be just hitting his stride.

By the time you read this, Ziglar's company, based in Arlington, Texas, will be closing in on Sweet Sixteen—more than a decade and a half of serving an exhilarating cocktail that is one part technique, one part adrenaline, and one part gospel. It was a sixteenth year marked by a best-selling book, a string of sell-out seminars, and general media fanfare of the kind normally accorded only to high-ranking politicos and high-priced movie stars. Zig, whose income is estimated to run well up in the six-figure bracket, is proving that the teaching of the golden rule can pay golden dividends.

Reduced to its nuts and bolts, the Ziglar regimen is basically standard TNS fare: You've got to believe it to sell it; you've got to know what motivates people in order to succeed; you've got to treat people well if you want to stay successful. Essentially the same message you can get from any of the hundreds of aspiring sales trainers who are eking out decent, if unspectacular, livings.

What distinguishes this particular trainer is his nonpareil delivery, and the God-serving context in which he couches his material. Ziglar's phenomenal hold on his audience—perhaps the most faithful audience in all of sales training—has been achieved largely through his easy-going spirituality, a quality that is also making him America's foremost "crossover" speaker. Zig's following, these days, is a curious amalgam of housewives and horticulturists, salespeople and saloonkeepers, lawyers and lithographers—people from all walks of life who, to an ever-increasing extent, are seeking to apply the precepts of sales training to their daily routine. No fool, Zig has chosen to go with the flow; without question, "Jean Ziglar's happy husband," as he is wont to refer to himself, has taken aim at the general audience with a fervor unmatched by anyone else so closely identified with the roots of the TNS movement.

Nor have Zig's efforts gone unrecognized. His "I Can" course in personal initiative is now taught in more than two thousand schools in all but two states. School spokesmen have variously credited the course with improving grades, cutting vandalism and drug abuse, and even bringing about a reduction in racial tensions. Similarly, *Zig Ziglar's Secrets of Closing the Sale*, quite likely the most ambitious effort at "mainstreaming" ever attempted in a work purporting to have been written for the trade, rode the best-seller lists for several months in the summer and fall of 1984. Among other things, *Secrets* offers tactical advice for employees, dentists, lawyers, husbands, wives, contractors, doctors, teachers, students, and—sales professionals. The book, says a promotional phrase guaranteed to bring a smile to the face of anyone who's big on puns, seeks nothing less than to present "a lifetime of experience and research between the covers."

Ziglar made his bones (as they say in the mob) selling pots for Wearever, where he rapidly rose to a preeminent position among the company's seven-thousand person national sales force. From there, after fine-tuning his speaking skills on behalf of Dale Carnegie, he struck out on his own, and was immediately successful. While Hopkins was still out on people's patios, smelling the steaks cooking, Zig was already a well-recognized face in the seminar-training movement, especially in the Bible belt.

But there has always been something mildly inchoate about Ziglar's offerings; borrowing heavily from realms that concerned themselves only marginally with selling, they never quite seemed as well packaged as Hopkins's for heavy-duty corporate use. Some of Zig's colleagues feel his success among the self-help set has come at a fairly high price: Not only has it prevented Ziglar himself from penetrating the hard-core, no-nonsense business market, it has adversely affected the image of training in general. At least one member of the movement thinks Ziglar's holy crusade tends to paint sales training as a less than wholly serious pursuit. "All he does is pump people up with visions of saving the world through selling," says this one critic. "Most businessmen don't see the relevance to what they're trying to accomplish on a day-to-day basis. It sounds too flaky."

Ziglar, naturally, claims the criticism is unwarranted.

"I never make a promise unless I can give people a plan for achieving it," he argues. "If you get all motivated, but you don't know how to go about implementing that motivation, it'll all slip away from you."

Apparently, Ziglar is determined that, at least in his own case, very little of it will slip away. Almost certainly the most

169

aggressive marketer of the current crop of TNS trainers, he mines his mailing list as relentlessly as the average collection agency follows a deadbeat creditor. Get on his mailing list and you will never get off. Order once and you will be deluged with subsequent offers. Take it from one who knows.

Zig's literature frequently arrives masquerading as a newsletter or an invitation. What it really is, of course, is a mail-order catalog, done with enough four-color panache to drive Sears Roebuck's marketing execs to drink.

Herewith, just a sampling from his 1984 Christmas catalog, which—as much as anything else—reveals the tenor of Ziglar's patented approach to the sales profession:

1. "Zig on Video." Three tapes: "The Winner's Attitude," ("30 minutes of the good, clean, pure, powerful and positive basics of the Zig Ziglar philosophy!"); "Selling: the Proud Profession"; and last but not least, "Using Voice Inflection," another half hour of coaching on the finer points of verbalized persuasion. A half-off special at only ninety-five dollars.

2. "The Family Focus." "The family unit," says the copy, "is our most important institution. Why is it collapsing? More important, what can we do about it? *Zig has the answer!*" Among this smorgasbord of books and tapes is Zig's new book, *Dear Family,* featuring letters Zig wrote— "or wished he had written"—to his family. Also included is Ziglar's tape on "Raising Positive Kids in a Negative World." (Catchy, no?) $27.95.

3. The paperback issue of *Confessions of a Happy Christian,* which offers the reader "fun and excitement mixed with tears, joy and humor. It's the kind of faith and trust Zig practices daily as he lays claim to all the benefits of serving God." You can lay claim to this one for just three bucks.

4. "Uncle Zig's Positive Lessons," in which "ole Uncle Zig" imparts his wisdom to young people. If your kids' allowance is five dollars a week, he can buy this goody after just one month.

5. The complete, unexpurgated "Born to Win" program, including sixteen cassette tapes "in two attractive albums," plus "the most complete goal planner on the market today"—you've got to write them down, remember?—plus *See You at the Top*. And, as if all that weren't enough, a "Born to Win" flight bag to carry everything in. Total cost, on sale: $99.95.

6. On the back cover are coupons good for one hundred dollars off the price of a Ziglar "Born to Win" seminar (priced regularly at six hundred dollars per individual).

All this fuss over "Born to Win" is actually an omnipresent feature of Ziglar's current publicity effort, for Zig is trying to redirect his energies somewhat. He has cut his barnstorming in half, assigning many of the speaking engagements to trusted proxies in an effort to concentrate on his three-day "Born to Win" extravaganzas, held on his home turf in Dallas. The "Born to Win" program is a motivational *tour de force* served up in a nontechnical format. Incidentally, the pricing of the elaborate eight-hour-a-day productions is revelatory, once again, of Ziglar's mainstream tendencies. If you go as a single, you pay six hundred dollars, but you can bring your spouse for just half price. No other trainer has approached the married market with such canny instincts for merchandising.

Indeed, there are those who feel that Ziglar's long-term strategy may lead him away from the professional end of the business entirely. Says management consultant Robert Scherer, a student of the emerging TNS phenomenon, "If anybody can bridge the gap between sales training and what televangelists like Jimmy Swaggart do, I'd have to put my money on Ziglar."

Danielle Kennedy

She could describe herself as America's foremost female sales trainer. But she doesn't. Instead, she'll tell you that she's the only leading sales trainer who has given birth. It is that kind of humor, at once offbeat and down-to-earth, that defines Danielle Kennedy.

Danny, as she is known to the industry, is the sole revenue-producing asset of Danielle Kennedy Productions of San Clemente, California. In 1984, Danny took in some five hundred thousand dollars, derived mostly from the hundred-plus training seminars that took her as far away as South Africa. A Kennedy seminar blends scores of homespun sale tactics with megadoses of reinforcement on the trade's more altruistic aspects. She is also one of the leading voices in the movement to eternally cleanse selling of its lackluster image. While many seminar trainers have their audiences chant *"Money, money, money,"* Danny exhorts them to shout, "Selling is not a dirty word!"

Danny is undoubtedly the "comer" among would-be challengers to Ziglar and Hopkins, expecially if the latter's forecasts on the strength of the women's sales market pan out. But make no mistake; this is no radical feminist. Danny is not kidding when she says she's the only leading trainer who's given birth; she's done it no less than six times. In addition, her household includes two children from the first marriage of her second husband, Mike Craig. (Danny still uses her first husband's surname for professional reasons.) What's more, last year, when I interviewed her, she was contemplating her most ambitious schedule to date while once again—at age forty—dusting off the old bassinet. Amazingly, she spoke of the impending birth as though she were twenty and just starting out. Even more amazingly, everybody—Danny, her new husband, her kids—seemed happy, prosperous, and well adjusted, amid enough turbulence to make Erma Bombeck truly hysterical.

The Kennedy saga is classic rags to riches; although, in her case, diapers to diamonds might be more apropos.

When she first started selling in 1974 she was an unemployed housewife in an unrewarding marriage. She had few skills and five kids, all of whom were under seven years of age, and one of whom was an infant. "I was selling real estate out of my house from a twenty-five-foot cord on my kitchen phone," she recalled. "That way I could roam here and there and see what the kids were up to. I had no sales training. I had nothing. All I had was a love for what I did. I loved the idea of finding a dream house for somebody."

172

So much so that at the end of her first three years in sales, she'd made the top 1 percent of all professional salespeople nationally. And she'd acquired a nickname: the Six-Million-Dollar Woman.

"They hung that on me because I sold six million dollars' worth of real estate one year," she said matter-of-factly. "This was back when Lee Majors was doing *The Six Million Dollar Man* on TV, so they started calling me the Six-Million-Dollar Woman, and it stuck. But I never liked it. It makes you sound like some kind of goddess or something."

It was around this time that she became part of one of Hopkins's experiments at building a staff of traveling motivators. Her theme was "Women Who Win." Though Hopkins staffers are evasive about Kennedy's impact during her tenure in the Hopkins camp, Danny herself claims her efforts were quite successful, despite her trepidations about public speaking. "I was terrified," she would later admit. "I kept picturing myself getting up and making a fool of myself in front of everyone. But, like Tom says, you confront your worst fears and you conquer them."

That conquest, in turn, led to a regional television show that revolved around the world of real estate. Before long, she'd self-published a book on the same topic, and even managed to convince leading bookstores to stock it, an achievement almost unheard of in publishing circles. (Her current effort, *Super Natural Selling for Everyday People,* is itself selling at the steady rate of forty-five per week at B. Dalton, says its author and publisher.)

Since then, however, Danny—like just about everyone else in the training business—has broadened her focus. One of her most popular courses at present is entitled "How to Sell Yourself in the Job Market." As a result of such offerings, her audience grows ever wider. Truth be told, one of her proudest achievements is that she outdrew Hopkins, the king himself, during a recent tour of Johannesburg.

Still, impressive as all this may sound, there's no denying that after a while, all the gaudy success stories start to sound alike. Does it really matter, after all, who earned a million and who clocked in at a mere nine hundred ninety-eight grand? What makes Danny noteworthy is less what she is than what she *isn't*. For, in scorning the trappings of her trade, she has established herself as the most unassuming of today's high-profile trainers.

The first thing you notice about Danielle Kennedy is her affinity for downplaying her track record. With respect to the sobriquet she earned during her real estate days, she says, "Lots of real estate agents do six-million-dollar annual business these days." True enough. But misleading. Today in California, six million dollars' worth of business can be generated by a dozen transactions or less. When Danny did it, before the real estate spiral, her average sale was for just forty-two thousand dollars. That's one helluva lot of houses.

Her life-style reflects similar modesty. She will call herself an earring freak, yet add in the same breath that the earrings she freaks out over "usually cost about eight dollars or something." She will say jewelry "is okay, but rings make my fingers itch." She is not a party person: "I don't socialize much at all." She does admit to a passion for clothes, yet she does not make regular forays to Rodeo Drive or Fifth Avenue (or even Park Avenue South). Rather, she shops "in a small place in a little industrial park in Laguna," a quaint suburban hamlet about fifteen freeway minutes north of her home.

"The lady who owns the store goes to New York all the time and comes back with these really nice things by some of the popular designers," she'll say, groping unsuccessfully for the names, "and she sells them for reasonable prices." That little shop is where Kennedy borrowed the five-hundred-dollar sweater she wears on the cover of her current book. The cover photo, incidentally, was taken not by some world-renowned studio photographer, but by her shutterbug son.

Asked why she borrowed the sweater as opposed to buying it, she blanched, clutching her bosom as if stricken.

"Can you imagine? I spill something every time I eat. What would a five-hundred-dollar sweater look like with fettucini all over it?"

The thought occurs, of course, that Danny's folksiness might be a guise adopted purely for the benefit of the visiting writer. She is very good with the media. She remains relatively unscathed by the kind of cynicism the press normally lavishes on those in her profession. (Even *People* magazine once dismissed the work of Danny's idol, Dr. Wayne Dyer, as "vapid" and "birdbrained.")

Yet you come away feeling that she is sincere, especially in light of the ample evidence scattered—literally—about her. Prior to our interview, I was taken on a tour of her house by Claudette Albert, Kennedy's young aide-de-camp. Granted, the house itself was gargantuan: a $750,000 maze of hallways that seemed to lead only to more hallways. Granted, it was carpeted throughout in an opulent hunter-green pile that, combined with a forest's worth of natural wood on doors, beams, and (monstrous) ceilings, gave the place a distinct palatial woodsiness.

But the bedrooms betrayed no sign of my having been expected (even though Claudette had not merely called, but *written* to confirm our appointment—so fiercely does she watch over her boss's schedule). Clothing and other personal effects lay as they were dropped, presumably by kids who abandoned ship in a mad rush to get to school, work, wherever. It didn't look slovenly, really. It just looked very . . . relaxed. Lived in. By lots of people.

"I have someone who comes in and helps me with the cleaning once in a while," Danny herself later explained, "but other than that, it's pretty much every man for himself."

She was consistent—simple and functional—down to the littlest things. We sipped our Diet Pepsis from unmatched, everyday drinking glasses that she herself had filled and then set down without coasters on the wooden piano stool. In every respect, Danny appeared to have forsaken the pretentious in favor of the sensible. The Kennedy driveway did not sport the near-obligatory trademarks of others in her profession. The family cars were just that—family cars. Suburban work-horses like Chevys and Datsuns. And not the sports models, either.

She attributes her homespun outlook to the lessons of what she calls "a year of tragedy and loss, the likes of which a lot of people don't have in an entire lifetime." That year—a personal disaster despite her blossoming career—taught her that true fulfillment lay not in what you had, but who you were.

"I know it sounds trite," she said, "but that doesn't make it any less true."

Not surprisingly, Kennedy's professional style gets back to basics. "Don't Go Nuts and Get Complicated on Me," warns the subheading of one chapter in her new book. The book was drawn, she insists, from her experiences as a housewife and mother.

"Kids are just super-natural salespeople," she says, giving some clue as to where she got the title. "There's this sales script in my book that goes, 'Wait until you see . . .' You use it to put people in the right frame of mind. If you're a real estate salesperson, it might be 'Wait until you see the tall trees!' Or a car salesman might say, 'Wait until you see the rear leg-room.' Well, I learned that from my kids. They'd come home, and if it was a good report card, they'd say, 'Hey Mom, wait until you see this report card!' If it was bad, they'd say, 'Ugh, wait until I tell you about this teacher I've got in English—what a jerk!'"

Besides providing her with ready-made sales lines, her home life has taught her that in order to do your best, you must be in the same place mentally and physically. She illustrates with the example of the woman who goes to work and gets twenty-five phone calls from the kids, then comes home and can't concentrate on that, either, because she's worried about all the things she left undone on the job. "So nobody really gets 100 percent of her," Kennedy observes.

"You can't let that happen. You have to have the discipline to focus your life. A lot of people live in the past. Or in the future. And because of that, what they're doing in the present suffers."

That's why, says Kennedy, career-minded women should never break a family commitment for the job. She claims to have passed up two-thousand-dollar speaking engagements because she'd previously promised one of the kids she'd come to a concert or a picnic. "You don't break promises to your family. That's a hard-and-fast rule."

Kennedy goes so far as to claim that the family environment, with its informality and general lack of gamesmanship, has really nurtured her success, rather than inhibited it. Fact is, she took the opportunity at one point during our interview to voice a certain disenchantment with the rigorously planned stimulus-response regimens taught by others, including her former mentor.

"What Tom does is wonderful, in its way," she began, clearly dancing among eggs, "because he's dealing with a lot of novice salespeople who need the tight structure." But she was quick to add, in the next breath, that many of today's "attempts to super-professionalize sales"—an oblique but obvious reference to what Hopkins is doing—are at least partly responsible for the trade's nagging image problems:

"If someone doesn't need my product, and I end up selling them something just for the strategy of it all, to me that's manipulation. Unfortunately, that is what goes on in a lot of sales training. People who are really successful at sales are skilled and disciplined, but they're not manipulative. Just like people who are successful at family life."

It's hard to listen to her without concluding that to Danielle Kennedy, the essence of The New Salesmanship is honestly and truly the essence of the family of man.

• • •

I'd read somewhere that an interviewer once suggested Danny call her next book, . . . *Yeah, But Who Watches the Kids?* A great title. And an even better question. Not that, having met her brood, you'd conclude they needed looking after. Young as they are—they range in age from twelve to twenty-two—they seem as established in their own ways as their mom is in hers. Each of them evinces a sense of purpose, and has already made strides toward fulfilling that early promise. So much so, that—again like mom—they all carry labels, by which Danny proudly refers to them. "The swimmer." "The gymnast." "The photographer." "The pianist." And so on.

Nonetheless, the question was too good to resist, so as our talk ended, I asked it.

Danielle flashed her toothy, Jane Fonda smile. "Aren't grandmas wonderful?"

She stood up and went right into a feline stretch, perhaps looking ahead to her exercise class (this, mind you, in her seventh month of pregnancy) or the meeting she'd said she had scheduled with somebody, after which there would be a dinner engagement, followed by a red-eye flight to the East Coast to begin a string of seminars the very next day.

It looked like another busy week for grandma.

Nido Qubein

Nido Qubein (that's NEE-do q-BANE) phoned me from the Atlanta airport; he had started out the day in Tarpon Springs, Florida, and was now on his way to Chicago. I asked him if I could reach him in the Windy City later in the afternoon. He said no, because by that time he'd be in Los Angeles.

Such is the tempo of Qubein's schedule.

Certainly one of America's most prolific trainers, Qubein typifies the wandering minstrel of motivation. He does two hundred short meetings each year, plus another fifty or sixty full-fledged seminars. "He's all over," says his secretary, Judy Ray. "There are days when *I* have a hard time keeping track of him."

Though virtually all sales trainers have inspirational stories to tell, Nido's tale is more inspirational than most.

With little money and less command of the English language, Qubein, a Lebanese émigré, arrived in High Point, North Carolina, in 1966. He was all of seventeen years old.

Yet within six years he had his MBA, was landing regular local speaking engagements and had formulated a solid blueprint for marketing a volume of cassettes that would enable others to follow his lead. Those tapes, and their offspring, now account for about a quarter of Qubein's yearly take.

"I figured if I could do it, given my background," says Nido, whose facility for the language now surpasses that of many native Americans, "certainly others, who had more of a head start, could profit from what I had to say."

Today, the machinery young Qubein set in motion produces gross revenues in the seven-figure-plus range. In short, he's come a long way, baby, despite the language handicap and a name that was a most unlikely candidate to become a household word.

What's intriguing is that Qubein does not really see the irony in his teaching Americans how to use his adoptive language for maximum persuasive effect. "In many ways," he says, "when you have to learn a language in an unfamiliar environment, you are forced to focus on what you must say to make things happen. It isn't the same as growing up with the language and learning it gradually among family and friends, people who are very solicitous of your needs. When you learn it as a crash course, so to speak, you must learn quickly how to make people respond to your objectives."

Nido, who developed an early appreciation for flexibility, offers three seminar lengths: two-hour, three-hour, or, for heavy-duty applications, a six-hour affair. Each of them is formatted individually; it's not a case of playing the same record on different speeds. Plus, for the man on the go, there's Qubein's forty-five-minute "talk," a fast dose of inspiration priced at an equally fast $2,500. And Nido does it all himself, as is customary with today's traveling motivator.

Say the last half of this last line in Qubein's presence, however, and you get an earful. "I hope you understand the distinction between Tom and Zig and myself," he admonishes. "In many cases, they're talking to people who are going out directly to consumers, and making their pitch, and that's that. I, on the other hand, am a corporate trainer. Or, you might say, an industrial trainer. My strategies are geared more toward overall corporate sales *policy* than toward training the direct salesman who goes out and knocks on doors."

One of Qubein's juiciest corporate accounts is Dole Processed Foods, the pineapple people. Others are Georgia Pacific and INA Bearing. All told, Qubein maintains a stable of approximately twenty companies, each of whom he sees "about a half-dozen times a year," and each of whom invests anywhere from twenty thousand to eighty thousand dollars in his "action plans." The precise figure depends on how much time Qubein himself must invest in the concept and implementation of the plan. Clients apparently don't argue much over cost. He quotes his capture rate—the percentage of companies who stick with him—at 70 percent.

That's a high number for any kind of consulting, but it's deceptive, too. In Qubein's case, repeat business is an assumption of his training philosophy. It is Nido's theory, shared by Danny Kennedy (and disputed by Hopkins and Ziglar and most others) that a single sales seminar will not make much of a difference in anyone's life. "It is very naïve," he feels, "to think that you can walk in one time and give a speech and change salespeople, or anyone, for that matter." (David N. White, director of the highly regarded sales-training program at Honeywell info-systems, has said that without regular refresher courses, the average salesman loses 90 percent of what he learns.) Thus, Nido's material is sequential, and organized to emphasize retention from one session to the next.

Aside from human nature, there are, Qubein notes, procedural and administrative hurdles that prevent salespeople from applying knowledge gleaned from open seminars like those administered by Hopkins and Ziglar.

"Salesmen will only really do what their sales managers let them do," he says. "And the sales managers frequently feel threatened by your presence. So you have to work with the higher-ups."

One thing Qubein shares with all fellow trainers is an abiding fondness for the pithy phrase. Among his favorites is "Motivation may be the cause of frustration without education and practical application."

Equally memorable is his advice on how to keep prospects from getting rid of you. "Don't stick your foot in the door to keep it from closing," suggests Qubein. "Instead, use your head, so you can keep talking." He attributes his own success to the diligent application of this particular approach.

A painful strategy, perhaps, but Qubein can afford plenty of aspirin. Keeping his head in the doors of some of America's biggest industrials should allow the intense-looking thirty-five-year-old to pocket half a million dollars for his insights this year.

180

Everybody's Getting Into the Act

Despite the frenzied itineraries of the heavy-hitters described above, there still aren't enough of them to go around. Thus, in the past ten years, the roster of the National Speakers Association has soared over twelve *thousand* percent, as opportunists like ex–car salesman Larry Wilson shuffle to fill the void.

Wilson has only recently gained wide recognition, via his 1984 hardcover best-seller, *The One Minute Sales Person,* but has been known to the trade for as long as two decades.

His dogma is rooted principally in the teachings of noted behaviorist Abraham Maslow (the father of "self-actualization") and others. Wilson is a leading exponent—some say *the* leading exponent—of the belief that a salesman must mentally segregate himself from the outcome of the sale. In other words, don't take rejection personally. His methods of overcoming negative thinking, one of which was outlined in Chapter 3, are considered classics in sales motivation.

Wilson's company, Wilson Learning (which became a subsidiary of textbook publisher John Wiley & Sons in 1983) counts among its alumni sales executives from Dupont, Alcoa, AT&T, General Mills, and Union Carbide. And it was Wilson who helped teach Sony salespeople why they're the one-and-only, and Bank of America how to stay ahead of the Chase. All told, his wisdom is imparted in nine countries to as many as two hundred thousand salespeople a year—or as few as ninety-two thousand, depending on whose statistics you use.

Larry Wilson, of course, is a veteran salesman with a successful track record. But your average TNS trainer lacks Wilson's long experience in the trenches. Incredibly, many of today's trainers lack *any* legitimate background in sales, for as the definition of what constitutes "salesmanship" grows ever broader, scores of people from allied realms join the crusade.

Consider, for example, celebrated radio commentator Paul Harvey, known for his upbeat, apple-pie outlook, his linguistic inventiveness (Harvey's contributions to the national vocabulary include both *Reaganomics* and *guesstimate*), and his nonpareil credibility. *So* credible is Harvey that prospective advertisers queue up months in advance for a shot at having him endorse their products during his freewheeling sermons. Harvey's formidable stage presence earns him a reported twenty thousand dollars per appearance on the motivational circuit.

Then there's Dr. Wayne Dyer. An early entry into the pop-psychology movement via his surprise runaway best-seller, *Your Erroneous Zones,* Dyer charges upward of ten thousand dollars for a short course in how to be a "no-limit-person"—his catchy term for someone who refuses to allow negative thinking to blunt his or her potential.

For hourly wages, though, it's hard to beat Denis Waitley, also an author-turned-motivator. Waitley is perhaps best known for his book *The Psychology of Winning*—a topic he's evidently mastered, given his rate of $3,500 an hour. Denis has been hired not only by the usual complement of *Fortune* 500 firms, but by contending football teams. And by the United States government. Which helps to explain how the deficit got so high.

Courting the professional audience is Loretta Melandro, whose courses are designed to show the members of the bar how to relate properly to their clients and purge themselves of their ambulance-chasing image.

"My workshop is going to make your shop work," promises Bridgit Maile of Innovative Management Technologies, a company designed to combat "listening mistakes."

Author Ken Delmar will tell you how to put *Winning Moves* on your business associates; the dapper Delmar will teach you how to look them in the eye, how not to look them in the eye, where to put your hands when you sit.

Denver's Debra Benton says you can tell if a given customer is ready to buy by whether or not he's "erect"; she refers, of course, to posture, and her company will teach you how to monitor same for optimum results.

Ken Clifford teaches "the equation of persuasion." David Sandler will show you how to "break the rules . . . and close more sales." Then there are the psychologists on the periphery of sales training, like Charles "Peak Performance" Garfield and Leo ("hug me") Buscaglia. Even television celebrity Art Linkletter does his share of motivational speaking; his sermons on the power of cooperation and sincerity go for seven thousand dollars a clip.

And on and on it goes.

In addition to the well-meaning (if not always well-equipped) souls who have answered the call from corporate America, there are also the charlatans.

"Regardless of the profession, you're gonna have crud," says Hopkins's partner, Tom Murphy. "In this business, you'll get a guy who prints up a damned brochure, and he'll charge a thousand dollars or more, and he'll go in and tell some jokes and stories, and the net result is that the whole business of teaching is affected."

As Hopkins puts it, "There's nothing in this life more satisfying than entertaining people. There's nothing more gratifying than having a thousand people in your hands."

But in the end, trainers defend what they're doing on the grounds that the free market is the ultimate crucible.

"Corporate America is not stupid," says Qubein, speaking less, he says, as an individual than as past chairman of the National Speakers Association. "If they didn't think they were getting value, they wouldn't spend the money.

"It's that simple."

Sales Miscellany

Just some of the headings besides "sales"
under which positions that turn out to be sales jobs
may be found in any local newspaper:
Advertising, Communications, Consultant, Consumer Relations,
Customer Service, Management Training, Marketing, Market
Research,
Public Relations, Public Speaking, and Supervisory.

7

A Corporate Case Study—
TNS at AT&T, or
an Interview (Sort of)
with Joe Carter

Spend a day high in the rarefied air of Aurora, Colorado, wandering the 194,000 square feet of AT&T's gleaming national training center with Joe Carter, and there's a good chance you may emerge a true believer. You will learn a lot about Carter's feelings on Lee Iacocca (very positive) as well as his feelings on Tom Hopkins (less so). You will learn bits of information that might come in handy during your next trivia game (example: There are fourteen mountains in the state of Colorado higher than Pike's Peak). You will learn to accept the word *she* as a personal pronoun of general reference. You'll even learn how to point your finger at someone without being offensive.

The town of Aurora, Colorado, is a Denver bedroom community fifteen minutes from Stapleton International Airport. AT&T's training facility is situated opposite the Ramada Renaissance, a very nice business hotel, which is especially deferential to those representing AT&T or there to see AT&T, perhaps because the place owes no small part of its yearly occupancy rate to the never-ending squads of sales trainees and veterans brought in by the giant company for refresher courses.

I arrived for my interview with Carter on Halloween, having

been told to expect "anything." Last year, it seems, one of Carter's thirty on-site course instructors showed up to teach his class dressed as a giant pumpkin. Another instructor, a technical consultant or "TC," had arrived with a pretty stewardess, which would have been nothing unusual except that they were wearing each other's clothes.

This year things are more decorous, if only slightly so. The back side of the building, where strategies are actually conceived, was draped in ghoulish ersatz webbing; all the walls and partitions were adorned with assorted beasties and ghoulies. "It's for the kids," said Carter, but he didn't hesitate to add that the informal atmosphere persists year-round, and is by design, not neglect. "These people [the trainees and their families] live here and don't really know anyone else in town. We try to create an environment that's as relaxed and friendly as possible."

Later on that afternoon, Carter explained, staffers would have a family trick-or-treat through the building—which itself has ghostly connotations. What has been dubbed "the Darth Vader building" is a gleaming monolithic structure of charcoal-gray glass that would feel more at home on Montgomery Street in San Francisco or somewhere in downtown Manhattan. In any case, it looks woefully out of sync in sleepy Aurora.

An avid New Salesmanship aficionado, Carter is big on morale-building social events. Last year he hosted a team scavenger hunt at a nearby dude ranch rented expressly for that purpose. There are also basketball games (Carter is a merciless competitor, say his co-workers), and from time to time the hallowed presentation room, where reps must sweat out a pitch before a buying committee as their final exam, is transformed into a banquet hall for a party or a luau. The general atmosphere exudes the kind of camaraderie you might find among enlisted men who know they're in for an eighteen-month hitch.

Or, perhaps, enlisted women. Carter uses the word *she* a lot; in fact, he is prone to using it the way most people use *he*. Carter will say, "If an account executive is having trouble mastering a certain financial skill, she might try such and such. . . ." He admits that his linguistic brand of affirmative action is part of a personal rebellion in general against the sales environment of days gone by.

"Years ago," he told me early in our talk, "everything in sales was Vince Lombardi. The attitudes, the mannerisms, and so forth. Now it's just as much Mary Decker." I looked over at Ric Morrison, the liaison to the company's PR unit, who would hold my hand throughout the course of the day. Morrison looked pleased.

The Aurora facility is the nexus of AT&T Information Systems. ATTIS is the company's distribution arm. The Brobdingnagian range of its high-tech office products seemingly outdistances everything except perhaps their ad budget, judging by the company's visibility in all forms of the media since the AT&T divestiture in January 1984. Everybody who sells for the ATTIS will pass through these doors not once, but several times, to experience the wide array of courses Carter oversees. Really, to say he oversees them is to trivialize his role. To a large degree, Carter invented them.

"They made me an offer I couldn't refuse," was Carter's explanation of how he wound up with the responsibility for formulating AT&T's training program. "The thing that was attractive to me was the notion of seeing how many ideas I'd put to work for us successfully at Baltimore could be translated to the marketplace in general."

Baltimore was Joe Carter's previous stop on the AT&T express. He has been with the company for twelve years—"I stopped here on my way to law school, and I've been here ever since," as he puts it. During that time he rose steadily through the ranks, and finally, a few years back, he landed in Baltimore, an office racked by a variety of problems. Under Joe's intense tutelage, the branch enjoyed a near-miraculous turnabout, quadrupling its productivity in just a six-month period and becoming the top regional office in the nation. This was possible, he said, "because we invested the time to teach the long-term, customer-oriented, consultative approach to selling."

Physically, Carter is very much the personification of the driven megadministrator. He is tall and slim, with thinning hair and piercing, importunate eyes. And one helluva grip. His repartee is ripe with allusions to the models of American business savvy; among his favorites are management guru Peter Drucker and Chrysler boss Iacocca, whom he calls "a maniac with a mission," sounding very much as though he aspires to the same sobriquet. Carter does admit that such intensity will take its toll.

"When I came here, I found that the most valuable resource they needed was an approach that would help reps translate their worth to their customers." Carter at first suffered the typical visionary's heartache attempting to get his special version of TNS off the ground. "Which is why," the thirty-two-year-old training director sagely noted, "I'm thirty years younger than I probably appear."

ATTIS makes for an interesting TNS case study, because the whole point and purpose of AT&T changed with its divestiture. The focus shifted abruptly from service to products, with the burden of communicating the new orientation falling to sales reps who might've had other things—like going head to head with established marketers like IBM and Xerox—on their minds at the time.

"Our whole corporate mission has changed from one of universal service in terms of the old AT&T mandate, to one that says, 'Hey, you've got to be successful in the marketplace by being innovative.' My sales instructors are the nucleus of people trying to shape not just the skills of people, but the hearts of people as well.

"We sold very well for a hundred years to commissioners, and then they in turn served our end-users. Now, competitively speaking [the commissioners] are just another customer."

Here he rose to use the blackboard, something he is wont to do quite often. Carter is very visually oriented, fond of making his points through drawings and pie charts and such (a quality he shares with some of the popular sales trainers he tends to deprecate in casual asides). He even had a computer-graphics package made up that depicts the AT&T training regimen and marketing focus.

"I'm gonna give you some really rough numbers," he began, "but let's say there's a fifty-billion-dollar telecommunications marketplace." He wrote the number on the board. "You'll get different figures defining it different ways, and this is the seventies we're talking about. We had a very dominant share of that, and there were a lot of people who were concerned. We brought some people in who said, You know, with the technology and the capability we have, if you broaden your definition of the market from one of telecommunications to one of information processing, that's probably a one-hundred-and-fifty-billion-dollar market." More numbers on the blackboard, with arrows. "And this was technology we were essentially giving away to others because we couldn't, under our former situation, compete in that market.

"So while we were concerned about eroding some of the telecommunications end, there was always the thought of what we could have if we simply were allowed to compete in the information-processing segment of the marketplace. With the explosion of opportunity in information management, it can be a five-hundred-billion-dollar market"—more and bigger numbers, this time with exclamation points—"by the year 2000." All of which points up that AT&T's decision to stop fighting the government and divest voluntarily was not, as many people believed, a totally magnanimous gesture.

It is Carter's belief that perhaps the greatest opportunity before AT&T is the integration of high-tech products. Companies, he feels, fall into niches: "IBM does mainframes better than anybody else, DEC does distributive software better than anybody else, Hewlett-Packard probably does special-purpose computing better than anybody else, then there's Wang for word processing." Thus, the market is flooded with products that were devised pretty much to stand alone. That is, the problem of how these components would interface with one another, and with the various other items composing the new electronic office, was given very little thought.

Carter, however, has given the subject much thought.

"Of course, we're not the only people in the integration end of the business. There's Team Xerox, for one"—just the slightest hint of sarcasm dances in his voice—"but we bring a history of communications and a networking background to this. You know, when you pick up a telephone and get a dial tone, that's one of six hundred million billion possible connections—and everything talks to each other."

Does Carter take this kind of long historical view in training his salespeople?

"When we have orientation day, we trace some of the global strategies of the company and the heritage of AT&T to equip them as professionals to articulate our business direction.

"Our salespeople are really the third wave in management in this business. The first wave achieved the mission of universal service. The second wave was kind of—I'm part of that. I moved the business from its regulatory focus to the idea of 'Let's get into the competitive end of it.' The people who come into the business today know little of the first two. And that's both good and bad. There's some heritage that I need to bring to them so they understand the foundation. But they don't have the constraints of the past two and that's very good."

Having finished his graphic portrayal of the evolution of AT&T's thinking, he segued into a discussion of his philosophy of building business relationships.

"There were other people who would've preferred to take the approach of moving the product out the door as quick as you can. In Baltimore, we took the opposite approach and we had the most successful branch in the country.

"You have to understand the customer; understand his objectives; understand the obstacles in the way of attaining those objectives." Pause. Wistful sigh, as though he were pondering the folly of salesmanship past. "You have to really *understand* how your technology can be instrumental in helping him achieve that.

"I'll give you a classic example. Something as mundane as an 800 toll-free number. Well, my view of the 800 number is that it eliminated Beechnut's concerns about the nutritional value of their baby cereals. If you understand that Beechnut was getting criticized about the nutritional and salt content of their baby cereals, and just through the miracle of a toll-free number . . . on every package of Beechnut cereal, there's a message that says If you have a nutritional question, call us toll free, we're concerned about you . . ."

Carter claims he is more than happy to sacrifice the short-term goal of "moving hardware" for the long-term goal of developing a "trust relationship" with a client (a client who will, presumably, spend a lot of money in the long run). Pass up the "quick hit," he counsels reps, and instead concentrate on getting a customer to "commit to AT&T architecture." (Leading salesperson François Levy uses this phrase often in referring to clients who have placed virtually their entire information-and-data-processing future in AT&T's hands.) Often, Carter observed, the quick hit and the architecture are mutually exclusive, since the strategic approach to a fast score differs materially from that used to engender a feeling of mutual trust.

"Selling to a person's threshold" is another of Carter's favorite catchphrases. He explained, "If you have a guy who used to work for one of our major competitors, he could be a Roman Catholic and I could come with the pope and he still wouldn't buy from us. You're not going to get him to throw over all those years of bias and suddenly believe that AT&T is the most wonderful company in the world. But you can at least establish some basic points of agreement.

"On the other hand, you might have a guy where all you have to do is show up, because his mom worked for AT&T for thirty years, so he'll buy anything. You really don't have to spend a lot of time because he's willing to buy from you on reputation alone. Sell to that threshold. *But not beyond it,*" he added quickly. He would go on to explain that one of the sales trade's biggest problems, in his view, is salespeople who oversell in the attempt to capitalize on a congenial business relationship.

"Just remember that the close, per se, isn't the goal. The goal is to develop a relationship. If I can move from a vendor, in the customer's mind, to a consultative resource, in the end there'll be a much greater return for both of us."

The latter part of the morning had been set aside for me to observe reps in the process of role-playing sales scenarios, one-on-one, with their course instructors. The AT&T facility has dozens of rooms set aside for this purpose, and each room is available to eavesdroppers via video camera.

It's a little embarrassing for Carter: We're in one of the

rooms set up for the purpose of monitoring the role-players, except that Carter can't get the damned video equipment to work, and the three of us—Joe, myself, and the ever-present Ric Morrison—are staring at a screen full of fuzz.

"We don't actually monitor that often," says Carter with an apologetic grin.

While waiting for one of the technical people to show up and rescue us, Carter vamps by telling me about AT&T's four-prong curriculum: initial selling skills ("which takes a newly employed person into the technical-sales population, and teaches them how we sell and how we bill"); advanced selling skills; computer-systems sales; and management. Carter seems to place his strongest emphasis on the second phase, advanced selling skills.

"Our sales force is getting pretty good at one-on-one across the table," he feels, "but to sell an integrated information system you're going to be doing buying committees, and that's a whole new set of dynamics." Like so many before him, Carter stresses that "the day of the one-sit close is over."

One factor Carter has woven into all of his courses is the necessity of distinguishing between a feature and a benefit. In an overall sales philosophy that Carter describes as "How-to, Hands-on, and So What?," this last point—the So What?—is the most critical.

"How-to is fairly self-explanatory," he says. "Hands-on simply means that it's not enough for an account executive merely to tell somebody something; he's got to be able to do it as well. What is So What? Well, for example, this computer over here has got an 8086 chip. It's got internal bus speed that's about 80 percent better than any computer on the market. But So What?"

Carter chuckles. If there's anything at all that might be mildly annoying about this man, it's his tendency to appreciate only humor that originates with him.

He continues: "It's a fun game to get your sales force to differentiate between a feature and a benefit. I'll walk into a course in advanced selling skills and I'll pull out a light bulb and I'll ask people, 'Okay, ladies and gentlemen, what are the benefits?' And you'll hear things like, 'Oh, it produces light.' Nah, that's not a benefit, that's a feature. You want to talk about features? Well, it's a high-impact tungsten filament that produces 2,300 Kelvin enclosed in a vacuum and packaged in an easy screw-in design. Now that we've gotten the features out of the way, what are the benefits? It tripled the gross national product of America by creating a second and third shift. It increased the life expectancy of the American male, and female"—Carter is ever careful not to forget the women—"by making night surgery possible. It made us a more mobile society. Et cetera."

A given salesman's—or saleswoman's—appreciation of benefits is enhanced by the parade of role models Carter recruits for the purpose. Top account execs will stand in front of their green counterparts and talk about their experiences on the outside, and why they're successful. This sort of input continues even after graduation. "We have an adopt-a-branch program where each of my instructors is personally assigned to one or two branch offices in order to maintain a constant level of support."

Carter's greatest coups may have been persuading honest-to-goodness executives from prospect companies to drop by and tell the class what sort of qualities and capabilities would enable a salesperson to sell them. For his part, Carter sees the cooperation of such executives as eminently understandable. "They know that in the long run, their help will come back to benefit them by improving the salesperson's grasp of the needs of the market."

We finally get the video cameras working and are able to watch a young woman make an earnest presentation to her role-playing instructor. Salespeople are videotaped for their own self-analysis as well as for evaluation by their superiors. The students have access to their tapes for study afterward on one of the roomful of Betamaxes Carter ordered soon after taking charge.

The instructors, Carter tells me, will portray different types of buyers—hostile, indifferent, quiet, talkative—and even different environmental situations; for example, they'll be sitting there eating an imaginary salad. The rooms themselves, eighty of them, have been designed by the New York architectural firm of Haines Lundberg Waehler to simulate twenty different office arrangements, lest the novice sales rep make a less than auspicious entrance by stumbling over the furniture. Think I'm kidding? Ted Hammer, a Haines Lundberg-Waehler partner, told *Industry Week,* "It's beneficial for new salespeople without a lot of experience to be able to anticipate and maneuver around various arrangements of furniture and decor."

The instructor we are watching is Elizabeth Elrod, "one of my best," according to Carter. She is very constructive at the end of the session. "This is a testing ground for you," she says to her student, who looks a bit demoralized. Elizabeth goes on to praise the young woman for her poise, but to discourage her use of closed-end questions, and to stress better organization of her material.

It is obvious that a definite "trust relationship" (a phrase Carter uses liberally in describing many different situations) has developed between instructor and pupil. Though Carter clearly finds this gratifying, not all would agree. It has been observed of role-playing scenarios that because salespeople basically know they are among friends, they react differently to their instructor's staged recalcitrance than they might in the real world. At AT&T, though, the pupils themselves don't see this as a problem—I asked—and they claim to feel just as intimidated as if they were out on the street selling to strangers. More so, if anything, because they're being judged. These are, after all, their employers.

Nonetheless, do students sometimes play upon this trust relationship and put on artificial personas just to get through the course?

No, says Carter, and he uses Elizabeth Elrod as an example. If she felt she were being duped by a sycophantic student, says Carter, "Elizabeth would cut [the student's] heart out."

We switch the dials and find a second session being conducted by "another top instructor," Jill DeStefano. (Is it my imagination or is Carter going out of his way to show me what a major role women play in the AT&T organization?)

As the intrigue between DeStefano and her flustered male pupil plays out, Carter ad libs: "AT&T's reputation is established every day, with every salesman, on every sales call. Everything we do—the advertising and the millions of dollars we spend—supports that, but it doesn't create it. Our heritage may give us entrée, so that, for argument's sake, Steve Salerno, AT&T account exec, can get to see people, if for nothing else than the curiosity about what they saw on TV last night. But the work that XYZ company places with AT&T starts with you, the salesman. The ideal account executive in my mind is viewed as a significant resource by his client."

Carter says he gets "very complimented" when his customers offer his salespeople jobs, something he says happens frequently, and may help to explain the steady flow of "new hires" filing through the building.

"I also get very complimented when our account executives are invited to join corporate planning sessions, or participate in internal training films, or to help write a position paper.

"Willy Loman is dead. We don't get by with a shoeshine and a smile anymore."

Does Carter think Willy's dead throughout sales? I ask.

"In any profession, there are people who retard, and then people who significantly enhance the profession's reputation. There are places where people live up to my expectations, and there are places where they don't."

Carter had earlier said he believed that only 10 percent of sales had to do with such factors as price, product, and delivery. The other 90 percent consisted of "defined values, the salesman's ability to tangibilize things like corporate reputation, service reputation, R and D, applications know-how, and so forth.

"If I had to graphically depict why a customer makes a buying decision, I'd do it like this." He drew an iceberg on the blackboard. "If you ask people why they buy, they'll always bring it down to price, product, and delivery. But there's a whole bunch of stuff below the waterline that adds up to final value. Or added value.

"Look at Perdue chickens. Frank Perdue is able to sell chicken thighs at a premium. How do you differentiate chicken thighs? But he did it. He went beyond the tangible goods and added other components to it. In 1973, when O. J. Simpson

197

gained two thousand yards, Frank Perdue had a higher recognition in inner-city New York than O.J. did. People would say, 'Hey, he's the chicken man! But who's that black dude?'"

Carter suggests to his sales reps that they use Bell Labs to articulate the worth of AT&T "just as Perdue used his marigold-seed diet to sell his chickens. We invented the transistor, the silicon chip, optical fibers, cellular technology, and it goes on and on. Bell Labs has churned out a patent a day since opening the door. Seven Nobel laureates. That's the kind of thing that you as a salesman have to understand in order to communicate the worth of AT&T to your customer." Reflectively, he adds, "You know, if anything ever breaks, we can ultimately get to the person who made it."

Carter's view of the essence of TNS, then, is the ability to communicate through one's physical presence the underlying worth of the company. "If a salesman or a saleswoman can say, 'The greatest piece of value you get by doing business with AT&T is me'—she wouldn't necessarily say that, but she would act in such a manner that conveys that—that's what makes sales success."

Up on the monitor, a salesman misses a buying signal. "I think we've got about all the information we need," said the role-playing instructor (the guy from Boston who came to last year's Halloween party dressed as a stewardess), "and we're ready to do something." Nevertheless, the salesman, intent on following his prescribed course to the letter, ignores the hint and proceeds with his regular presentation as if nothing had happened. Carter tsks.

I ask if maybe the AT&T regimen, with all its emphasis on company heritage and interpersonal relationships, doesn't concentrate quite enough on the hard realities of closing. Carter almost winces at the word.

"Typically, to the outsider, closing implies a kind of I-win, you-lose scenario. I would rather define what you call 'closing' as a reaching of agreement." He says the difference is not just semantic. "The thing is, you don't close at the expense of the customer. In fact, we have a step in our presentation that we call

198

'testing feasibility.' And you have to get concurrence from the customer on what you think you want to do before you do it. So before you get to the closing piece of the sales call, you've already tested it out," presumably so that the close seems less harsh to the customer than if it came like a bolt out of the blue.

To illustrate, Carter tests feasibility with me: "Steve, if what I've heard you say is that you're interested in somehow connecting all your personal computers together—if I can provide you with a software tool to do that, you are willing to pay up to x amount, right? Fine. Do you agree with that? Fine. You would like to see us deliver that by the end of the year, correct? Fine.

"If you've done all that, it kind of makes the closing more natural and less tension filled. And what also happens is that during the testing-feasibility stage, I learn more about ya."

After we've spent about forty-five minutes watching various people role-play, Carter hands over the podium to the women he had earlier identified as two of his top instructors.

Jill DeStefano says this particular class is not really representative of the general mix, in that a lot of the people have some sort of track record in electronics. Carter had said the company hired most of its people directly out of college (he estimated that a mere 25 percent had had some computer background), but Jill claims the present class contains only five raw recruits.

"The perspectives are real interesting and varied," says Jill. "You have people who are street smart, and then you have people who are just so naïve and . . . trusting." Everybody laughs except Carter. "But they're wonderful," she says, referring to the trusting types, "because they're like little sponges. Their attitude is Tell me what to do and I'll do it. It's easier for them to learn than for someone to relearn, to have to do away with bad habits."

Jill on role-playing: "I think one of the things we try to do is, we let them tell us how they think they did, first. It's important for them to vocalize what they feel about their performance. If for some reason they think they did a wonderful job—and they didn't do such a wonderful job—it's important for that to come out initially. Then the instructor can think quickly"—she rolls her eyes up in a gesture of awkwardness, like the girl who's been asked to the prom by someone she doesn't want to go with, but whose feelings she doesn't want to hurt, either—"and be able to give that person constructive criticism without destroying their self-confidence. Confidence is so much of this." (Notice that this is another case of TNS being applied to the teaching of TNS; rather than telling the students how they did, the instructors first ask them.)

Jill on the "trust relationship" between teacher and pupil: "They see us in the classroom, they see how we respond to certain situations. They know we've been in the field. We give them examples of what we did in the field, or how we'd handle certain situations, so there is a lot of trust involved."

Elizabeth Elrod describes the role-playing scenario she's using today: "We're having an interview with a tactical manager. It's based on a real case. Certain financial details have been changed, but it's basically a representation of an actual business situation. The tactical manager is the one who's been designated by the president of the company to assemble the information they need in order to make a decision. It's customer service that's basically the company's largest problem. The students are trying to get from us the flow of order-processing: how orders go throughout the organization, and where the problem is in that processing line."

Is it ever set up where the students discover halfway through the presentation that they're talking to the wrong person?

Jill: "They did that yesterday. They determine before they ever really start who they need to talk to, who would make the ultimate decision, and who would be the people to get the right information from. [It is seldom the same person in all three cases.] That's a very big part of the strategic meeting, in determining what the buying process is, what are the criteria they use to make a buying decision, who would be influencers and who would have the information they need to study the situation."

Elizabeth: "What they're trying to do today is get some costs. Usually the strategic manager does know what the problem is costing his company. The students today have to get at that information"—she slips easily into a sales dialogue, playing both salesperson and client—"'Well what's that costing you?' 'Oh, it's costing us about three lost sales a month from what I've been able to figure.' 'Well what impact does that have on cost per sale? How many of those could you recoup if I could take care of that problem?' . . . That's what we're trying to get from them today.

"Tomorrow," she continues, "they test feasibility with the same person they're talking to today. In other words"—back into character—"'If I change your operation in this way, is that acceptable to you? If I can show you that it's cost-justified and I could recoup one lost sale a day, would you support me in a proposal to the president?' That's what they do tomorrow. Then they make a presentation, the next day, to the president of the company."

Do they really think the students are being totally natural, or is there a tendency to patronize the instructor?

Jill: "I think there are some isolated situations. But our job is to make it real clear, in the classroom, that this is their trying grounds. This is where they find out what works for them, and when it works. And it's not gonna work with every client. So this is the opportunity for them to try new and different things until they find a comfort zone. But then they still have to be sensitive enough to know when they have to modify according to the client."

Elizabeth, who, you may recall, keeps her classes in line by cutting out the hearts of would-be snow-job artists, adds: "I try to play different personalities on them. Yesterday I was very— you know, if they didn't ask me exactly the right question, I was quiet. If they asked me a close-ended question, it was no or yes. They had to dig. Today, I've been playing very, very expressive, and if they ask me an open-ended question they can barely shut me up. And that's hard for some of them to deal with, too. Last week I had a group of incumbents, people who'd been in the company awhile, and I played very analytical. I numbered 'em to death, which is the hardest client for me, personally, to deal with."

Jill: "And it may differ from student to student. Because these people may go out and say, 'Oh, she's just spillin' her guts

201

today. You ask a question and she's off on a blue streak.' But you have to be able to play a different client or a different style with different students. That helps the realism, I think. They can't think, Oh, I'm goin' in to see Elizabeth, or I'm goin' in to see Jill, 'cause they know *us* by now. This way, they have to react to the client."

Carter interjects, "I would say we've got thirty unique personalities on this staff." He laughs. Jill and Elizabeth laugh, and as if on cue—Carter has spoken, the talk is over—they head for the door.

"Have fun," says Elizabeth, leaving, "but not too much fun," adds Jill.

• • •

Alone once again with the silent Ric Morrison and me, Carter shares his philosophy on the meaning of the word *customer*.

"One of the things we try to create a different attitude about is the word *customer*. Our first definition, at the Bell System, was *subscriber*. We've moved from that heritage to one of *customer*"—he says the word with an almost holy reverence that sounds sincere—"and to move it a step further, we're going from customer to *client*." It's a bit of a head trip, Carter concedes, but "*client* implies a higher level of trust. If you're a doctor, you sometimes refer to your patients as clients. Or if you're a lawyer . . ." Carter smiles, realizing that lawyers do not have as good a connotation as doctors, and aborts his sentence.

"Do you think it'll evolve to where you start calling customers *patients*?" I ask. Carter allows a smile in return.

There is no formal policy on semantics at AT&T. According to Carter, sales phraseology is the province of the individual instructor. Personally, Carter considers the use of so-called red-flag words—words like *buy, sign,* and the like—a subtlety, not a major underpinning.

This is not the only respect in which AT&T's brand of selling differs from that promoted by Hopkins, Ziglar, and their scores of Johnny-come-lately imitators. The company's reps are encouraged to take an intensely rational approach to the customer; a typical ATTIS presentation leads the buyer through a *logical* sequence of steps that, hopefully, culminates in a sale. The italicized phrase is important, because TNS trainers who make their living on the lecture circuit preach that buying is a virtually 100 percent *emotional* process. Hopkins has often said that people make decisions with their hearts and then look for intellectual reasons to justify those decisions; the salesperson's use of logic is important only insofar as it helps the customer find a rational pretext for a choice that has already been made on a more visceral level. The following list of alleged "real reasons why people buy" comes from *The Equation of Persuasion* by West Coast trainer Ken Clifford:

greed	security	health
prestige	ambition	peer pressure
love	price	the next door neighbor
vanity	comfort	spite
hate	status	style
	ego	

Yet nowhere in the role-playing scenarios I observed, or in my discussions with Carter and members of his staff, were any of the above motivations (save for price) even touched upon.

This is actually symptomatic of Carter's attitude toward the evangelical wing of TNS. In his opinion, a lot of today's sales training is "self-help nonsense" in which "all they're trying to do is create a sense of self-worth in somebody who calls himself a salesman." He says the feedback he gets from AT&T's corporate audience supports his contention. Carter's feelings on the subject grew more blunt as the day progressed. When I challenged him, shortly before I left, with some of the more inspirational verbiage from one of Hopkins's recent seminars, he retorted, "I've got more confidence in my testimonials than in Tom and his toupee."

So it was that as we sat there in the aftermath of observing the role-playing sessions, Carter insisted, "Some of the clichés of sales training are just that. No more than that." He pursed his lips, then scowled slightly. "I can remember an insurance salesman trying to sell me 'a financial plan'—that's the new cliché for life insurance. And I was watching him go through the steps and he said, Would you mind if we used the kitchen table? And I had to stop him. Because that's just such a cliché—all the major decisions in the family are made in the kitchen.

"I told him flat out. I said, Look, you've been okay up to here, I can stomach it. But I'm not going into the kitchen. I don't *make* the major decisions in my life in the kitchen. We make those decisions in the bedroom. That's where we have the most fun.

"There's cognitive skills that you teach salespeople. And there's things that you tell 'em to avoid, and things that you tell them to do. But, the interpersonal intensity of the professional . . . well, the last thing I want to do is rob them of originality.

"I'm convinced that if you had the right sales relationship with a customer, if you truly build a relationship, you could sell them Nehru jackets. If you could identify an application you could sell them *anything*. As long as there's some trust that's built into it.

"Look at the complexity of what we're marketing. Office automation products. Terminals. Work stations. Networking. If you take the wrong approach, you'll sell the onesies and twosies, but you won't build a long-term relationship."

Not surprisingly, Carter is also strongly opposed to the kind of assumptive reasoning that has a salesman taking as many liberties as possible until the customer stops him. In one role-playing episode, a salesman had asked his "client," "Do you mind if I take notes?" At my observation that the salesman's question had been wrong on two counts—first, he opened himself up to the possibility of a no answer, and second, he should've just gone ahead and begun taking notes in order to establish control of the situation—Carter came close to flying off the handle.

"What you're telling me is that in some cases, you violate your customer's rights. . . . There's a lot of stuff that gets into assumptive closing techniques that's almost—high pressure." He said the phrase as though he were a doctor describing a malignant tumor. "AT&T's value to its marketplace is in a total architectural sense. If I sell a terminal and it costs me the trust and the opportunity to sell what else is behind it, I may have won the battle but I've lost the war.

"We have a presence in every office in America," says Carter, pointing to his phone, "and now we need to expand that. I won't lose a customer at the expense of dropping some hardware." His eyes flashed. "Our focus is to understand the customer, the information flow, to define customer needs. We're focusing more open-ended. Give us more, let us sift through it and then feed it back to you. I mean, 'Do you want it in red or blue?' is a great close-ended strategy in selling certain commodities. But *It . . . does . . . not . . . work* in selling systems."

From there, he launched into a facetious adaptation of Hopkins-esque alternative-choice questions, spewing technical jargon seemingly out of both sides of his mouth at once. Sort of, *Do you want a ramsiframansis or a whosicallsis?* He punctuated his monologue by insisting that "you don't sell computers that way. What you're seeing here is a systems approach to sales, which is what our market requires."

Warming to the task, Carter continued in a sterner tone of voice than I'd yet heard from him. Morrison, meanwhile, looked nervous. "In fact, if you laid some of those high-pressure assumptive closes on me, I'd look you right in the face and say, *So what*, Steve?" He sounded contentious, almost incensed at the suggestion that Hopkins-based techniques could—or should—be applied to selling computer systems. To him, they're little or no better than the old shtickiness.

Carter glanced at Morrison, whose eyebrows appeared to flicker a bit, possibly as a subtle reminder that all this was being recorded. Whereupon my host mentally regrouped. When he continued, he was once again affable Joe Carter, voicing the company line in an even, businesslike tone: "What this type of selling requires is a benefits-oriented consultative approach to systems design, and what we're trying to do is establish worth and trust on a long-term basis. And the products will just fly outta here."

A Case Study in Helping the Products Fly Outta Here: François Levy

Levy signed on with ATTIS at a training salary of twenty-two thousand dollars in 1982. He recalls feeling, at the time, that his new employer didn't have much confidence in him—perhaps because of his uninspiring background. The world of retail clothing is not exactly known as a hotbed of new-generation selling skills.

"In my old business," he muses in his disarming Jean-Claude Killy accent, "I was selling five-hundred-dollar suits. It was more of a social event than anything else."

Consequently, when Levy joined AT&T, he was assigned "the dogs," as he puts it, accounts from which the company had never derived much income in the first place. "I guess they figured if I couldn't be much help, at least I wouldn't do any harm there."

Like all new hires, he spent the better part of his first six months in training. It was this six-month exposure to ATTIS's comprehensive sales philosophy that made the difference, giving Levy the confidence that seems present in all super-achievers. He says, "I knew that once I went on commissions I'd come out just fine."

Levy was right. Between June and December that first year he booked fifty thousand dollars in commissions, to finish his freshman season at a respectable sixty thousand dollars. The next year, he crossed the six-figure mark, and he continued his uphill climb at the same torrid pace in 1984. He declines to provide too many specifics about what he's been able to achieve, saying, not with undue modesty, "Some of the percentage increases sound too high to be realistic. People would say, 'He's not only a good salesman, he's a good liar as well.'" But the facts are that when Levy was handed the American Express account in March of 1983, billings lolled at around one thousand dollars a month. By year's end, says Levy, "we were doing over one hundred thousand dollars a month with them."

Nor was the Amex account Levy's lone triumph. "In January of last year they gave me First Interstate Bank, which was tough, really tough. They hadn't done much business with us in over seven years." Now, says Levy, the bank is on the verge of "committing to AT&T architecture," the high-tech equivalent of what a real estate agent gets when he signs an exclusive listing.

Levy says the biggest change he sees in selling overall has to do with an emphasis on service over hardware. Symptomatic of this change is the fact that "two of the biggest phrases you hear now are 'MTTF' and 'MTTR'—mean time to failure and mean time to repair. Companies need to know how reliable the equipment is, and how fast you can get it back on line when something goes wrong. Downtime is incredibly expensive." In language that would make Joe Carter proud, Levy defines selling as "an exercise in communicating your company's sincere concern for the performance of the machinery they buy, and how that relates to the long-term goals of the client."

This ability to perform has superseded the lowest bid as the major concern among corporate purchasing agents, Levy claims. He uses an analogy to the space program to illustrate his point.

"Do you think the astronauts who go up in the space shuttle want to know that their equipment went to the lowest bidder?" he asks rhetorically. "They want to know that the job was done by people who took pride in what they were doing.

"You cannot any longer take your magic box and do a song and dance for the customer and expect to be successful. In the old days, the salesman would show up and hope to dazzle the client into buying something he might or might not really need. But today, with all the sophisticated equipment and the complexity of business, these businessmen depend on solutions to survive. Their whole corporate profit structure is dependent on what the salesman is able to come up with."

Levy sees this, in turn, as having wrought a salutary change in both the image of and conduct of selling.

"The balance has shifted," he says, summing up. "For the first time, the customers need us as much as we need them, and they know it."

•   •   •

Meanwhile, Back at the Ranch . . .

Sales training at AT&T is a bit of a departure from much of the sales training that goes on elsewhere, in its painstaking emphasis on the salesperson's mastery of matters financial. So much so that the uninitiated might think he'd mistakenly wandered into a room the company had leased out to Merrill Lynch.

Herewith, the scheduled curriculum for the week of my visit, as listed on a blackboard at the front of a class being conducted by TC Marc Sherrell:

> MONDAY: FINANCIAL STATEMENTS; COST OF CAPITAL; DEPRECIATION; PROFIT VS. CASH FLOW; CASH FLOW; and something simply designated by the acronym ITC (short, perhaps, for It's Too Complicated)
> TUESDAY: THE VALUE OF MONEY; DISCOUNTED CASH FLOW; FINANCIAL OPTIONS; COST-TO-COST ANALYSIS
> WEDNESDAY: EQUITY POSITIONING; PROFIT IMPROVEMENT; INVESTMENT ANALYSIS; CALCULATIONS; ABBREVIATED ANALYSIS
> THURSDAY: SPREADSHEET SOFTWARE; REVIEW FOR FINAL
> FRIDAY (in ominous bold letters): FINAL EXAM

It is the measure of the average trainee's preparedness for all this that when Sherrell asked his class what they thought of the course so far, he was fairly deluged with remarks about the breadth and volume of work expected of them.

Carter's earlier tirade notwithstanding, one female student demonstrated her mastery of TNS's euphemistic vocabulary when she told Sherrell, "We're not complaining, we're just *sharing our concerns*." She said it playfully, with a twinkle in her voice. The instructor nodded as if to say "Touché."

Sherrell is in his element. Having come to AT&T by way of management careers at both a savings and loan and a private mortgage company, he knows the financial ropes backward and forward. He thinks most companies are basically very unsophisticated financially, and says he wants his reps to be able to be a "true resource" in their quest to upgrade their client's financial-planning capabilities. Toward that end, he explains, a lot of new hires are MBAs (though Carter says his only real criterion for hiring is a consistent record of achievement, whatever your background. "If you were a boy scout," he says, "I hope you were an eagle. If you were a girl scout, I hope you sold the most cookies").

Sherrell's partner, Dennis Clevenger, spent four years in the air force, got into digital technology, and wound up piloting

208

AT&T's approach to the two largest utilities in Indiana. Sherrell and Clevenger are among the thirty on-site instructors who took about a 50 percent pay cut to move in-house ("My wife thought I was just a nutty salesman," says Clevenger) for the prospect of unending upward mobility through the ranks.*

But both Sherrell and Clevenger claim to feel it is their duty to help expand the financial horizons of their colleagues.

"More and more sales involve buying committees composed of people with different fields of expertise," says Sherrell. "You can't fake your way through it, especially where the dollars are concerned."

Many of the reps who emerge from AT&T training will "in all likelihood be more solidly grounded in financial considerations than the people they begin their negotiations with," says Sherrell. But he adds that seldom will a deal be finally consummated without the input, on the client side, of someone who's "very attuned to the financial workings of the situation."

The information is not presented merely as raw data, but in a sales context—how it benefits the client company. Fittingly, the salespeople must learn not only how to do cost-benefit analyses, but how to pick the best one for a hypothetical client and then defend their choice.

Sherrell: "In running what is, truthfully, a very detailed cash-flow analysis, and in trying to find the best solution for our customer, we're doing something that probably most of our competitors have never done. We're truly trying to determine what is best for our customer based on his financial position. We're focusing on the So Whats.

"Price of the product is not necessarily the issue anymore. If a rep says he's having trouble selling because of price, then it's probably because he doesn't understand financial marketing." Carla Estes, the training division's resident hacker and keeper-of-the-stats, says reps using Multiplan, the financial marketing formula that she conceived, have beaten bids that were as much as 25 percent lower.

The AT&T compensation package of 70 percent salary and 30 percent commission can provide a top-notch account executive with a six-figure income; Clevenger says he heard of one Tennessee superstar who was pulling down around $165,000.

Says Carter, "The technology is changing so fast that financial questions other than the initial cost of acquisition become that much more important. Clients are saying, 'Give me a way that I'm not locked into something for the next forty years so that I can update and yet still protect my investment.'" In today's arcane world of leasebacks, depreciation schedules, and overnight obsolescence, flexibility is of paramount importance.

But couldn't this curriculum be devastating to some otherwise talented salespeople? Aren't there individuals who are good sellers, but just don't quite have what it takes when it comes to hard numbers?

Better to have them screw up here than on the street, says Sherrell, and there's always help available for those who can't actually dot all the *i*'s and cross all the *t*'s themselves—"We just want them to be able to recognize the factors that may impact a given purchasing decision." Besides, adds Clevenger, "We evaluate, but we don't judge. We try to enhance their sense of self." (Excuse me, Dennis, but isn't that what your boss just finished criticizing Hopkins for?)

Students can avoid some of this through a test-out option; that is, they can take an exam at their branch to see if they've already somehow come upon all the knowledge AT&T would ordinarily impart to them through its Aurora curriculum. In practice, few salespeople choose the test-out option; few pass, anyway.

However, even if a given rep is really up on his facts and figures, he can't test out of the entire week, because it isn't just a bookkeeping course. Instead, the emphasis is always on application.

"At a certain point, even those who have an accounting background are still going to need some information on how you run a cash-flow, how you target as a sales-closing tool as opposed to just a number-crunching exercise," Clevenger notes.

Carter says growth over the course of the course—"How much better does a student do at the end than at the beginning?"—is more important than performance in an absolute sense. According to Carla Estes, the average class grade at the end of "financial week" is 87.

Final-exam scores and other facets of the student's behavior are relayed back to his local branch manager together with overall class averages, so that the manager has some idea how well each of his people did in relation to everyone else.

"A bad final-exam score is not necessarily death," says Carter pointedly, "but a bad attitude can be."

•   •   •

After an unexpected fire drill sends everyone in the building out into the pleasant 50-degree late afternoon, we reconvene in Carter's office with an additional cast member: western regional sales manager Joe Flannery.

I mention that my general impression of the ATTIS training operation is that it is heavy on attitude, real heavy on data, but relatively light on specific strategies. Am I correct, or did I miss something?

Carter explains that the pendulum at AT&T had earlier swung too far toward technique, and now has probably swung too far in the opposite direction. "A necessary adjustment," though, he claims, "in light of the wholesale changes in marketing philosophy and the plethora of product introductions. We released thirty-two products last year alone, and the most pressing priority was equipping the sales force with product knowledge. We figured it would be nice if the account executives knew what they were selling." Carter expects the overcompensation to be corrected "when the market settles down, if it ever does."

Before long, we have drifted into a discussion of what makes a salesperson a salesperson.

"In my opinion," says Flannery, whose answers tend to be long, circuitous, and syntactically remote, "there are some inherent abilities that a person must have in order to be a successful salesperson. Qualities they must not develop, but must have, not the least of which is the ability to understand where they are in relation to a given point in time. In other words, a problem-solving ability, where they have a direction that they have to go after. They have to have an awareness of themselves, and others. I think that, in varying degrees, exists in certain people better than others. . . .

"What can, I think, be trained are those things that—if you have those inbred abilities—what other types of information do you need in order to accomplish those goals? All right, so, I think there are some certain qualities that a person must have naturally, but I think it's my function to give them the technical tools, to be able to go out into a competitive marketplace and be able to optimally utilize those inherent qualities."

"In Iacocca's biography," chimes in Carter, "he says that he was definitely not a born salesman; he had an aversion to public speaking, he didn't really enjoy interpersonal relationships, and he was trained, initially, as a mechanical-industrial engineer. So he feels that it was through personal coaching that he became proficient in sales.

"I think there are people that have interpersonal skills to make the foundation of a good salesman. I think you can cognitively recognize what you can do to make those things better. But I think there are other people who would just rather work with machines than people. And to ask them to be a salesperson is to ask them to work against their natural inclinations.

"You know, if you don't like some of the theatrics associated with the sales profession . . . if you don't like the *intense,* interpersonal requirements . . . if you don't like the verbalization of what you have to do . . . if you don't like the immediate feedback cycles"—Carter laughs—"You know, one thing about the sales profession is you know where you stand. . . . Quite honestly, if you can't handle [or redefine?] failure and rejection, if you don't have some resiliency . . . we could do it, we could cognitively equip you with the skills. But you'd never be successful."

Do you think that a salesperson needs to be a little more amoral than the average person? Needs not to come to such firm judgments about right and wrong as the average person does?

"The sales profession is a relative behavioral science," says Carter, "and as such, there's not a lot of absolutes. I mean, one of the things that they have to demonstrate is an almost unbelievable flexibility. Customers expect different things. And I think a salesman—through his or her ability to respond in a flexible manner—has to be able to deal with that very relative value system, to be honest with you."

Flannery, with uncharacteristic forthrightness, says, "I think your very, very good salesmen are very moral people. I think if you're gonna get to the top of this profession, I think you have to have that quality. I think it's a requirement, because I think people buy from people, and eventually it's gonna come down to that relationship, and people can sense that. Now, that's not to say that you can't be a good salesman if you are immoral, but I think if you're going to go to the top of the profession and be very professional about it, it's a requirement."

Carter, apparently having thought better of the import of his original answer while Flannery was talking, decides to add: "Because of that relativeness of values they're exposed to, they have to have an internal clock that's probably greater than some of the other structured professions where the rules are always defined and never change."

I ask Flannery about whether the sexual equality I've seen at the company today is truly representative of the rank and file.

Flannery says, "It's weighted towards males—"

"But the gap is closing," notes Carter, who would, on more than one occasion, finish sentences begun by his colleague.

Apprised of another executive's observation that "women just can't sell in certain executive settings," Carter's eyes seem genuinely to flash.

"How far do you take that?" he demands, barely waiting for me to finish the thought. *"Blacks can't sell in a certain environment? Hispanics can't? People that are old or young can't? People of Jewish persuasion can't?"* He sighs. "I think those biases exist—and incidentally, I think from a sales-management standpoint, what you try to do is minimize them—but I see those biases waning."

Carter asserts, "First of all, most of the customers at the level that we've been talking about all day—people making six- and seven-figure decisions—they're above and beyond simple prejudices. You'll find isolated pockets of it. But my experience is that women have been very successful." Reminds me of something said by Marvin Edelstein of Burroughs. Asked whether an upper-echelon male executive might feel somehow threatened by a female salesperson, Edelstein replied, "First of all, I think that when you're threatened, you don't stop to look at the gender of the person who's threatening you." He went on to say, "The assumption at higher levels of performance is that people got there because they have a right to be there. The stereotypes—though they may exist—just don't apply."

What about the stereotypes of the sales profession? How long do you think it will be before *they* no longer apply?

Carter smiles his executive smile. He has lost none of the clear-eyed intensity he had at 8 A.M.

"I don't have any problem identifying that I'm part of the sales profession," he says, without a trace of qualification in his voice. "In fact, I am enamored with what this profession can do."

• • •

It's hard to say how things will turn out for ATTIS. Notwithstanding the company's enormous investment in training, as well as in advertising aimed at raising public consciousness, the marketplace still seems confused about AT&T's postdivestiture role in the scheme of things, a confusion evidenced by the stagnation of the company's stock during 1984. (The issue closed out the year within a point of the price at which it had opened on January 1; originally, many analysts had predicted a volatile year for AT&T common stock.)

But I'll say this much: if you've spent any time at all with Joe Carter—gotten to know him and his highly intellectual interpretation of TNS—you're inclined not to bet against him.

• • •

P.S.

To answer the question you've been wondering about since the beginning of this chapter: How do you point your finger at someone without being offensive?

You hold the palm of the other hand perpendicular to the end of the finger you are pointing with, sort of like a football referee's time-out sign. Carter says this procedure blunts the sinister overtones associated with the pointing gesture.

Sales Miscellany

Average (median) income of American salesperson
(approximately, as of 1984): $32,777

8

The Selling Life in the Age of TNS

But what about the salesperson's life in the age of TNS? Has it changed all that much? After all, the essential realities of selling remain ever the same, do they not? Salespeople must still pound on doors; they must still work long, often irregular hours (if they truly aspire to the kind of success TNS makes possible); they must still beat the bushes in search of new business. Granted, you say, today's sophisticated strategies have changed the way the presentation unfolds and affected other facets of selling dramatically—salaries, for instance, which in certain industries have skyrocketed; but then, better salespeople were always able to stay well ahead of the economy, even during periods of runaway inflation or ice-cold recession. Granted, you say, salespeople can now rely on technology for many of the mundane functions they once had to handle, but the actual selling of the product still requires that same degree of human investment. The personal touch.

Doesn't it?

Not necessarily.

While there's no denying that the actual closing of a sale is still handled by humans, you'd be amazed how much of the groundwork has now been entrusted to computer chips. Technology has evolved from a process that passively supported the sale to an actual factor in it. It is not unusual these days for the preliminary "discussions" to take place between the salesperson's computer and your computer. You may be qualified or disqualified as a prospect without even knowing it. Further, by accessing your data base, the salesperson can make great strides toward determining your needs, capabilities, and corporate direction, all of which fall into the category of "preapproach planning," as Xerox calls it. He will use this information now to determine what product or service he feels would benefit you; later, he will use it in question form to shape the probes he hopes will get you to say, "three of diamonds."

While this is a relatively far-flung example involving high technology, the nature and conduct of the sales business has also changed in dozens, perhaps hundreds, of subtle ways—ways that affect every facet of the salesman's professional life cycle, from how he gets his job to how he may lose it. Then, too, there are aspects of the selling life that are and have always been either unknown or incompletely understood.

What we take here, then, is a comprehensive look at the selling life, as it is lived by the new salesperson, circa 1986.

How Does One Get to Be a Salesperson, Anyway?

It depends for the most part on what level you're talking about. For the majority of entry-level positions in nonskilled capacities, the newspaper is still the first resort, although at all levels, fewer and fewer sales jobs are obtained by dealing directly with the employer. You certainly don't walk in off the street, clutching your finger-smudged, coffee-stained copy of *The New York Times* classified section (with nineteen different ads circled in red), and interview for a forty-five-thousand-dollar-plus-bonus-plus-car-plus-fringes job as a sales engineer. Chances are you'll land that kind of job through the divine auspices of a major executive-search firm, increasing numbers of which are devoted exclusively to sales.

Search firms have all the openings right there at their fingertips (or rather, the fingertips of the people running their IBM XTs) and all the names right there in their autodialers, and know everybody in the world who's anybody. They can get you fixed up at A Real Blue-Chip Company—where again, chances are, you will repose just long enough to catch your breath (and justify the search firm's 30 percent fee) before they have you back on the street once more, interviewing for Something Bigger and Better. Like a maniacal broker churning an account, the typical sales-recruitment agency is a marvel of incessant activity. By aggressively headhunting the market—playing musical chairs with those in the upper echelon of the trade—they manage to effect a virtual 100 percent turnover among key staff members every few years.

(What this does, in turn, is produce a decided, if fundamentally illogical, paranoia among management of top sales outfits. Loath to lose their most valued producers, they don't court publicity, and they shun it even when it comes walking their way. During the early phases of my research, at least three major firms—Harcourt Brace Jovanovich, Xerox, and Pfizer—turned down my requests for interviews with sales reps, citing the fear of identifying them to competitors. Overlooking for a moment the issue of why they think their employees would be so easy to steal in the first place, there are three basic flaws in such arguments: (1) the competitors already know who the top producers are, and what they're making; (2) so do the search firms; (3) the firms giving me these arguments should be well aware of points (1) and (2) because in many cases, they got *their* sales reps by headhunting the competition.)

With respect to those jobs that will be placed out of the newspaper, however, it's worth noting that TNS has definitely made its mark on sales help-wanted advertising. The copy often reflects the tenor of today's salesmanship. I recall scanning the classifieds one day shortly after I had gotten out of college in 1972, and seeing this one sales ad whose heading, in bold caps, read WE'RE LOOKING FOR A WILD BULL. You don't see much of that anymore. Words like "sincere," "analytical," and "friendly" are gradually replacing old standbys like "take-charge" and "aggressive."

Interestingly, the ads themselves show an increased tendency to actually *apply* TNS strategies. If your classified section comes from a paper such as *The New York Times,* you'll note that in many instances, probing questions have supplanted the extravagant claims that once typified sales advertising. MAKE $250,000 THIS YEAR! is giving way to ARE YOU EARNING WHAT YOU'RE WORTH? In fact, it's safe to say that in 1985 a good deal of classified advertising of all types—in particular the glossy work done by the recruitment divisions of major ad agencies like J. Walter Thompson, U.S.A.—pays tacit tribute to the principles espoused by leading TNS theorists. Understatement is replacing overkill. Not only have companies stopped looking for the wild bull, they're less inclined to throw it, as well.

• • •

After you're hired, chances are you'll receive some modicum of sales training—unless you go to work for a car dealership.

"The car business,' says Tom Murphy, Tom Hopkins's business manager, "is in a time warp. By and large, their approach to the customer has not changed at all in fifty years." Murphy's point is echoed by leading mergers and acquisitions specialist Mike Brown, who simply says, "When you're talking about car sales, all the horrible stereotypes are true."

Surprisingly, "entry-level" aircraft dealers (those who sell the likes of used Cessnas to people who are buying their first plane), whose product costs triple or more what even today's inflated street machine does, may be even worse offenders. Or so says commercial jet salesman Dave Cresti, at any rate. Cresti's observation is supported by a recent issue of *Flying,* which describes in painful detail the exasperating experience suffered by—get this—a Houston car dealer who was out to purchase his first airplane.

"If I ran my shop like that," the magazine quotes the car dealer, "no one would come back, and I'd deserve it." Which, I suppose, proves that even car dealers need someone to sneer at.

For most reps who are trained, the intensive instruction lasts either three to six weeks or three to six months, with the latter becoming the norm in service firms, high-tech industrial manufacturers, and financial institutions. Training programs at some insurance companies and investment houses run for a year or more. For reasons that are unclear, training regimens lasting from six weeks to three months are relatively rare throughout the sales industry.

Oddly enough, training programs at companies that distribute high-tech *consumer* products may run as short as a week or two. This suggests that the guy or gal who's trying to sell you a personal computer was trained only a sixth as well as the guy or gal who's trying to sell you your office desk top, though the two products may be virtually identical.

There are indications, however, that even among the top blue-chip companies, sales training is not as effective as some would like it to be. A survey by McGraw-Hill, which is noted for its comprehensive statistical explorations of the sales universe, found that a full quarter of sales executives at major industrial companies believe the bulk of their sales reps incapable of articulating the company's basic message.

In their never-ending efforts to surmount problems like that, sales organizations, particularly those listed among the fabled *Fortune* 500, devote great amounts of time and energy to analyzing customers' buying habits. The hope is that by getting a solid line on why people purchase the things they do, they can pretty well lay out the most probable buying scenarios for the salesman, and by laying out the most probable buying scenarios, they can reduce the potential for his mucking things up by ad libbing counterproductive spiels.

One of the most highly prized of such analytical tools, revered by sales managers everywhere, is:

The Sales Meeting.

Sales meetings were originally conceived as broad theoretical forums for the exchange of empirical data that would enable the salesman to gain a far better understanding of his company's precise role in the marketplace. In theory, salespeople would take the opportunity to rehash recent sales calls that had gone less than spectacularly, and perhaps rehearse some alternative methods of dealing with the situation should it come up again soon. That was in theory. In practice, in the past, that aspect of the meeting usually lasted about five minutes. Thereafter—sales being the almost exclusively male preserve that it was—the conversation tended to degenerate into a frenzied rap session with a decided locker-room flavor.

There are indications that the microchip may change all that. The much-maligned sales meeting has lately shown signs of fulfilling at least some small part of its noble promise, thanks to the use of videodiscs, voice-stress analyzers, and other high-tech paraphernalia. Nor has the growing female presence in the national sales force hurt. As in police work, women seem to have had both a sanitizing and a stabilizing influence on sales staffs. Men are more inclined, when in mixed company, to maintain some semblance of decorum and tend to business.

Concern about the efficacy of sales meetings is genuine and warranted because they're so damned expensive to run. Especially given the current trend of holding them at posh resorts. It cost Master Lock thirty-five thousand dollars plus travel expenses to entertain fifty-six of its leading sales reps at a "Shoot More for '84" sales meeting held at the O'Hare Marriott in Chicago. The theme stemmed from the company's commercial in which one of the company's products refused to pop open despite being shot clear through by a marksman's bullet.

Naturally, the lusher the venue, the more expensive the gig. Some of the favored places nationally are the Pointe, a Mobil five-star resort in Phoenix; the Sheraton in Steamboat Springs, Colorado; Wayne Newton's Tamiment in Pennsylvania; and Miami's Doral Country Club. Penny conscious? Las Vegas and Atlantic City—where the per diem expense allowance is presumably paid out in quarters—offer the best dollar-for-dollar value, say insiders. Or you can have your meeting at Grossinger's, which has, in recent years, shed its provincial, ethnic image, and get off for just sixty-seven dollars per room, double occupancy, off-season, including all meals and access to a twenty-seven-hole golf course. If you're planning such a corporate getaway, you may want to consult *S&MM,* which, usually in its February issue, presents an itemized breakdown of all costs and amenities in a variety of popular hotels and country clubs across America, complete right down to the cost of morning coffee rolls and whether or not you can get a limo to the nearest airport. (Don't assume you can; Birmingham, Alabama, and San Diego, California, are just two of the cities that don't offer this particular convenience, says the magazine.)

Of course, sales companies incur expenses all the time, not just when they're entertaining the troops in faraway places. In 1984, the median cost of making a single sales call was variously

pegged at between $150 and $205, with certain major markets—
notably New York and San Francisco—as much as 60 percent
higher than the national average. Bear in mind that in high-
powered industrial selling, five separate calls may be required
before a sale is finalized. Even *S&MM,* which adopts a more
conservative formula for figuring cost-per-call (only those factors
that are under management's control are considered), reported
that a typical week in the field cost the average company $681.45
per salesperson.

Overall selling expenses, expressed as a percentage of gross
sales, run from a low of 1.4 percent for the petroleum industry—you obviously don't have to work too hard to get people to
buy gasoline—to a high of almost 17 percent for the drug/sur-
gical supply industry. All sources agreed that the cost figures are
gravely inflated by poor productivity resulting from careless
scheduling, bad work habits, and the general climate of inefficiency indigenous to the selling life.

In fact, indications are that the average salesperson may
spend less than 15 percent of any given eight-hour work period
in front of a customer, selling.

• • •

Understandably disturbed by this sort of lackluster productivity, more and more companies are turning to the "front office" system of managing their staff's daily itinerary. In the bad
old days, a salesman was pretty much on his own. He made his
own contacts, scheduled his own appointments, and was responsible for tracking his prospects after his initial presentation.
The problem was—and is—that most salespeople tend to adopt
an overly conservative view of their own workload capabilities,
the result being fewer completed presentations each day. The
solution was to take the scheduling responsibilities from the
salesperson and entrust them to a third party who'd been trained
to watch over management's interests. Thus, the origin of the
front office, which acts as liaison between salesperson and customer. Like American Airlines, sales outfits who've gone the
front-office route are wont to overbook their salespeople's daily
schedules on the assumption that a number of appointments will
be lost daily for a variety of reasons, chief among them the

salesperson's own lack of initiative. One day soon, of course, all salespeople will have become walking incarnations of TNS and such attitude problems will disappear by themselves; but while we're waiting for Utopia, says management, we'd better tighten the reins.

A second factor in the front office/no front office question is the method by which a given company obtains its customers. Outfits that, like IBM, devote a great amount of time and energy to cold canvassing are more inclined to dump the game in the salesperson's lap. (Outfits like IBM are also more inclined to devote a great deal of care to selecting their sales reps, so that they wind up with a staff that can be trusted to fend for itself.) Conversely, outfits like the small company I worked for, who derive virtually all of their leads from direct consumer response to "sale" advertisements, tend to go with the office staff.*

The thinking in the latter case is that there's no better time to set an appointment than when the customer makes that first, tentative inquiry, especially if the product is kind of frilly or frivolous. Thus, some minimal commitment—the commitment to at least see the salesperson—is exacted right off the bat.

My former employer's own computer studies clearly demonstrated that the greater the interval between the first inquiry and the actual scheduling of the appointment, the lesser the chances of a successful close. There are many reasons for this. Enthusiasm wanes. The initial burning desire for a given item—particularly something like a wall mirror—palls before sober financial realities. Tyrannical spouses get wind of the planned purchase and throw a tantrum. And so on. Taken together, these contingencies justified the added overhead of maintaining a full-time front-office staff to schedule appointments as the prospects phoned in.

Further, the greater the interval between scheduling and appointment, the lesser the chance the salesperson will even get to make a presentation. "Ideally," my boss used to say, "the best time to see people would be the exact moment that they called up to make the appointment." It used to frustrate him no end

*Yes, IBM runs ads, too, but they are institutional—glossy and quality-oriented—in nature. What they essentially do is bolster the company's image so that the next time the IBM rep comes a-knocking, you won't slam the door in his face.

that logistics and other considerations prevented this idyllic scenario from being realized.

It's a strange truth in home-improvement circles that if you set a hundred appointments, an hour later you'll have already lost two or three. And that's only if you wait for them to call you to cancel. If you were to take the initiative and call each of them back to reconfirm the appointment you'd just set an hour ago, your odds of holding the full hundred would be appreciably worse. For this reason, there exists in sales circles an admonition that goes as follows:

NEVER CALL AHEAD TO CONFIRM A SCHEDULED APPOINTMENT.

Better to take the relatively small risk of showing up at an empty house—or calling on some company mogul only to be told by his secretary that he left yesterday for Mozambique—than to blow all chances of making a sale, now and forever, by giving the customer a chance to rethink his decision to do business with you over the telephone. At my company, in fact, it was less an axiom than a hard-and-fast rule: Get caught calling ahead to a confirmed customer, and you turn in your sample case. Simple as that. During the early years of my sales career, I was told a story about a very fine reupholstery salesman who nonetheless insisted on breaching this cardinal rule. He would call just about every customer before going, ostensibly to get directions. "I don't want to waste valuable selling time driving around aimlessly in the fog," was his justification. The front office complained repeatedly and bitterly to management; appointments were being lost left and right. Management repeatedly broached the subject, though solicitously, for the man was, after all, a star peformer if and when he did manage to get into someone's house. Therein, by the way, lies another cardinal rule that has applications in many arenas besides selling— star performers can generally dispense with all the other cardinal rules and get away with it.

Finally, though, when the star salesman lost three consecutive evening appointments in a traditionally hot-selling area three weeks before Christmas, he was called into the office and given a symbolic Christmas present: a pink slip nestled within the pages of a Hagstrom road map.

Who Is the New Salesman?

For one thing, the new salesman is, increasingly, a woman. Nationwide, women now compose between 20 and 25 percent of the industrial sales force (much more in retail) and are particularly strong in high-tech fields. At Xerox, for example, nearly 40 percent of the reps are female, and Burroughs's Marvin Edelstein says—without a trace of the patronizing ring the sentence usually carries—that some of his very best salespeople are women. Edelstein asserts, "A woman, when she puts her mind to something, is often more dedicated than a man. She's less open to distractions."

Be that as it may, statistics suggest that saleswomen are simply not earning what their less dedicated, more easily distracted male counterparts earn. An unpublished study done by the Bureau of Labor Statistics in 1983 revealed that saleswomen were making only 65 percent of what salesmen at the same level earned—$305 weekly for women, compared to $466 for men—a ratio that gave sales one of the worst equal-work–equal-pay scores among all jobs that were not highly esoteric. (Female astronomers, for example, made just 24 percent of what their male counterparts did.) Part-time saleswomen—those who juggled households as well—fared even worse, earning an average of just *a quarter* of what their full-time male counterparts banked.

Interestingly, the ratio of women to men in sales management (28 percent of the total) exceeds the ratio of women to men in the general sales population, a statistic that supports the notion, expressed by Edelstein and others, that women who do go into sales are quite good at it, and rise quickly through the ranks. What makes the statistic that much more impressive is that the bulk of saleswomen are concentrated in real estate, retail, and so-called party-plan (or multilevel) sales, whereas female sales managers are distributed more or less evenly throughout the sales universe. So, adjusted for professions (that is, throwing out the two or three fields from which the majority of saleswomen hail), the ratio of women in management is astonishingly higher than the ratio of women in sales.

The myth that women are, by nature, inferior salespeople is only one of many stereotypes to come tumbling down in the past ten years. It took awhile, but management is finally awakening to the realization that some of the best salespeople come from unexpected backgrounds. François Levy, AT&T Information System's standout performer in the western United States, came to the company after several years selling men's clothing—a realm whose alumni were long blacklisted by high-profile industrial firms. So pernicious were the habits formed in retail apparel sales—so it was believed, at any rate—that anyone who worked there for any length of time could not possibly emerge without being tainted for life; bring somebody like that up to the major leagues and he'd infect your entire staff before long. Needless to say, Levy is but one of the many top-drawer sales executives nationally who have proved the old dictum wrong.

Hiring criteria have changed in other ways as well. A few years ago, a sales executive at IBM—known for its analytical approach to both hiring and selling—told *Money* that the company had begun hiring college music majors because of their "logical minds." Bethlehem Steel says that nearly a quarter of its sales recruits come from the field of liberal arts. Other companies report stellar performances by people who, outwardly, at least, would have to be described as milquetoasts.

It would seem that finally, a mere hundred-odd years after the emancipation proclamation, sales has begun evaluating people as individual human beings.

Technology having advanced to where it is, it was inevitable that the world would one day encounter salespeople who were neither male nor female, nor ex-musicians nor clothing salespeople, nor even human. For a while during late 1982 and early 1983, computers equipped with voice synthesizers were busily phoning people and making their programmed spiels. The FCC would later crack down on this practice, insisting that people be informed, early in the call, that this was an automated survey (Do salespeople sound so much like robots that an average individual might not know the difference without being told?).

More recently, several Ford dealerships were testing a new Ford Selection Center, a computer that provides potential customers with all the dope on model availability, options, comparative benefits, and so forth. When you find what you want, the computer prints it all out for you. You can't yet actually consummate a purchase by interfacing with the machines, made by San Diego's Cubic Corp. But on the plus siae, you don't have to listen to them say, "Tell ya what I'm gonna do," either.

The Pit Crew

The unsung hero of the sales organization is the marketing support rep. Playing Robin to the sales rep's Batman, the support rep (SR) quietly does much of the legwork—gathering statistics, assembling reports, putting in library time, sealing written proposals inside those neat-looking glassine folders—that frees the outside salesman's mind to concentrate on the task before him as he pulls up to his next appointment in his Batmobile.

But, says Don Hanson of McDonnell Douglas, it is hard to provide a succinct description of what an SR does without trivializing his role, making it sound as though support people are just glorified gofers: "Selling in a high-tech or heavy industrial setting today is a team effort. Without the marketing support people and the others who do the detailed analyses you need to make a comprehensive presentation, you can't compete in this arena." Hansen adds, "When a sale is closed, the credit belongs as much to the support team as to the rep himself, and the rep knows it."

Support people may have some face-to-face (or at least, ear-to-ear) interaction with their counterparts in the client's organization, the flunkies in accounting or manufacturing or shipping-and-receiving who are responsible for tracking facts and figures that the higher-ups need in order to make an informed purchasing decision. Their jobs usually include doing their reps' paperwork—"discwork," actually, since everybody other than the local candy store has gone to automation as a way of monitoring productivity and having all the figures available for instant analysis.

While support reps are unsung, they are not necessarily unpaid. Recent surveys on trade compensation reveal that many support personnel in major industries earn as much as salespeople in lesser industries. In fact, many of today's support personnel earn as much as sales reps in their *own* organization were earning as little as three or four years ago. Twenty-five-or-thirty-thousand-dollar salaries are not uncommon. Further, many sales support specialists go on to become analysts or consultants, a pair of fields that pay quite nicely in today's increasingly service-oriented business environment.

Like the newest telephone salesperson, the newest support person is not a person at all, but a computer. Raytheon, a major supplier to the government and the heaviest of heavy industries, relies on terminals in remote locations to hook their salespeople up with the home office and allow more things to be done on the fly. Complicated proposals and analyses can be worked out from the field, eliminating the wasted time involved in returning to the office.

What Do Salespeople Really Earn, or Venice, Anyone?

Sales earnings have risen substantially in recent years, and are continuing to do so despite the unpredictable economy. A nationwide survey, done in 1984 by Roth Young Personnel Service, reveals the following median salaries for various levels of sales achievement:

Trainee (unspecified product line): $17,150
Consumer sales: $21,125
Key-account manager: $25,350
Technical sales: $25,600
Sales engineer: $28,500
Branch manager: $31,833
Regional manager: $38,500
National-accounts manager: $38,500
Vice-president, sales: $66,700

Bear in mind that some of the numbers factored into the above categories were probably compiled as long ago as 1983; incomes have certainly risen since then. Equally certain is the fact that even when the above figures were current, they were low for any number of major business centers, including parts of both coasts and Chicago. Both *The New York Times* and the *Los Angeles Times* regularly advertise trainee positions, in various industries, that pay at the "technical sales" level quoted above; in the Silicon Valley, engineers are hired straight out of college, given a modicum of sales training, and then sent on their merry way with compensation packages that top $30,000 per annum, exclusive of fringes.

And in almost any market—East, West, or wherever between—those who toil for major corporations blow the above figures right out of the water. Xerox's Myron Howard is rapidly closing on the six-figure plateau; AT&T's François Levy passed it two years ago in just his second season with the company's Information Systems division. Up in Alaska, where everything runs high, Don Wilson chalks up annual commissions that hover at the half-million mark, selling the New York Life story.

Nor are the major firms' second tier of challengers any slouches. Typical is Burroughs's Rob Hoertz who, at barely thirty years of age, was well on his way to a seventy-thousand-dollar year when we spoke in late 1984. In a top market, even sales support personnel can bank forty thousand dollars per year.

The securities industry produces some of the sales world's top wage earners, of course. A study done in 1984 by *Working Woman* showed average retail brokers bringing home nearly $83,000 and their institutional colleagues—those working with banks and corporate finance departments rather than mere mortals like you and me—earning upward of $212,000. But these figures are by no means near the upper limits. Jim Hansberger of Shearson-Lehman American Express earned $650,000 in 1984, working primarily retail accounts. And then there is the illustrious Mike Brown of Newport Beach. Brown's name may not ring a bell, but you almost certainly read of his handiwork at least twice in 1984: first, Saul Steinberg's courtship of Disney Productions, followed by T. Boone Pickens's efforts to wrest control of Gulf Oil. On the strength of such efforts, Brown, the West Coast M and A (mergers and acquisitions) man for Drexel Burnham, is among the handful of sales professionals who've reportedly cracked the hallowed seven-figure plateau.

There are some fields that are less lucrative than most of us have grown to believe. Real estate, for instance. There's a tendency to identify the sale of real property with sky-high earnings, but that's not always the case. The truth, as Tom Hopkins's volatile early career amply demonstrates, is that real estate tends to be a boom-or-bust trade. When it's boom, though, realtors can earn incomes that dwarf those of their white-gloved counterparts from the land of the *Fortune* 500. In 1974, Hopkins's disciple Danielle Kennedy rose to the top of the world of professional selling—with no prior sales experience or training—as a housewife with six kids. Last year, fifty-three-year-old Joan Harding of U.S. Home Corporation capped off a decade of $50,000-plus earnings with an $180,000 performance—thereby belying the old myth about a salesman being only as good as the market for his product. If you're really good, you earn consistently, despite the market.

Don't assume from all this that you can't pull down big bucks unless you work for an IBM or a Century 21. Helen McVoy, a sales supervisor with Mary Kay Cosmetics, finished 1984 just shy of four hundred thousand dollars. The colossal paycheck included overrides on the commissions generated by her underlings; still, her own performance with volume buyers was nothing to sneeze at. Perhaps next time the Avon lady rings your bell, you'll see her in a new light.

Actually, "the least prestigious sales jobs sometimes pay the best,"—so said *Money* magazine, at any rate, in a special report on careers. The report went on to brand sales in general, "one of the few fields that can yield a six figure income without executive responsibility."

What's interesting is that the executive responsibility may come anyway. In major United States industrials, the sales branch produces a higher percentage of CEOs than any other division. A notable case in point is new IBM chief John Akers, who began his career with Big Blue as a thoroughly green sales trainee in 1960.

Not that those who fail to make it out of the sales division into general administration must panhandle after hours. A really top sales executive—like Irving Rousso of Russ Togs (a clothing manufacturer)—will bring home paychecks that come within a hair of seven digits.

• • •

More interesting, perhaps, than what a salesman makes—which is fairly cut and dry—is how he makes it. For years, the system by which salespeople were paid has inspired constant debate among corporate executives. Pay a man salary, the reasoning goes, and you give him security—but on the other hand, you remove some of his incentive to excel. Then again, pay him on commission, and you give him a very strong incentive to excel—it's called survival—but you put him in a frazzled state of mind. (Although technically, most companies help their commissioned reps to unfrazzle a bit by evening out the flat spots through the "draw" system explained earlier.)

About one fifth of all salespeople these days are paid straight salary; another fifth are on full commission. The remaining three fifths receive some combination of salary and commission.

Given his druthers, a salesperson would want as high a guaranteed salary as possible, right? Not always. Generally, the higher the salary, the lower the commission, a reality your more accomplished, confident sales reps find despicable. Rumblings of discontent at IBM, where the pendulum has recently swung more toward the salary end of the scale, are reportedly due to a drop in earnings among top pros who've lost out on some of the fat commissions to which they'd grown accustomed. (Headhunters, take note!)

As a rule, the opposite is equally true. The higher the commission rates, the lower the base salaries. In the pharmaceutical industry, for example, where the commission rate is a trade high 23 percent, base salaries may start as low as seventeen thousand dollars. Which may also explain why the turnover rate in the sale of health service ranks among the highest for all sales disciplines. In the world of high-commission selling, you either produce or pack it in. Darwinism at its most extreme.

Within the last five years, hiring salespeople as independent contractors has been steadily gaining favor among direct-sales organizations. Under such an arrangement, the salesman is more or less in business for himself. The cost of all the normal employee benefits—medical insurance, vacation time, and the like—is shifted from the employer to the employee, as is the responsibility for taking care of taxes and social security payments. Companies like this system because it simplifies bookkeeping and cuts expenses. Salespeople like it because it provides fatter (i.e., gross) paychecks. Of course, the salesman is supposed to take care of that end of it on his own. But in practice, the number of independent sales contractors who report the full extent of their income is probably comparable to the number of waitresses who report the full extent of their tips—even though, at least in the case of sales contractors, it's a fairly easy item for the IRS to double-check. The employer, after all, is going to keep accurate records of all payments to its salespeople-cum-contractors in order to justify *its* write-offs at the close of the tax year.

Nonetheless, even salespeople who play by the rules seem to like getting paid in gross rather than net dollars. It's a question of the psychology of the deal.

"I brought home a check for a full seven thousand dollars last week," says one such salesman whose company recently made the accounting switch. "Before we went to the contractor system, that same check would've been for about forty-five hundred." He says he knows damned well that he's going to have to make up the difference out of pocket at some point, but he still can't help feeling "like I got a twenty-five-hundred-dollar-a-week-raise.

"How's that for an incentive?" he asks.

• • •

Not all incentives come in the form of commissions on jobs sold. The sales contest, a vestige of the profession's Willy Loman heritage that fell out of favor when the trade first began upgrading its image, is now coming back in a big way. Whether the contests actually do revitalize a lackluster staff or stimulate long-term habits is moot; productivity results of contests are often ephemeral, with participating sales reps settling back into complacency until the next contest arrives. Nonetheless, one recent survey revealed that nearly 30 percent of American industrial companies were budgeting between $50,000 and $250,000 for special incentive programs in 1984. The rewards might include all-expenses-paid trips to the Bahamas, a new car (the familiar Mary Kay pink Cadillac comes to mind), or direct cash payments. A not too surprising offshoot of all this is that manufacturers of items that might constitute likely rewards are spending a fortune running ads in trade magazines for no reason other than to remind the heads of sales organizations that their product is, indeed, "the perfect gift." "Apples make great carrots," says the clever copy of an advertisement run by Apple Computer Inc. The copy concludes by noting sagely that "using Apples as carrots could easily mean more leafy green stuff for you."

A typical sales contest run by National Linen Service assigned points for each new customer, with the point categories borrowed from bowling: For signing up a new customer who spent *x* amount, a salesman would receive a "spare"; for a customer who spent a bit more, he'd get a "strike"; and so forth. The name of the promotion, imaginatively enough, was "Strike It Rich."

Since not everybody can win such a competition—and the risks of actually *lowering* staff morale in the anticlimactic aftermath of such a promotion are real indeed—many firms have taken to establishing a regular awards program that recognizes more intangible aspects of sales performance. These honors may include: "Sale closed in the shortest period of time," "Sale closed after the highest number of repeat calls," and "Most interesting sale of the week." The latter award is a special favorite of XLS president John Franco because (a) it's charming, and (b) it's sufficiently noncompetitive, from a productivity standpoint, and so a salesperson who's had an otherwise lousy week can still qualify. (It's analogous, I suppose, to telling your date she has a nice personality; she'd rather be called pretty, but it's better than nothing.)

Interestingly, the sales contest, in all its various permutations, seems to be a phenomenon occurring chiefly in companies with gross incomes that are very small—under ten million dollars—or very large—over a hundred million dollars. Enthusiasm for this type of motivational program falls off markedly among what has been dubbed "the *Inc.* magazine set"—companies with between ten and fifty million dollars in gross annual revenues.

So, in an effort to motivate salespeople, we've got salaries, commissions, bonuses, gifts and prizes and trips to faraway places, direct cash awards . . .

Jesus, *is money everything?*

The experts say no. At least, not to the new breed of salespeople, and especially those gravitating to the high-tech fields, which have provided so much of the impetus for the TNS movement in general.

"As a rule," says industrial psychologist Donald Moine, who is also president of Los Angeles's Association for Human Achievement, "[high-tech salespeople] are not particularly attracted by huge commissions. . . . Many high-tech salespeople derive more happiness working toward average-sized commissions for a 'Rolls-Royce'–quality company than working for fatter commissions for an average-quality company." Moine claims his insights are based principally on research done by the H. R. Chally Group, which not long ago analyzed the personality profiles of over forty thousand salespeople in a variety of settings.

Slowly but surely, the awareness that people can be motivated by things other than cash has begun trickling down from the corporate elite. The sales brain trust is paying unprecedented attention to the necessity of building a salesman's "psychic income" as well as his more traditional paycheck. One result of this is the movement, now clearly afoot, to make sales more fun, to encourage camaraderie in a cute—rather than a mercenary—way.

The firm known as Undercover Wear achieves this by extending the metaphor of its product line, which is sexy lingerie. Undercover Wear's saleswomen are "agents." They receive their basic training at whimsical sessions known as "SALT (Successful Agent Learning Techniques) Talks." A hardworking rep can advance to "CIA"—Captain of Independent Agents. The corporate operator in North Reading, Massachusetts, answers the phone by cooing, "Undercover Wear—nobody does it better!", an allusion to the popular Carly Simon theme song from the James Bond thriller *The Spy Who Loved Me.*

And guess which three digits the corporate phone number ends with?

The fun and games have paid off, I might add. Top Undercover Wear agents, known as "first ladies," enjoy a mid–six-figure income.

Nine to Five . . . or Six . . . or Seven . . . or . . .

The top salesman earns his pay. He is seldom "unreachable." His average workweek may exceed sixty hours. Even when he is not technically working, he remains on call. (Remember the furor a few years back over the medical-supply salesman who had to come into the operating room on his day off to bail out a top surgeon who'd incorrectly implanted one of the salesman's products in a patient's hip?) When approached with the kind of diligence sales managers like to see, selling can be a most grueling form of work, a reality reflected in the attrition figures, especially from those industries where the salesperson is forever pitching new business. One survey taken by the insurance industry in 1979 suggests that 85 percent of life-insurance salespeople quit within four years (or when they run out of relatives, whichever comes first).

If that sounds like an astounding statistic, consider the following testimony from top life rep Joe Gandolfo, as told to author Robert Shook:

> "I had a young man come to see me recently . . . who wanted to know how he could double his production of two and a half million. Well, I asked him to tell me something aboout his typical day. He replied, 'I get up about six-thirty or seven in the morning, have breakfast with my wife and the kids, then I take the kids to school and get to the office about a quarter to nine.'
>
> "'We don't need to talk anymore,' I said. 'Why?' he wanted to know. I told him he was wasting half his life. I explained that he doesn't sell his wife and kids at breakfast and he won't get paid to take them to school. . . . It takes sacrifice, and unfortunately, it is sacrificing your family."

Gandolfo tended to breakfast with clients—often more than once in a single morning. He willingly adapted his life-style to the requirements of the customer, meeting them whenever they could be met. In fact, because Gandolfo sought to make optimal use of the prospect's "dead time," which frequently occurred during meals, it was not uncommon for him to go through a day having multiple breakfasts and lunches. Expedient, if somewhat fattening.

For the average salesman who takes his work seriously, there is really no such thing as lunch time, not in the sense of being a respite from one's activities. If a salesman isn't meeting a client, he's calling him. The attenuated closing cycle—as noted earlier, it now takes an all-time high of five tries to nail down the typical industrial order—has focused attention as never before on the call-back. There are no more disposable customers—as in use once, and throw away. Every contact must be mined repeatedly in order to bear maximum fruit. Thus, salespeople budget ever larger amounts of their "free" time for telephone work, as anyone who has ever attempted to get near a phone in a diner during lunch hour is painfully aware.

Nor does the workday end when the workday ends, at least where the telephone is concerned. The trend today is toward giving out your home number, something that was unheard of when I joined the profession back in the early seventies. The reasons, in those days, were eminently understandable. Who wanted to field phone calls from customers who'd concluded they'd been hoodwinked just as you were on your way to a fancy restaurant with the deposit from the job? Why would you want to risk having some irate husband ruin your evening by phoning your wife to tell her about the pass you made at *his* wife? Give customers your home number? Hell, if there were a way the average salesman could've avoided giving customers his *office* number, he probably would have.

Today's go-go approach to professionalism has its inevitable side effects. No figures were available as of this writing, but my own informed opinion is that sales marriages may be only slightly less fragile than police marriages. Part of this is probably attributable to what selling does to a person's psyche—the constant "on" behavior is likely to grate upon a mate after a while—but certainly work load has at least something to do with it, too. Many lower-level salespeople work the hours of an obstetrician for the pay of a janitor. It's even worse than that when you consider that janitors are on salary, whereas your run-of-the-mill shoe salesman has to hustle to come up with his ten dollars per hour aggregate of salary and commission. It takes a special kind of husband or wife to put up with the long hours and interruptions in normal family routine for such a relatively little amount of money.

Besides marriages, the sales work load also takes its toll on sanity. At about nine each evening, after ten or more hours of fervent selling, a conductivity problem arises in the synapses connecting mind and mouth. The brain closes shop for the day, and those fluid, adroitly crafted responses that had distinguished one's speech earlier in the day dissolve into disjointed nonsense. It is at such times that I myself have authored such malaprops as "Keep in call with me," and "Give me a touch when you decide." Once, at 8:30, I closed the sale of an extremely complicated bathroom job, and spent the next three hours groveling among the pipes leading from wall to toilet to sink in a futile bid to get accurate measurements. As I left the man at nearly midnight, I turned to him in utter exhaustion and said, "Enjoy the rest of your wife for me."

•   •   •

Selling has not remained altogether untouched by the national tendency to shorten workweeks, stagger shifts, and make other civilized concessions to quality of life. In high-tech industries (and, for that matter, most fields where a client would be unlikely to still be at the office past 6 P.M.), salespeople are no longer expected to return to the office after the close of business to make some sense of the day's activity. Many firms have even abandoned the daily "shape-up": Rather than report to the office first thing in the morning, salespeople can simply hit the road directly from home. Progress reports and other necessary data are phoned in as time permits during the course of the day.

Technology has also helped to streamline the salesperson's efforts on several fronts. Computers have allowed reps to make great strides toward eliminating that perpetual backlog of paperwork. In addition, the computer's ability to provide rigorous, nonbiased statistical analyses offers the salesman a scientific way of appraising his game plan for any given client; trial and error can be kept to a minimum. Instead of knocking on doors, the salesman can turn to his terminal for a detailed breakdown of the demographics, with customers ranked and cross-referenced by their conformity to current customer profiles, their annual purchasing budgets, their D&B rating, their zip codes (a big help when it comes to scheduling), and their overall potential as prospects. At his fingertips a salesman, or his support rep, has available the latest scoop on products sold, anticipated customer needs, competing products, and the number of probable buyers in a given territory.

As wonderful as this all may sound, not every salesperson is titillated by technology. Your more mediocre reps—who, remember, constitute about four fifths of the national force—consider computers a mixed blessing at best, since management can now track a salesperson's performance with stunning up-to-the-minute accuracy. Malingerers, or those who are simply mired in dismal slumps, can be dispatched from the squad without the customary lag that, in days gone by, would have allowed them to collect as much as an extra month's worth of pay.

One of the newest trends capitalizes on the nation's rapidly expanding cellular mobile telephone network, which was either up and running or in the final stages of preparation in each of America's top one hundred markets as of this writing. With a portable computer (like an Apple IIc) and a dedicated modem (i.e., usable for that specific purpose only), a sales rep can effectively transform his car into the functional equivalent of a business office. Theoretically, at least, he would never have to return to base. By interfacing with the other standard components of the modern electronic office—mainframe, data base, E-Mail, Telex, printer, and so on—he can accomplish everything from a remote location that he would have been able to do sitting at a desk. And he can do all this while in transit from one appointment to the next. Talk about productivity!

Corporate executives are cautiously optimistic about such arrangements, which do not come cheap. Right now the phone/computer package runs five or six thousand dollars per person, per setup. (Like everything else that was once brand spanking new, prices are expected to drop as time goes by; look at what's happened to the home computer.) But early reports from the field suggest the setups may be more than cost-effective even at the inflated opening prices. Ron Yary, former all-pro NFL tackle and present lithography salesman and entrepreneur, says his cellular phone "pays for itself just in the business it brings in the first day of each month."

• • •

In marked contrast to the bulk of what you've just finished reading, there is one aspect of the salesperson's daily routine which, through the years, has been discussed enough to become a genuine part of American folklore. The subject of salespeople's sex lives has been the inspiration behind innumerable films (from Hollywood, as well as from less glossy sources), stories, plays, dreams, fantasies, and party jokes. You'd be hard pressed to find a single issue of *Playboy* from the last ten years that did not feature either a joke or a cartoon glorifying the subject.

What is the present status of the sex-and-selling relationship?

The harsh truth is that even in its more benign forms, hanky-panky in the office or on the road can still lead to lost sales, lost commissions, artificially sweetened business deals, sullied reputations, and a host of other undesirable aftereffects. Case in point:

"Don" was short and slim, and he worked in Manhattan for a major manufacturer of office equipment. Given the close-knit fraternity of industrial salespeople, fiercely protective of their territories, that's about as descriptive as we can be without divulging Don's actual identity. Which we wouldn't want to do because just a few years ago, Don got himself involved in a rather untidy situation.

Secure and happily married, Don nonetheless got drawn into a fling with a bouncy young thing who we'll call Anne, an administrative assistant for one of his client companies. It was not a decision he made with casual detachment, for the sober-minded Don was not given to casual decisions. The fact is, his young paramour had been baiting him—and none too subtly—for weeks.

"It seemed that whenever I walked into their office, the slit in her skirt would somehow find its way to the side of the room I was standing on," Don recalls. "And then there was the eye contact. I thought salesmen were supposed to be good at that stuff! Christ, she was a master." Thus encouraged, Don met Anne first for a drink, and then for lunch, and then, one slow afternoon, for sex.

They were in the midst of things in Anne's midtown apartment when there suddenly came a knocking at the door. While the intruder let himself in with a key, Don shot up out of bed.

And, it was standing there, stark naked, that Don met the six-foot-five-inch hulk named Harry.

"There really weren't any pretenses or anything," as Don remembers it. "They told me I'd been set up, and then Harry reached inside the liquor cabinet and began playing back a tape of what had been going on just before he walked in on us. It was damned embarrassing. She even made sure to say my name about eleven times—'Oh, Don! Ooohhh, Don! That feels so-o-o-o good, Don!' She managed to get my wife's name into it, too." Listening to the tape, and realizing, a bit late, what Anne had been up to, Don was a little surprised she didn't mention his shoe size or his social security number. Numbed by the thought that he'd been had by the oldest trick in the book, he simply sat on the edge of the waterbed while Anne and Harry "decided" his penance. Finally, they told him he could prevent his wife and employer from hearing the tape for $2,500—an amount that coincided almost to the penny with the commission Don had banked from his last sale to Anne's employer.

Top management at most major sales firms live in perpetual fear of scenarios like the above. Setups can indeed have repercussions that extend far beyond the salesperson's private little universe. More than one libidinous salesman has inadvertently involved his employer in a kickback scheme or similar business entanglement. The feeling is that even when uncomplicated by sinister threats of one form or another, trysts between buyers and sellers are generally unhealthy for business.

Even the occasional one-nighter can be hazardous to a salesperson's professional health. "Helen" sold paper products in San Diego. She met a man for dinner, after which they went back to his place and made love. He saw their physical involvement as a commitment; she saw it for what it was—an impulsive, thoroughly enjoyable roll in the hay.

He began phoning her constantly. "It got like that movie *Play Misty for Me*," says Helen. "He was obsessed. It got to be a standing joke. I'd phone in for my messages, and one of the secretaries would say, 'You got three messages and five Georges.'"

Unfortunately, George had begun calling other people as

well. It so happened he had a number of friends among Helen's clients, and the unfavorable gossip (is gossip ever favorable?) began spreading.

Before long, Helen noticed that her predominantly male customer base had gotten suddenly and remarkably smaller. People who had never before thought of "shopping" her suddenly began to do so in spades. "I'd been selling to some of these people for a year or more," she says, "and all of a sudden they tell me they'd have to check my price." Eventually, a friendly competitor clued her in as to what was going on.

Confronted with the situation, George was impassive: "His attitude was, You screwed me, so I screwed you back." Helen claims it took her months, and several tense presentations, to overcome the negative inertia George's spiteful stories had gotten rolling.

Damning as such evidence may sound, cynics ascribe corporate America's antisex sentiments to a peculiar asceticism that is part Billy Graham and part Knute Rockne.

"Don't believe them when they talk about protecting the salesman from himself," says Roger Barris. "It's just pure Victorian b.s. Either that, or they honestly think having sex robs you of your motivation to excel. It's amazing how much like the old rah-rah football coaches some of these characters get."

Whatever the underlying reasons, the fact is companies devote a not inconsiderable effort to policing the libidos of their sales staffs. Salespeople have been dismissed for behavior as innocuous as sharing an after-work drink with someone employed by a client company.

However, several of the more enlightened organizations, fearing the old forbidden-fruit syndrome, feel that the best way to prevent untoward occurrences is to pretend sex doesn't exist. IBM—which has long regulated lesser areas of employee comportment such as dressing and drinking—is conspicuously silent on the subject of sexual misconduct. A spokesman refused to get drawn into an analysis of corporate morals (sounding very much as though the mere acknowledgment of sex were somehow an affront to the company's good name). He would commit only to a single all-purpose sentence outlining IBM's impeccable standards of professional behavior. Apparently, the company hopes its salespeople will take their cues from the unerringly correct example trickling down from on high: "Asexuality by osmosis," as one IBM saleswoman phrased it.

In the end, perhaps the most illuminating words on the subject of setups and such come from a sales executive at a New Jersey electronics firm. "Always remember that in sales, most of the people who make it up here [to the managerial level] have also been out there. We know what goes on; we've lived through it. There's no point in making too big a fuss about it. You just hope your salesmen will use discretion."

Still, many salespeople feel that despite career risks, you can't help running into a passionate customer from time to time, and one, Dave, offers yet another variation on the classic anecdote to support this theory:

"I had this buddy who worked for a roofing contractor in Queens. He went to one of those row houses in Richmond Hill for an estimate. Now Richmond Hill, by the way, is the absolute epitome of a middle-class neighborhood. He knocked on the door, and the lady who answered was wearing nothing but a bikini-underwear outfit and a big, friendly smile, as they say.

"In fact, she was so friendly that she had the guy really nervous. It was much too easy, he figured. She was good-looking, too, supposedly. One of your typical thirty-five or fortyish women—slightly plump with a real, hot, womanly look, if you know what I mean. Anyway, by the time he got back down off the roof she had his folding ruler out, and she was rubbing herself with it."

He pauses briefly here.

"Now you have to realize something," he continues. "This lady had no idea who or what was going to show up on the other side of that door. It could've been Albert DeSalvo [the Boston Strangler] for all she knew. But there she was . . . ready, willing, and three-quarters naked. That tells you something."

Exactly what it tells you is debatable. A forty-five-year-old sales dropout named Tim says, "I think that in a good many cases all you're really hearing is the ego of the salesman involved. You have to remind yourself when they tell you all these wild stories that it's *salesmen* you're listening to. Their whole life consists of conning people, painting rosy pictures of very ordinary things. Some guys just don't know when to turn it off. You know that old saying about people taking their work home with them? Well, salesmen don't just take their work home. They become their work."

•　•　•

What about today's enlightened breed of salesperson? Are they taking the TNS movement's love of humanity to its logical conclusion?

Not long after I moved west, I sat in on a sales seminar attended by a number of high-powered pros. I knew these guys were good as soon as I pulled into the driveway; it looked for all the world like the parking lot of a dealer specializing in exotic cars. I had been retained by their boss to do some promotional work for the company, a solar-energy firm, and management felt it behooved me to have an understanding of how the sales team actually functioned.

Listening to them confirmed my first impression. These guys had the mechanics of true interactive selling down cold; they were a far cry from the types after which I had patterned myself in the formative years of my career. Proof of the pudding—the company sported a 66 percent closing rate, meaning that more than two out of three qualified leads, or prospects, ultimately bought. That is a phenomenally high ratio for any kind of selling, let alone in-home, big-ticket selling.

But as the meeting drew to a close and the conversation (as it inevitably will) turned to sex, something funny happened. The salesmen spoke of their conquests with great gusto—gusto that was to progress to a semineurotic game of can-you-top-this? Details were cast about graphically and comprehensively, but the overall effect was oddly devoid of sensuality. The focus seemed to be the joy of proselytizing, of taking a woman who was basically blasé or uninterested and convincing her that she *had* to have sex, then and there, with this particular salesman. The flavor was not at all that of a locker-room conversation; the loudest noises of appreciation were reserved not for the sexual specifics, but for cleverly constructed ways of overcoming objections to having sex in the first place.

Sometimes the narratives ended abruptly at the place most sexy stories begin—the entrance to the bedroom. Nobody seemed concerned about these gaps and omissions. I remember thinking that if they were golfers, they might have been more concerned with the trajectory of the ball than whether or not they finally sank it. It left you with a strange and discomfiting feeling.

It reminded me of a confession I once heard from someone I'll call Rick, a salesman I met exactly once in my life, several years ago in a bar in Forest Hills, and whose testimony I try here to reconstruct for its startlingly trenchant insights.

"It used to be fun," Rick said. "It used to be a challenge. Now, it's a quota." He added that he tried not to look at it that way, but he couldn't help it.

In the beginning, Rick said, he chased women for the sheer joy of it, savoring his nightly rewards. But somewhere along the line, things got perverted. Rick began to demand more and more of himself, so that a yes a day no longer sufficed. "It got to the point where I'd be on my way to the motel with one, and I'd be looking in the rearview mirror at another chick who was crossing the street."

Rick concluded, "My father used to say, 'You know, son, you can't have them all.' But in selling, you're not taught to think that way. You're taught to believe that every door you knock on will result in a sale."

Rick's quandary is a not uncommon occurrence among supercompetitive sales pros, who thrive on *the battle* itself. The thrill of battle *is* the thrill of victory. The result is almost superfluous, irrelevant. The end becomes the means.

This raises some questions about TNS's much-ballyhooed advancement of the never-ending quest, especially as it spills over into one's personal affairs. It's fine, in a sense, to dispense with the notion of failure; but without failure, there is no release from the burdensome obligation to *keep on trying*. Similarly, if each success is viewed merely as a stepping stone to an even greater success, then when does a salesman ever get the chance to step back, relax, and savor what he's accomplished thus far?

Donald Moine has written of the selling game, "At the top, it's the challenge that counts, not just the win."

That may be fine when you're talking about selling cases of industrial-strength Ty D Bol. . . .

But is it really the kind of attitude you want to take with you to bed?

Sales Miscellany

*Number of sales-oriented productions that played to Broadway audiences in 1984: three (*Death of a Salesman, Glengarry Glen Ross, *and—albeit briefly—*Play Memory).

9

Beyond Selling:
Back in Your Own Backyard

Feeling a little short on charisma these days?

A firm called Ventures in Self-Fulfillment (its ad lists offices in San Francisco, Los Angeles, Newport Beach, and San Diego) offers courses in Charisma Training. THE ULTIMATE IN PUBLIC SPEAKING AND LEADERS' TRAINING WORKSHOP, says a bold-faced heading above the ad copy, which goes on to promise "an unorthodox two-day master class . . . where you learn once and for all how to get out of your own way."

The course is to be conducted by one Dave Braun, who, we're told, is fresh from five years of "leading his Painless Public Speaking" workshop. Drawing on that experience, Dave will "show you who you really are." One suspects that a Braun seminar must be a sight to see. Can you imagine a room full of people who don't know who they are and can't get out of their own way?

Anyhow, the ad concludes by telling us that the course has been designed especially for "those who want to lead, teach, manage, sell or entertain." This last, by the way, is a familiar marketing technique used to make the offering sound somewhat more exclusive than it really is. More on this momentarily.

The West Coast in particular abounds with laissez-faire applications of self-salesmanship and pop psychology. "What passes for serious thought in California is usually scraped off the bottom of your shoe everywhere else, if you get my meaning," says one Manhattan sales manager.

Ken Keyes of Coos Bay, Oregon, spends much of his time in California conducting seminars on "The Power of the Human Spirit." Keyes is the founder of The Science of Happiness Center. Ken's theory basically poses that the on ramp leading to the freeway of happiness is accessible only to those who take what life has given them without complaint. Among other things, Keyes tells his audiences that he loves tomato sauce, but since he gets a negative result from eating it, he must forego the infernal stuff to be happy.

And you thought you had problems.

Sometimes the merchandising of self-improvement gets truly baroque. Last summer, fairly large numbers of Californians were paying one hundred dollars each to be taught how to walk over burning coals without hurting themselves. This could be accomplished, said their mentor, twenty-four-year-old ex-salesman Tony Robbins, through the attainment of a self-hypnotic state in which one's pains and fears were doused by the refreshing psychic imagery of the phrase "cool moss." Robbins referred to the mechanism of his regimen as "neuro-linguistic programming."

The young entrepreneur, who bears a general resemblance to Tom Hopkins, complete with Tom's fluffy hairstyle, has christened his venture "The Firewalk Experience." The subtitle, "Turn Fear into Power," suggests that Robbins has indeed spent some time reading the more evangelical passages in Hopkins's work.

According to one Orange County newspaper, at least five thousand local residents had been raked over the coals, as it were, by Robbins in 1984.

Before you rupture yourself laughing, though, consider that very, very few of the firewalkers reported any adverse effects.

• • •

As hordes of hopeful trainers forsake their strict trade affiliations for the untold promise of a mainstream audience, TNS creeps gradually into every corner of social conduct. In 1985, this was becoming a busy two-way street, with equally large hordes from the mainstream (or from professional realms besides sales) scurrying to update their daily routines to conform with the basics of state-of-the-art selling. To put it in crass capitalistic terms, the market's hunger for this new exciting product was fast approaching the seller's hunger to sell it.

Not that all of the instruction was paid for. A lot of the strategy is absorbed osmotically, through association with people who've gained their knowledge under more formal circumstances. It's becoming genuinely hard to get through an entire day without (a) directly encountering some form of TNS, or (b) directly encountering someone who's been exposed to some form of TNS, and has unconsciously begun to apply its principles. Just one f'rinstance: Have you gone to a seminar or other type of structured meeting lately? Not necessarily sales—any kind of meeting will do. Tax planning, real estate, business counseling, money management or investment strategy, even dating advice. Each of them qualifies because lecturers of all descriptions have been paying close attention to their siblings from the world of sales training. Anyone who does the slightest amount of public speaking nowadays is using tie-downs to secure audience agreement (and, not coincidentally, to build momentum for the sale of collateral materials). The introductory phrase "Don't you agree that. . . ?" pops smoothly and often out of real estate guru Paul Simon's mouth.

This heightened awareness of TNS applies at the most exalted levels of American life. The presidential media consultants who took wing during the waning days of Ike's administration and then flourished in the aftermath of Kennedy's nationally televised trouncings of Nixon (the first case, perhaps, in which the issues themselves were overshadowed by the totally apolitical matter of *how the two candidates came across*) are really just a specialized breed of sales trainer.*

One reason why it is essential that a politician acquire at least a cursory knowledge of modern selling is that you never

For a lively but insightful treatment of the subject of how today's politicians finesse the facts, you might want to go to your local library and look up Mark Davidson's "A Thinking Person's Survival Guide for Campaign '84," in USA Today, January 1984.

know when you're going to run up against a Robert K. Gray. Lobbyist extraordinaire—his 170 employees are pledged to protect the best interests of CBS, NBC, and United Artists, among others—the erudite Gray attributes most of his phenomenal success to qualities that essentially reduce to sales skills.

"If you've got a good case, and you can communicate it properly," Gray told the Murine crowd during a recent broadcast of CBS's *Night Watch*, "that's what makes you successful. It comes down to being a communicator." He claimed the notion that better lobbyists are successful because they're "wired" (not in the sense that Belushi was wired, but in the sense that they have access to all the right people) is a case of putting the cart before the horse: "You don't get access unless you first communicate—the greatest misconception is that it's all done by who you know." Sounding very much like a Xerox trainer lecturing a group of novice salespeople about work habits, Gray added that one must be willing to invest hours' worth of research in order to ensure that a ten-minute presentation goes as it should.

"In the end," he concluded, "we [lobbyists] are persuasive only because we have a penchant for accuracy, and we know how to articulate our case well."

Thus, politicos must learn the ropes of TNS simply for self-defense. Pay close attention to the interviews you see and hear these days; more and more, public figures accosted by journalists who try to wedge them into an unpleasant corner are skillfully turning the tables.

I had to laugh some months ago when I noted the following exchange during a local news broadcast.

A crusading reporter had buttonholed a Los Angeles public-health official and demanded, rather brusquely, to know what the city government intended to do for the downtrodden denizens of the "tent city." (At the time, a group of LA's homeless had sought refuge from the unusually severe winter temperatures by erecting makeshift shelters not far from the downtown business district.) The mayor was talking about evicting his "tenants," and the media had seized upon the story as an opportunity to resurrect one of its favorite recurring motifs: the insensitivity of government to the pain and suffering of the disenfranchised members of society.

Hardling missing a beat, the official sighed, fixed the reporter with a most sincere look, and said, more or less, "Given the financial constraints we face today, why don't *you* tell *us*"— he gestured broadly toward the minicam rolling in the foreground and the vast viewing audience beyond—"tell us what you would do?" I marveled at the fellow's voice—he sounded neither piqued nor impatient but, rather, as though he were genuinely soliciting the reporter's help. As I marveled, I could clearly hear the insurance agent responding to his client's question about endowment policies by saying, "Do you think the endowment policy is something that would suit your needs at this time, Mr. Jones. . . ?"

The Hot-Potato Parry rides again!

• • •

Of course, most of us are not politicians. If you're a sales trainer, and you orient your material toward that or any other specialized market segment, you severely cut your draw. True, those who are really good may go further in the long run by defining their focus. It worked for Denver's Loretta Melandro, who earned large fees teaching lawyers part-time how to relate to their clients. The competition is brutal, however, and as a prospective livelihood, it ranks with acting. Either you're eating filet mignon, or you're not eating.

Faced with such sobering realities, the bulk of one-person ventures that strive to expand the boundaries of sales training are aimed not at any specific audience but, rather, at you and me. Drawing their momentum from the success of the current self-help craze, they promise to teach us—life's Everymen— how to get along in this cold, cold world.

Assuming the Suit
Attitude is 75 percent of the ball game.

Sales trainers and motivators who teach you nothing else will at least leave you with this one lasting impression. You don't have to walk on fire to appreciate how far blind conviction will carry you. Even when you're dead wrong. And here I can not only agree, but offer a vivid illustration from my own experience.

Some years ago my wife and I went to Macy's on Thirty-fourth Street, New York City, in the hopes of picking up a sport jacket for our then-fourteen-year-old son. At the time, we lived just outside Huntington, Long Island. Huntington had a perfectly good Macy's of its own, but that particular store was out of stock on the jacket our son liked. So on a crisp weekend in late fall we took the one-hour-and-ten-minute drive to Manhattan.

Once inside the huge New York Macy's it took us only minutes to locate the right sports jacket, a gray herringbone design by Stanley Blacker. One problem, though. The New York jacket was selling for $75, whereas its Long Island counterpart had been on sale for just $49.95. My wife and I grumbled between ourselves, graduating from puzzlement to incredulity to indignation.

I collared the nearest saleswoman and demanded an explanation.

Although she said she was as befuddled as I about our dilemma, she also insisted in a rather stiff tone of voice that the price on the Blacker jacket was correct as marked. I suggested she summon the manager. She said he was on his break. I said that if I could make the seventy-minute drive from Long Island to New York, he should be willing to make the three-minute walk from the sandwich wagon to the boys' department. Sighing heavily (I'm quite sure she dismissed me as just another lunatic suburban cheapskate), she relented.

The manager was even younger than his young saleswoman, but no less condescending. I told him my story. He assured me that the Blacker jacket did, indeed, cost seventy-five dollars. "And comparable value would be over one hundred dollars, at many other fine retailers," he added airily, purposely not naming Bloomingdale's and Sak's and Bonwit, I felt, because he believed my wife and I—culturally deprived hicks from the hinterlands that we were—would not recognize the names.

I was unfazed. I told him I had no intention of leaving the store without getting that jacket for $49.95. I told him I'd been a loyal Macy's customer for years, during which time my Macy's charge had known thousands of dollars' worth of apparel. I told him I thought it was awful that Macy's would try to hoodwink people like that, especially before the Christmas holidays. I told him I intended to write letters to the chairman of the board and the newspapers and the New York City Department of Consumer Affairs and David Horowitz and Ed Koch and anyone else I could think of to let *them* know how I felt, too.

By this time my voice had risen a few decibels and a small crowd of observers was forming. I started retelling my tale, to no one in particular, bemoaning the injustice of it all—"Can you *believe* this? We came here all the way from Long Island just for this lousy jacket . . ."—and making sure I was bemoaning loudly enough to attract the attention even of those across the aisle who might be absorbed in men's underwear.

We got the jacket for $49.95. I didn't use my Macy's charge, because I didn't have one. (All right, so I'd overdramatized a bit. It was for a noble cause, I knew.)

But I was wrong, and that's what makes the story interesting. When we returned to our own Macy's a few days later for a shirt to go with the jacket, we realized the mistake had been totally and completely ours. The fifty-dollar sport jacket was on a rack right next to the Blacker rendition, and looked remarkably similar, but it was not itself a Blacker garment. We'd gotten a full one-third discount we were not the least bit entitled to.

We assumed our way into that discount. Because we believed, at the time, in the justice of our cause. And, as trainers will tell you, when people begin to sense your degree of resolve, they often begin to doubt theirs.

Why that happens is a moot question. My former boss had this theory that most people basically fear responsibility. Faced with a situation where they're asked to assume control, they'll look for an out, a scapegoat, someone to usurp or negate their authority. No doubt, if and when the department manager at Macy's got called into somebody's office to explain why he sold a seventy-five-dollar sport jacket for barely 65 percent of its value, he said he had to do it or else I might have made a scene and spooked the other customers. He *had* to do it, notice. *I forced his hand.* He can't be held responsible for things he had to do. If you're not responsible, then you're not accountable, and if you're not accountable, then you can't be blamed for things. So people submit to the will of others as a form of subliminal buck-passing. And you, opportunist that you are, can make this work in your favor, if you are so inclined.

I'm not necessarily advocating that you take this sort of approach to everyday living, by the way. I'm simply telling you that ethics aside—and this is very precarious ethical ground we're treading here—it works.

• • •

Other than having a Positive Mental Attitude, how might someone like yourself knowingly put the high-powered logic of TNS to work for you in your daily regimen? There are any number of possible ways, involving various combinations of the outlooks and techniques explained in Chapters 3 and 4. But the experts feel the two aspects of TNS that can be most readily adapted for use by laypeople are (1) The Hot Potato Parry, and (2) the axiom that goes *Don't tell them everything, just enough to get by.* We'll take the second one first, since it's more straightforward.

I recall, when I was a youngster, walking into a bank with my father. This particular bank had large signs with bold yellow letters on a blue background that said AT CHEMICAL BANK, ALL OF OUR ACCOUNTS ARE FULLY INSURED FOR UP TO $40,000.

When we got back out to the car I told my dad I thought he was pretty smart for doing business with that bank. When he asked why, I told him how impressed I'd been by what the signs said.

He laughed, and told me that this bank wasn't quite as special as its signs implied. I could, said Dad, find the very same security at any of the thousands of banks that were members of the FDIC or FSLIC; actually, he continued, there were only a handful of banks that didn't offer such insurance.

Even at that tender age, I remember feeling a little . . . manipulated. Weren't those signs misleading? I asked my father. Didn't the wording suggest that Chemical was offering its depositors something other banks didn't have? My father shrugged. "Not at all," he said. "They're just being good businessmen. They're selling themselves." You can't blame them for that, he added.

It's true. Sure, the folks at Chemical could've elaborated and told their customers that as an FDIC member bank, they were doing what every other member did by offering people forty thousand dollars' (now a hundred thousand dollars') worth of deposit insurance. But why *should* they help the competitor siphon off some of their own business? Where is it written that if other banks are doing a lousy job of publicizing the FDIC arrangement, Chemical should step in and help them out?

Why make the other guy's case for him?

The same holds true, say, when you're trying to sell your house. Take your cue from what the better real estate agents do. They limit their discussion of features and benefits to the house they think their buyer is interested in. They will not say, "Oh, this *whole development* was put up by a contractor with a reputation for building well-insulated homes." Do they expect the buyer to purchase the whole development? Of course not. Then why say something that dilutes the impact of their praise, and diverts the buyer's attention away from the specific property in question? They should simply say, "This is a very well-insulated house," instead of phrasing it in a way that makes the buyer think he can find the same benefit in any of the two hundred or so other homes in the tract.

People who are trying to sell their homes privately make this kind of mistake all the time. (One of the best arguments, say Hopkins and Kennedy, for not trying to cut the real estate broker out of the picture.) In glowing detail, they'll tell people who come to see their house that "the builder really outdid himself on this development" or that "the whole neighborhood has access to the community pool" or that "homes go quick around here because a lot of them have assumable mortgages." Or, better still, that "the view from the top of that hill over there is breathtaking." What's the first thing people do when you tell them that? They leave your house, drive up to the top of that hill over there, and start looking for FOR SALE signs.

A slightly different slant on the same idea comes from sales trainer Harry Fried. Fried, who says he knows "next to nothing" about cars, explains what happened last time he went out to buy a second-hand car for his son from a private party:

"This guy took me out to test-drive his Mercury Cougar. It was almost ten years old, and it had a lot of miles on it, but it seemed to run real strong. Almost like driving a new car. So I told him he must've really taken care of it. And do you know what this jerk says to me? He says, 'Well, the 351 Cleveland Ford was making in those days was just one hell of an engine!'

"I couldn't believe it," Fried continues. "I mean, that's almost like telling me that he did his best to run the car into the ground, but the engine managed to hold up anyway. And in effect, he was also telling me I could get the same kind of performance and durability from any car with that same 351 engine. Why didn't he just answer me by telling me what I wanted to hear? He should've just told me that he'd treated the car with a little TLC, and let it go at that."

Fried uses the story as an illustration of his belief that, without being asked, people volunteer all sorts of extraneous information that is actually counterproductive to the sale.

Harry bought the car, by the way, and that old 351 Cleveland is still running.

The translation of the Hot-Potato Parry to everyday life is a more complex subject, but the technique's utility is the moral of a story related by the sales manager for a top midwestern industrial firm. It concerns two men, a would-be community office holder and the influential investment banker from whom he sought support in an upcoming election.

They were at lunch when the banker happened to notice the headline of a newspaper being read by someone a few booths away. It said PLANNED PARENTHOOD CLINIC FIREBOMBED. Turning to his lunch companion, he said, "It looks like they got another abortion clinic."

Whereupon the hopeful candidate replied, "Serves 'em right. They never should have legalized abortions in the first place."

The rest of lunch passed uneventfully. Nothing further was said about the newspaper headline. The candidate did not realize until weeks later that he'd self-aborted as soon as he'd opened his mouth about the firebombing. As it develops, the investment banker, his pinstriped suits, understated ties, and custom-made English shoes notwithstanding, had been an early supporter of the local pro-choice movement. In the wake of that luncheon meeting, the banker began a quiet but authoritative campaign aimed at thwarting the election of the man who had foolishly opened up a window to his soul over crab salad.

Sales trainers insist that most of us commit comparable (if less spectacular) faux pas almost on a daily basis. We do it by responding decisively to the questions or statements of others before we've had a chance to get a fix on their thinking. A second, more routine example:

Say your name is Matthew, and that you're a harried junior vice-president for one of those ostentatious financial firms at which employees are either a vice-president or the guy who stands vigil over the eroding deodorant wedges in the men's room latrines. You're seated after work at the counter of the coffee shop located in the bowels of your Manhattan office building, trying desperately to enjoy a cup of coffee that's as tepid as your career.

Suddenly, *she* walks in: the proverbial vision of loveliness, every man's ultimate fantasy fulfilled.

She sits next to you, and you savor the way her blonde curls nibble at the nape of her neck, sigh at the way her lean, temptress's body strains against the silky confinement of her burgundy dress. Her eyes find you, linger briefly and discreetly, then turn away. Your heart sinks; she strikes you as utterly unattainable. But seconds later, she cocks her head for a second look—this time less brief, less discreet—and the quickest flicker of invitation dances elusively across her brow.

Having never been one to resist an invitation, no matter how flickering, you lean over and say hi.

She turns toward you, swiveling gracefully on her squeaky stool, and favors you with a magnificent, sensual smile. Then, noticing your attaché, she asks if you wouldn't by any chance happen to be a member of the legal profession. You fairly gag on your coffee, having just been through a difficult divorce, made all the more difficult by the relentless dedication of your ex-wife's attorney.

"A *lawyer*? God, no! I swear I've never chased a single ambulance in my entire life!"

By the time the words are half out she has stiffened, recoiled, and you regret your impulsive venting of rancor. But it's too late. She gets up and moves about a mile and a half down the counter from you. Presently, your waiter clues you in.

"Hey, Valentino," he chides, "*she's* a lawyer."

The lesson of anecdotes like the above, sales trainers point out, is that there are many dangerous topics in this world besides politics, religion, and sex. Any given conversation, says Zig Ziglar, is ripe with the opportunity for you to destroy yourself. Which is why you might find it expedient to forestall making a commitment on a given issue until you have drawn out your companion regarding his or her own feelings—hence, the Hot-Potato Parry.

Admittedly, the Parry is not a panacea for everyday living. You obviously can't go around answering everyone's questions with a question of your own, unless you want to cultivate a reputation for being (a) argumentative, (b) flippant, or (c) retarded. The successful use of this method of probing presupposes a certain amount of discretion and sensitivity. You must be able to identify the crisis areas that warrant a high-powered response. One would not, for instance, waste this technique on a question like "Would you please pass the salt, Harry?" ("Would passing the salt meet with your needs at this time, Eunice?")

Furthermore, as the lunch-with-firebombs story demonstrates, not all—not even most—questions arrive with question marks at the end. This is where the sensitivity comes in: sensitivity to body language, to phrasing, to thoughts or observations that, while innocuous enough in and of themselves, relate directly to substantive *issues*. Trainers advise you always to ask yourself if there is an issue—a bias, a peeve, a tradition—lurking in sinister ambush behind the seemingly straightforward remarks that come your way.

As complex and unfathomable as some of this may sound (How the hell are you supposed to know what people are thinking when they say the things they're saying?), TNS trainers have, happily, provided some ground rules to guide you.

First and foremost, there are essentially two categories of questions: those that are rooted in a single affirmative thought; and those that are rooted in multiple possibilities, known or unknown (to either the listener or even, perhaps, the speaker). "Would you please pass the salt?" is really just an interrogative and polite form of the assertion "I want the salt." This should be clear enough to most people, but if you want to prove it to yourself, next time you're at a dinner party and your mate asks you the polite question, ignore it; you'll get the direct statement soon enough. In other words, there is one and only one thought in the mind of the person asking the question.

Sales trainers stress the importance of grasping this deceptively simple concept, for in most cases, to greet a single-affirmative-thought question with an advantage-seeking reply is to incur the wrath of the questioner. Hopkins feels that parents, especially, are masters of perverting the thrust of brilliant questioning techniques by implementing them at the most ill-advised moments.

CHILD: So, Mom, can I get that new model airplane?
MOM: If I buy it for you, do you promise to be a good boy from now on?

Naturally, the kid will say yes. The yes may come in the form of a half-hearted grumble, but it will come nonetheless. He *wants* the plane, after all. But if you think about it, mom hasn't won any points. The child is apt to leave the check-out counter thinking, *That old bat—every time I ask her for something, I get a sermon.* Thus, mom's manipulative instincts have cost her not only the $7.98 for the plane, but an incalculable amount of her child's esteem as well. All because she attempted to trade on a single-affirmative-thought question.

So, say the experts, when you're in a "selling" situation—which, as Danielle Kennedy is wont to say, can be anytime, at anyplace, with anybody—you're advised to carefully appraise the questions that come your way. One of the easiest and most productive ways of doing this is to simply ask yourself, How many things could he possibly be thinking when he asks me that? How many potential answers are there, and which of them is, in all likelihood, the preferred one? If you're not fully cognizant of the circumstances surrounding the asking of the question—its psychological context, so to speak—then you toss it back. Matthew should've asked the young lady in the coffee shop why she was asking if he was a lawyer. It was, after all, her very first question; there *must* have been some special import to it.

In the family environment, says Danielle Kennedy, there are plenty of instances in which the Porcupine Technique (she calls it that because she trained under Hopkins) can be used to circumnavigate the usual bickering between parent and child. How? By taking an issue that would normally be a parental responsibility and tossing it into the child's lap. Kennedy explains,

"How many parents scream after their teenagers just as they're about to walk out the door, 'Wait a minute! I want you back in this house by eleven P.M. sharp!' And the kid groans and sulks off, slamming the door. If you've got a child who is basically a responsible person, you can avoid those kinds of fiascos by putting the burden of setting the limit on the child. Then you guide them or, if its absolutely necessary, correct them.

"If your kid comes up to you and says, 'What time do you want me home?' why be an ogre and insist on a time? Instead ask, 'Well, what time do you think is reasonable?' Or, if they don't ask you what time they should be home, you should ask *them.*"

Danielle claims that a surprising percentage of kids will name the same time parents were going to say, or will not be much more than an hour off. This way, you bolster the child's sense of self-worth—you're treating him as a rational human being capable of making his own decisions.

More important, adds Kennedy, is that you're giving your child a self-imposed curfew to adhere to. "If they violate it," she says, "you're in a much stronger position than if you insist on a time like some dictator, and they stalk out the door just itching to show you up."

In addition to improving one's skills at argumentation, questioning savvy can probably save—or earn—a lot of money for you. A perfect illustration might be the familiar American phenomenon known as the garage sale. The holy fathers of TNS insist that the common practice of affixing tiny price tags to all the merchandise is terribly misguided. But before venturing into that, a bit of background from the world of structured selling is in order.

Each day in America, the same scenario repeats itself many thousands of times. Joe Average wanders into a car lot, or a carpet warehouse, or a furniture store, or an antique gallery, or any retail environment in which he's likely to encounter trained sales staff. One such salesperson comes over, and after exchanging pleasantries with our hero, asks some version of the following:

"So tell me, Mr. Average, about how much were you looking to spend?" A higher-caliber salesperson would present the question in veiled terms, perhaps, or in any case might render the remark more positive/less threatening by substituting *invest* for *spend*. But that's not really material here.

Having been asked the momentous question, what does Joe do in response? He tells the salesperson. Truthfully. Thereby surrendering about 90 percent of the leverage he had when he walked in.

In their more candid moments, sales trainers and top pros are unanimous in the belief that one of the worst things you can do to yourself, and your chances of getting a square deal, is answer questions like "How much were you looking to spend?" It's interesting, by the way, how much joy trainers seem to derive from working the other side of the game; like pitchers who prefer to spend the postgame interview discussing their hitting exploits, sales trainers delight in talking about their own efforts at confounding the persuasive efforts of the sales reps with whom they do business. Danielle Kennedy tells of the time she and her husband, Mike Craig, went out to buy a new car. The salesmen kept hitting them with assorted hard-sell clichés; typical might be "So would you consider buying this car for fifty-five hundred dollars today?" Though they let the remark pass unchallenged, Craig came away thinking, Next time some clever salesman asks me that, I'm going to turn it around—I'm going to ask him, So would you consider selling me this car for fifty-five hundred dollars today?

Contrary to what people believe, there are few fixed prices in this life, save perhaps for those prices illegally fixed across the board by consortiums of profiteering manufacturers or distributors. Even "sale" prices have been known to fluctuate in accordance with the buyer's consumerist acumen, as perceived by the alert salesperson. It's funny how sale prices sometimes don't include things for Mr. Schlepp that they included ten minutes ago when Mr. Shrewd wrote out his check. Back in the days when I was selling, it was common practice among shop-at-home firms to portray your guarantee—which was, officially, a freebie—as an optional service contract. If the buyer was sharp and you had to throw it in, you threw it in. But depending on the customer, you could ask for, and frequently get, hundreds of dollars for it. Dollars that were commissioned at the overage rate, not the much lower base rate.

If the price you own up to is high, large numbers of salespeople will "sell" you items that were actually meant to be included at no extra charge, or they may inflate the cost of the product, or load in unnecessary extras. If the figure you quote is low, the salesperson could either lose interest and give poor service, or try to overcharge you on a super-cheap model that's been lying unattended in the warehouse for eons.

This happens not necessarily because salespeople are immoral, but because they need to eat. Promotional items usually carry slashed commission rates. Only by tacking a premium onto the price of low-line merchandise can your average salesperson make ends meet. Remember, we are talking here about the salesperson you are most likely to encounter, one of the 80 percent who remain unenlightened and correspondingly unwealthy. If you walk into the store and admit to a budget of a thousand dollars, your salesman is far better off overcharging you by a couple of hundred dollars on an item meant to sell for eight hundred dollars than he would be giving you your money's worth.

In sum, then, when a salesperson asks how much you want to spend, you can take your cue from the Kennedy-Craig family and reply, "How much did you want to charge?" The line usually gets a laugh (I've tried it several times myself lately) while at the same time communicating the fact that you're not a babe in the woods. More important, it saves you from committing yourself prematurely, that is, *before you know the dimensions of the ball park*. The more the salesman thinks his product is worth to you, the farther away those center-field fences can get.

Which brings us, finally, back to the garage sale. A West

Coast sales executive named Ed tells the story of an open house conducted some years ago by him and his wife. Early in their marriage, they'd acquired a pair of drapes that looked for all the world as if they'd been designed by a Renaissance painter on acid. (Ed treads carefully here, for the drapes were acquired from his mother-in-law.) For many years, those drapes lived out a reclusive existence in a box toward the rear of his garage. When he got an irresistible job offer in another state, he decided it was about time to make them one of the headline items at his mammoth garage sale.

Problem was, he couldn't decide how much to ask for them. Ed's wife thought ten bucks was fair; he thought it was exorbitant. Indeed, it struck Ed at the time that they'd probably have to pay someone to take the damned things off their hands.

In the midst of their confusion on that first morning of the sale, a little old lady who just happened to be driving by spotted the drapes, hit the brakes, and careened into Ed's driveway. She flew out of her seat, making just a haphazard swipe at closing the door, and buttonholed Ed's startled wife directly in front of the card table on which the colorful drapes reposed.

"How much are these drapes?" she demanded in an urgent tone of voice.

Ed's wife was stymied. How much should she say? As reported by her husband, her reply came out, more or less, "Uh, well, howboummm . . . I dunno—errr—what'd you have in mind?"

The elderly woman paused in thought for just the briefest instant. She then asked if seventy-five dollars would be enough.

Standing just within earshot, Ed gulped. "Sefetykjlsdatlrs?" blurted his astonished wife.

"Well, it's all the cash I've got with me," said the old woman, sighing. Ed's subjective impression was that she felt her offer had been insultingly low.

Ed's wife—bless her heart—replied that seventy-five dollars would be far too much. And in perhaps the only known case where a garage-sale proprietor actually bargained a customer *down,* she made the matron a counterproposal of twenty-five bucks. She confided later that, fearing the woman was senile, she didn't want to lose sleep over having taken advantage of someone who was in no shape to make decisions involving money, let alone draperies.

The point is that Ed's wife's inadvertent use of the Hot Potato Parry paid off handsomely. By letting the woman indicate what the drapes were worth to her, Ed and his wife took in 150 percent more than he'd expected (and stood to pocket as much as 650 percent more, if he'd accepted the lady's original offer). Had the pricing issue been finalized before that old woman planted her tires in their azaleas, those drapes would've fetched ten dollars or less, because that was their value to Ed and his wife. But where was the logic supporting the notion that everyone else's appraisal would tally with their own?

Now, it so happens the old woman had a very good—and very arresting—reason for buying those drapes. A reason that left Ed and his wife feeling more than mildly uncomfortable, in retrospect. As Ed helped her get the gauche window dressings into her car, the woman told him the drapes reminded her very much of ones she'd had during the newlywed years with her husband of three decades, who had just passed away. She rambled on and on about how having those sweet memories back, in the form of the drapes, might somehow help her get through this most distressing period.

As Ed and his wife listened to her touching reminiscences, their hearts sank. Ed's wife was on the verge of giving her back her money, but she didn't want to offend, embarrass, or patronize the woman.

I add this footnote because it raises a moral question, worth exploring, about the use of TNS strategies with people who are ill equipped to defend against them. In the business world, there's an unspoken assumption that everybody plays to win. If your competitor isn't up on all the latest sophisticated strategies, that's his tough luck. But in the course of day-to-day affairs, most of us back off from that hard line; we dislike taking advantage of people who are not functioning on our level. Until this last paragraph, the majority of people reading the above anecdote would've been amused. They would've more or less identified with the effort by Ed and his wife to get maximum return.

Until, as I say, the last paragraph. Then things changed. All of a sudden, the old woman underwent a total metamorphosis, from a doddering character to a sympathetic figure, a martyr.

Right?

I asked some of the trainers about it. Most were squeamish, uncomfortable about coming down hard and fast on one side of the issue. The consensus seemed to be, Jesus, how were Ed and his wife supposed to know the lady's husband just died?

So I made the vignette more compelling. Suppose Ed and his wife *had* known in advance about the woman's recent loss? Should they have felt obliged to part with the drapes for free? Or for some token amount, perhaps? In the larger perspective, to what extent is a salesman supposed to consider the circumstances of his prospect?

Still, indecision reigned supreme. Speaking for the majority, an insurance executive said, "I guess there's a time to be a salesman and a time to be a human being." He meant it at face value, by the way; I don't think he ever gave a thought to the ironic implications of the remark.

One trainer was adamant, however. He objected to the maudlin tale as a bizarre diversion from what were, are, and ever shall be the cold realities of American merchandising.

"Our whole system is based on the fact that you need what I've got," he said. "A car dealer who gives away cars to people because they don't have any means of transportation is not going to have a viable business for very long. And while we're on the subject of death, what about funeral directors? Should they only take money from customers who aren't bereaved?"

A salient argument, to be sure. But not as salient, perhaps, as the fact that although this person is identified elsewhere in this book, he refused to be quoted by name here.

The Subscription Letter, Etc.

If you can't see yourself actually making TNS a regular part of your daily routine, you might at least find it useful to know where, besides selling, you're most likely to run up against it. Many of the TNS applications that don't come directly at you from salespeople will come indirectly from a closely allied field: the world of advertising.

Not long ago, I received an intriguing note from *Esquire*. It seems I had not only neglected to renew my subscription, but I'd compounded the offense by failing to acknowledge their previous half-dozen reminders. This time, the publisher himself was writing to find out just what exactly was the problem.

"Recently, our Circulation Department notified me that there was a small group of subscribers—including you—who had not renewed their subscriptions. . . . According to their records, you've received several opportunities to keep *Esquire* coming . . . yet we haven't heard from you."

The remainder of the letter was filled with tart phrases like "don't put it off any longer," "unless you act immediately," "let us have your renewal instructions by return mail," and "*one final chance*" [italics theirs]—phrases, all of them, that strongly suggested Phil Moffitt had farmed out his subscription service to a loan shark rather than an ad agency.

As I read along, half amused, half incredulous, I half expected the strange little note to threaten a personal visit from someone in the Compliance Department if I didn't renounce my errant ways and return at once to the fold. I should mention that enclosed within the folded letter was a FINAL ACCOMMODATION NOTICE that reminded me yet again of my precarious subscription status, and admonished me to SEND TODAY (or else?).

Despite its tendency toward overkill, the mailing piece represented one of the most remarkable single instances of assumptive selling I'd come across in a long while. Note the presumption that runs through it: *Where have you been? Surely, you can't be serious about failing to renew your subscription . . . It's an oversight, right?*

(After all, what kind of addle-brained Neanderthal would knowingly allow his *Esquire* subscription to lapse?)

Certainly, there were softer, less intrusive ways to get the same point across. But don't be too hard on Phil Moffitt; the letter was simply a reflection of Madison Avenue's perspective on modern salesmanship, taken to its outer limits. Tom Hopkins has said, "The best way to convince a prospect to buy something is to make him feel he already owns it." The *Esquire* letter, distilled to its raw essence, evinced the feeling that the best way to keep a customer was to make him feel he had yet to (or couldn't) leave. The logic is pretty much the same throughout the world of contemporary selling; tough as it is to find new customers in today's unpredictable economy, companies will be damned if they'll give up the ones they've already got.

Once upon a time, advertising's goal was simply to make the marketplace more comfortable with the client's product.* That has changed. Now, the object is to make customers feel decidedly *un*comfortable without it. Or, if not uncomfortable, then intellectually delinquent, or sociologically remiss, or otherwise guilt-ridden. You might call it *angst appeal.* The message has been refined from "This is a product you may want to try," to "This is a product you probably cannot do without,'" to "Wake up, shmuck, this is a product any self-respecting imbecile would have had long ago."

Since that's not the kind of thing an advertiser wants to say straight out, the message must be conveyed subliminally, or at the very least, obliquely. Which is why contemporary advertising lends itself so well to the tenor and methodology of TNS.

In their efforts these days to plumb your soul and get at your innermost angst, more and more ad campaigns hinge on clever questions rather than statements. Have you driven a Ford lately? Do you know what you're missing? Then again, Wouldn't you really rather have a Buick? And what about that fancy women's cologne—What will it remind you of?

These questions can never be as effective as those delivered in personal sales pitches because there's no interaction. The TV can't answer you when you concede that you do, indeed, feel a twinge of inadequacy coming home from work in your beat-up VW only to watch all your neighbors' electric garage doors closing on their brand new Buicks. But it starts the juices flowing, which is all a good ad is supposed to do.

(Unfortunately—for the advertisers—when you get down to the car lot, the salesman usually couldn't care less whether you've driven a Ford lately. All he wants to know is whether

---

*The one profound exception was the brainchild of early ad guru Stan Freberg. In a moment of sardonic brilliance, Freberg decided to sell air travel by poking fun at the public's fear of plane crashes. Perhaps in today's jaded, post–Mr. Bill society, the campaign might have succeeded, but Freberg's 1960s audience was not amused.

you plan on driving one *now*. It's unbelievable how much time and money major automobile manufacturers spend on refining their ads, compared to the niggardly sums they invest in refining their sales force—the very people on whom they depend to finish the job begun by their advertising! One of the ultimate ironies of American merchandising is that a brilliantly conceived twenty-million-dollar ad campaign more often as not winds up at the mercy of an untutored, indifferent, ten-dollar-an-hour salesperson.)

Besides being at the core of high-powered, high-cost national ad blitzes, TNS has trickled down to the local level as well. A very successful Southern California hair salon runs an ad that is set up as follows:

(headline over art:)

YOU MAY THINK YOUR PRESENT SALON IS THE BEST IN THE BUSINESS . . .

(art work)

(tagline:)

. . .BUT HOW DO YOU KNOW IF YOU HAVEN'T TRIED US?

A second boutique selling expensive self-indulge-wear shows a pretty, fashionably dressed lady about to open the front door of her apartment, presumably to greet her gorgeous hunk of a date. The caption, just beneath her sequined derriere, asks:

DO YOU EVER GET A SECOND CHANCE
TO MAKE A FIRST IMPRESSION?

The proprietor of the store told me she had previously run the ad in statement form—YOU NEVER GET A SECOND CHANCE TO MAKE A FIRST IMPRESSION—and the response was measurably smaller. She attributes the difference to the fact that, besides being inherently more interesting, questions are far less likely than direct statements to sound pompous or clichéd.

And so, seemingly, the crux of TNS is once more reaffirmed. In 1985 America, people want to be asked, rather than told.

By carefully nurturing our innate sense of underinsuredness and piquing our subconscious dread of the unknown, the insurance industry has been one of the most frequent and successful purveyors of angst appeal.

"If you, or someone you know, are fifty-five or over, I urge you to get pen and paper and prepare to respond to this announcement," says the intense male voice, sounding much like Jack Palance with an ingrown toenail. What the listener hears is more to the tune of, You'll get that pen if you know what's good for you. This is the opening line of an ad that goes on to ask its target market, "Can you really afford *not* to have this coverage?"

Note, while we're on the subject, that the advertiser has carefully targeted its pitch to (a) those who are fifty-five, or (b) those who know someone who is. Without checking the demographics, I think it's reasonable to venture that, with the possible exception of six second-generation Exxon oil riggers out somewhere off the coast of Newfoundland, there is currently no one alive who fails to qualify for one of the two categories above. Yet the copy is worded and delivered in such a way that it implies exclusivity—that the listener is privy to a special announcement aimed at a small, very select group.

Historically, many sales shticks have relied on a similar approach. It may have taken a variety of forms—*this is a limited offer; only if you order tonight; exclusively for our regular customers*—but the import was ever the same. Always, there was the implication that you belonged to an exclusive inner circle (although more often than not, if the truth be known, that exclusive inner circle would have had to hold its meetings in the Houston Astrodome).

The fifty-five-plus insurance-policy ad is not strictly an appeal to ego, since not too many of us pride ourselves on knowing someone who is age fifty-five. Nonetheless, it is an appeal to our sense of individuality. We all like to think of ourselves as special in some way, and many of the most effective sales lines are designed to tweak that sense of self-identity, that perception of our singular place among mankind:

"Have you thought of how *you* might use our new sixty-four K word processor, Mr. Jones. . . ?"

Now realistically, what the hell can Jones do with a word processor that fifty million other people can't do just the same? Try as he might, he's not going to get the blessed machine to clean his pool. Still, Jones—like the rest of us—is just narcissistic enough to revel in the "personal" applications he devises for items he has bought. Even if he can't think of a single imaginative use for his new toy, he'll be unable to resist the feeling that word processors weren't quite real until he owned one.*

"One of the most effective things you can do as a salesman," says Danielle Kennedy, "is just to treat your prospect as an individual, a unique human being. Talk to him as if he matters. While you're with him, you should feel that your product was made for him, and him alone." Kennedy eschews the more mechanical, complex aspects of today's training in favor of downhome "relating." You don't have to stroke someone, or reel off volumes of fulsome rhetoric. Just make him aware that you're talking to him as a person, and not as just another potential client, and you're halfway home.

The insurance industry was among the first businesses, after the big sweepstakes outfits like Publisher's Clearing House, to orient this aspect of TNS reasoning toward its own advertising purposes.

Shortly after my mother became a senior citizen, she began receiving myriad solicitations from insurance companies that read basically as follows:

"How can you, YOLANDA SALERNO, afford *not* to be eligible to receive $250 each week, mailed directly to your APARTMENT 2B in beautiful JACKSON, should you suffer the loss of your left eye and your right hand in some tragic NEW JERSEY traffic mishap. . . ?"

The most glaring problem with the above pitch, as with all "personalized" messages, is its cloying superficiality. But people continue to respond with enthusiasm to such announcements.

---

*Think of some gadget you've purchased recently; maybe it was a computer, or a Cuisinart, or a garage-door opener, or a big-screen TV, or what-have-you. Despite your awareness that any number of other people before you had used that same appliance, didn't you get a special kick out of watching it go through its paces the first time you used it—almost as though it were something you had **invented**, rather than bought?

272

An old friend who once wrote copy for the prestigious J. Walter Thompson agency assures me that the vast majority of us are indeed naïve enough—to put it kindly—to be flattered by "personal" attention of this sort. Frankly, it always struck me as slightly bizarre that anyone could take seriously a brochure in which the main body of text, printed in slick, offset characters, stood in brilliant contrast to the tacky dot-matrix relief of the personalized particulars, punched in courtesy of an 8088 microprocessor.

In any event, the language of the insurance company's appeal suggested to my mother—as it presumably suggested to millions of other senior citizens who received their "personalized" mailings—that by having not yet subscribed to their policies, she had foolishly breached some unwritten law. Her failure to have purchased to date was thus a transgression of sorts.

"Those who acted six months ago are protected today against the hazards that still threaten you, YOLANDA SALERNO," one particularly ominous passage observed, just before noting that "our offer will not be repeated for another six months, so you will need to act *now*." In the same way, my friend the magazine publisher felt compelled to remind me at one point that my very existence as a functioning human being had been imperiled by my failure to reorder his magazine.

"Do you truly wish to give up . . . all the people, places and events that figure so prominently in your everyday life?" he wrote.

Potent stuff. A leading question and an ownership question rolled into one. The temptation is strong to say, Ah what the hell, and get out your checkbook. After all, what's fifteen dollars or so, in the context of such heady considerations?

I got out my checkbook.

What all this means to you, as one who lives in a world full (and getting fuller) of TNS derivatives, is that you ought to pay closer attention to the constant assault on your psyche. Be alert to questions, especially rhetorical questions. Ask yourself, Is it legitimately a question in the first place? Or is it merely a statement dressed in question form? Are you being asked for your honest opinion, or are you simply being called upon to affirm a thought that might not stand up to scrutiny were it phrased in a more forthright manner? Is there a tie-down involved? (As in, Wouldn't you really rather have a Buick?) If so, watch out.

More important, to whom or to what is the question directed? Is it speaking to your conscious mind—or is it calculated to slip beneath your guard and reach far deeper, in the hopes of arousing a reaction over which you have little voluntary control?

The New Salesmanship is here to stay, folks. If it hasn't as yet paid you a personal visit, it will one day soon.

You might as well be ready for it.

•　•　•

If I've tended, in this last section, to paint TNS as something sinister, that was not my intention. My own feelings on the subject are akin to the controversy over firearms.

On the one hand, you have the National Rifle Association telling you that the gun is less the issue than the person who's holding it. On the other hand, guns are so inherently dangerous that it requires a very special, and probably very rare, kind of responsibility to maintain and handle them without eventually hurting somebody.

TNS is much the same way; it holds the potential for both great good and great harm, depending on the circumstances, and on who's using it.

What concerns me is that the underlying framework of TNS makes it too easy for salespeople to rationalize the intent of their persuasive efforts. For the most part, redefining failure as success is no big deal. Redefining bad as good is another story.

It is all too easy, given the built-in self-aggrandizement of TNS philosophy, to lose sight of the distinction between right and wrong. The notion that you've entered sales as a holy crusade to "help people" does not absolve you of the moral obligation to make some effort at determining the worth of what you're selling. In their rush to confer upon all of humanity the means of ever lasting fulfillment, TNS's enlightened despots sometimes forget that when you strategically bypass the normal decision-making processes, you've tampered with one of humanity's most sacred privileges.

If you're going to do that, you've got to be certain—absolutely certain—that you're doing the right thing. I worry when I hear Hopkins tell me that "as long as a salesman believes in his product, that's enough." Doesn't it depend on what his product *is*?

Sure, it would be wonderful if we could all be enlightened and prosperous and "happily involved" with all the great things on the market today. But suppose a given product isn't so great? Suppose you don't really need it? Or can't afford it? Then are the salesperson's sophisticated methods of overwhelming your defenses still justified?

As a former colleague of mine put it, "Seduction may be less traumatic than rape, but I'm not sure that makes it less wrong."

For the salesman, the danger is of becoming so involved in the process that he overlooks such considerations. There's a tendency, when you've been trained to believe so strongly in your cause, to tune out "abstractions" that are extrinsic to the task at hand. Viewpoints that fail to coincide with your own become irrelevant. I've seen it happen.

Worse still, you tend to absorb the process. Like a hammer, TNS can be a great thing when it's regarded as a tool; but tools need to be put away at the end of the job. The problem is that TNS is less a technique than a comprehensive philosophy. In the end, too many salespeople actually become full-time hammers.

To a certain extent, this was always true, but it never mattered as much in the days before TNS. Given the stylized abrasiveness of most old-school salespeople, it was relatively simple for the consumer to differentiate between those who could help him and those who might do him harm. Usually, the nice guys seemed like nice guys; the bastards seemed like bastards. Now, as consultant Robert Scherer says, "The more somebody impresses you as a super-salesman, in the traditional sense of the word, the less chance he actually is one. And vice versa."

Everybody seems nice. Everybody seems to be on your side. Even the salesman—once he's become fully immersed in the world of modern selling—sees himself as your best friend. It's not a con job. He really and truly believes it. Which is why it's all the more important for you to recognize his attempts to

275

"help you decide" so that you can defuse them and instead come to some objective evaluation of his offering.

Not that a little "help" now and then isn't welcome and warranted. As I noted quite early in this book, even in the bad old days, many customers who were prevented from canceling by intransigent salespeople later wrote letters thanking those same salespeople for taking such a hard-nosed attitude. And surely we've all had the experience of being "talked up" by a salesperson, whether it be with respect to buying extra options on a car, or a stereo with an extra fifty watts output, or a house with an extra bedroom. In most cases, after the initial discomfort wears off, you grow to appreciate the decision the salesperson guided you to. When you cruise down the freeway with the sunroof open—the sunroof he repeatedly pushed for, despite your qualms over price—you realize that you would've been less happy with the car if he'd let you off easier. In the long run, when judged against the pleasure that step-up affords you, the money becomes almost meaningless. *The salesperson was right,* you say to yourself, as you enjoy the gentle breezes on your face, or as you listen to Mantovani at two hundred watts, or as you sit in your favorite chair in your library—the extra room you kept telling the salesperson you didn't need.

As also noted, TNS has much to offer those who aren't professional salespeople. We might all employ some of its tenets and techniques to improve relationships and avert many of the bitter confrontations that wring so much of the joy out of day-to-day living.

But the key in adapting TNS to one's daily affairs is to keep things in perspective. Salespeople and nonsalespeople alike would do well to remember that TNS works best when it's regarded as an aid, not a life-style, as a means to an end, not an end in itself.

When all is said and done, a passage written long ago with respect to what it took to be a salesman in post-Revolutionary times has probably never been more true than it is today in the age of The New Salesmanship—especially when read on a figurative level. Said Leonard Fischer in his book *The Peddlers:*

No particular experience was necessary for peddling Of course, a peddler had to have a good head for business and for driving a sharp bargain. And he needed a strong back and good muscular arms in order to carry his goods. He had to have sturdy legs for walking long distances. He had to be able to find his way in the wilderness without getting lost, robbed, or attacked by hostile Indians. And he had to guard against poisonous snakes, wild animals, frostbite, or drowning in a desolate, misty swamp . . .

Index

281